LIVING THE MINDFUL LIFE

LIVING
THE MINDFUL LIFE

CHARLES T. TART

Foreword by
SOGYAL RINPOCHE

SHAMBHALA
Boston & London
1994

Shambhala Publications, Inc.
Horticultural Hall
300 Massachusetts Avenue
Boston, Massachusetts 02115
www.shambhala.com

9 8 7 6 5

Printed in the United States of America
⊗ This edition is printed on acid-free paper that meets the
American National Standards Institute Z39.48 Standard.
Distributed in the United States by Random House, Inc., and in Canada
by Random House of Canada Ltd

Library of Congress Cataloging-in-Publication Data
Tart, Charles T., 1937–
Living the mindful life/Charles T. Tart
p. cm.
Includes bibliographical references and index.
ISBN 1-57062-003-2
1. Meditation. 2. Attention. 3. Awareness. I. Title.
BF637.M4T36 1994   94-6192
158′.12—dc20   CIP

BEGINNING DEDICATION

HO! Mesmerized by the sheer variety of perceptions, which are like
the illusory reflections of the moon in water,
Beings wander endlessly astray in Samsara's vicious cycle.
In order that they may find comfort and ease in the Luminosity and
All-Pervading Space of the true nature of their minds,
I generate the immeasurable Love, Compassion, Joy, and Equanimity
of the Awakened Mind, the heart of Bodhicitta.

—Jigme Lingpa (1730–1798), translated by Sogyal Rinpoche

CONTENTS

FOREWORD

There is a story that I remember hearing in my childhood in Tibet, about an old woman who came to the Buddha and asked him how to meditate. He told her to remain mindful, present, and aware of every movement of her hands as she drew the water from the well each day, knowing that if she did so, she would soon find herself in that state of alert and spacious calm that is meditation. The practice of mindfulness, simple yet powerful, is the heart of meditation, and the supreme antidote to distraction. For, as the Buddha taught, the root of all our suffering is ignorance, but the root of ignorance itself is our mind's habitual tendency to distraction. So mindfulness is the gateway to liberation. Buddha said:

> The practitioner who focuses on mindfulness
> Advances like a fire,
> Consuming the chains of bondage
> Both great and small.

What is it then that mindfulness brings? It allows all the warring and fragmented aspects of ourselves to settle and become friends; it gradually defuses our negativity; and it removes the unkindness in us, revealing our true nature, our compassionate Good Heart. One of my masters, Nyoshul Khen Rinpoche, calls mindfulness "the fortress of the mind" and "the friend of wisdom," for in its magical simplicity come a presence and a peace which are sane and grounded, clear, joyful, and awake, and full of compassion and wisdom.

When I first began to teach in the West, I found to my surprise that many spiritual practitioners today lack the knowledge of how to integrate their meditation practice with everyday life. But nothing could be more important. It cannot be said too strongly or too often: to integrate meditation in action is the whole ground and point and purpose of meditation. Here too mindfulness holds the key, for the true discipline of meditation is to maintain the thread of mindfulness throughout our everyday life. It is the continual application of that presence of mind that can bring about a deep change in a person's life, and become a source of real healing. Isn't it extraordinary though, how difficult it is, as we go about our lives, simply to remember to be mindful and to bring the mind home whenever we catch ourselves lost in distraction? I created a slogan which my students find helpful: *Remember to remember, when you remember.*

So to integrate meditation with life, the Buddhist masters tell us, there is no substitute for regular practice, for only through real practice will we be able to taste unbrokenly the calm of our true nature of mind and so be able to sustain the experience of it in our everyday life. This is why developing stability in spiritual practice is so important, through first practicing in the right environment and in proper practice sessions, and then mixing the experience of practice with everyday life.

I have known Charley Tart for many years now, as a friend, as a student, and as someone whom I meet at conferences around the world. He is someone who has always impressed me with his humor and eloquence, but above all with his sincerity and spirit of indefatigable inquiry. I have always admired his clear-sighted desire to help make the wisdom teachings more accessible to Western minds and to build bridges between the scientific and spiritual communities. We both share, I think, the belief that these teachings can be practiced and understood at the deepest level by people born and brought up in Western culture.

In *Living the Mindful Life,* Charley Tart shows, from his own experience with the teachings of Gurdjieff and of Buddhism, the tremendous benefit of applying mindfulness in everyday life. He presents his ideas and findings in a deceptively casual way, though in fact the effect that more and more people living a life of mindfulness would have now on the world would be nothing short of revolutionary. We live in a world governed by mindlessness and dominated by distraction, where people are deprived of spiritual nourishment and given little help to explore their true nature, the innermost nature of their minds. I am sure that the exercises Charley Tart presents here have much to offer people of any kind of background or spiritual inclination, in enabling them, throughout every aspect of their lives, to live in that most powerful and wonderful and healing of places, the present moment. I am sincerely moved by his aspiration to help others, and I pray that his work may reach and benefit as many beings as possible!

Sogyal Rinpoche
April 1994

ACKNOWLEDGMENTS

This book would not have been possible without the help of many people. Special thanks should go to Patricia Morgan for her secretarial help, to my wife Judy for her general support and editorial help, to Irene Segrest, who has assisted my research and writing for many years, and to Henry Rolfs and the Institute of Noetic Sciences, who inspired me to begin writing about G. I. Gurdjieff's ideas.

Many people have acted as teachers to me and so made this book, and what understanding I have, possible. As I do not know how to exactly weigh each teacher's contribution to this book, I will thank the more prominent ones here under the socially acceptable convention of alphabetical order: James Baraz, David Daniels, Lama Anagarika Govinda, Henry Korman, Jack Kornfield, Claudio Naranjo, Jacob Needleman, Sogyal Rinpoche, Kathleen Riordan Speeth, Tarthang Tulku, and Shinzen Young. I want to also thank my various Aikido teachers, who patiently and repeatedly forced me to learn the vital importance of body knowledge and body intelligence, usually by throwing me, lovingly but forcefully, across the dojo, until I got some understanding. Robert Frager inspired my wife and me to begin Aikido, and Alan Grow, Bruce Klickstein, Steve Sasaki, and Pietro Maida trained us well.

LIVING THE MINDFUL LIFE

INTRODUCTION

There are many times when I, like all of you, feel deep pain and sorrow about the sad state of our world. Is the end of the cold war to be nothing more than an opportunity for the horrors of "ethnic cleansing," the chance for each little social group to slaughter its traditional enemies without interference? And are we, our children, and our very earth to die slowly as the toxins accumulate and we mindlessly overbreed?

Making the pain of this perception worse is frustration. I want to help, but nothing seems to work! What can I do to help? Do my actions mean anything? What can the community, the nation, the world do? You read the papers or watch TV and there are all those wonderful plans to save the world that raise our hope and energy and then . . . do little or nothing. I, like all of you, sometimes get excited about movements, leaders, programs, and plans that look like they can help, but they then usually turn into bureaucracies that at best accomplish nothing and too often make our problems worse.

It is tempting to despair about the state of our world, our nation, our community, our friends, our very selves. Yet despair won't accomplish anything either, and the problems won't cure themselves. How can we accomplish something, even a *tiny* something, that will actually help and not just be another one of those good ideas that go astray?

An old question asks, What is the best form of government for an insane asylum? A republic? Democracy? Socialism? A monarchy with an enlightened ruler? A meritocracy? Communism? A dictatorship?

Our mind can start to get caught in this question, but it quickly becomes clear that it's not really a relevant question. An insane asylum does not lack for ideas, passions, and creative energy. The real problem is harnessing the available human energy. The place is full of crazy people! No matter how good the ideas and intentions, their execution invariably becomes warped, crazy, and destructive.

1

What we need to do is cure the widespread insanity, to bring people to their senses, to help them live in reality instead of illusion. If we could do that, probably any one of those forms of government could be made to work rather well in promoting the general good, and a sane community could then discuss intelligently the issue of the best form of government.

Sometimes ideas and movements accomplish some good in our world, at least temporarily, but since in too many ways our world *is* a big insane asylum—complete with insane ideas about what constitutes sanity—things and people keep going bad. I speak of the world at large here, but this statement all too often applies quite well to our personal world as well.

Personally, I do not have a sense of social vision, a feeling that I know what national or global programs will solve the world's problems. But I am convinced, from personal experience as well as my psychological studies, that anything that helps individuals become a little saner, a little more perceptive, a little more awake to reality and to our deeper spiritual nature is bound to help. People who are less asleep, less intoxicated by ideas and feelings, can be more effective when they act in the world while trying to help, can stop contributing to the vast reservoir of negative feelings that fuels so much destructiveness, and can inspire others to also come to their senses.

In the course of my personal development and professional studies of human consciousness and potentials, I have learned some useful things about helping people to become more awake, more mindful, more sensible. Sharing these in this book is, I hope, at least a small contribution toward helping our suffering world.

Let's think about four ideas, four human conditions, namely, sleep, mindlessness, mindfulness, and awakening.

Sleep. A person can be inert to the world about him or her, just lying there. That is a fairly harmless state, as long as the world makes no demands.

But a person is not always completely inert. About 20 percent of ordinary sleep is occupied with dreaming. We are inert on the outside, but inside we are going places, doing things, hoping, fearing, triumphing, failing. Dreaming is a very active condition, even if the vast majority of dreaming is forgotten by most people on waking.

The outside inertness is actually a forced paralysis. If you dream of walking, for instance, or grabbing something, all the necessary nerve impulses are sent to your muscles to walk and grab. Fortunately, as soon as you go into the dream state, a special part of the brain sends signals to the muscles that paralyze them, which keeps them from responding. Otherwise the night would be impossibly dangerous, with people's minds in another world but their bodies acting in this one.

Suppose the paralysis were broken, so you acted in this physical world but with your senses perceiving only the dream world and with your mind operating in the common dream manner that often seems strange and irrational by waking standards. Suppose our ordinary state of consciousness has a lot more in common with dreaming than we believe. Suppose there is a very real sense in which our minds and senses are far away, while we nevertheless act in the physical world. Suppose this is at least partly true for many people when they think they are working to help our world.

Mindlessness. A word, a string (I mistyped "sting," which is very apropos) of letters that calls for considerable contemplation. The word refers to a real class of actions that creates immense suffering in our lives.

Let me give three personal examples of mindlessness, roughly in order of intensity.

The other morning, while getting some breakfast food from a kitchen cabinet, I started to turn around and stepped on my cat Sparky's tail. He meowed loudly in pain and kept clear of me for a while after that. I felt terrible about it, a supposedly superior human being like me inflicting pain on a tiny creature! And, unfortunately, it's not the first time I've done this. After my mind finished mechanically running its standard excuse—that cats should know better than to get underfoot of big, clumsy humans like me—I remembered, for the umpteenth time, that a little mindfulness—remembering I'm in a room with Sparky, who isn't smart enough to not get underfoot—and taking half a second to glance around before I turn would prevent this.

It's not the first time I've vowed to be more mindful and not step on either of my cats.

A few weeks ago in my university class on humanistic and transpersonal psychology, I made a comment on a woman student's remark that came out sounding quite sexist. I realized the possible implications of what I was saying about three quarters of the way through the sentence, too late to stop it effectively. Several students immediately made other remarks about the topic we were considering, and the discussion went on. I intended to come back and apologize as soon as an appropriate moment occurred, but I got involved in the discussion and forgot about my intention.

A few days later, another student came by my office to tell me that she had been upset by my sexist remark, and that several other women in the class had been, too. It was not only upsetting in and of itself but totally out of character from what they had come to expect of me. I apologized in class that afternoon and was able to use my slip as a salient example of the suffering caused by mindlessness, but meanwhile, several people had felt bad about it for several days.

I rate this second example as causing more suffering. My cat seems to forget my stepping on his tail after a few minutes, but the pain we cause other humans through mindlessness, through lack of simple, basic consideration of others' feelings, can go on for a long, long time. I inadvertently added a little to the reservoir of human suffering. Did some of those I hurt take some of their feelings out on others, thus multiplying the suffering even more?

A couple of weeks later, I joined several other transpersonally oriented psychologists and psychotherapists, a scholarly Christian bishop, and a noted scholar of comparative religions in a discussion that touched on the nature of evil. Now *evil* is not a word with which I'm comfortable. There's no doubt that people occasionally act in terrible ways and hurt each other badly, but I try to see and encourage the higher possibilities in people, their better sides, as much as possible.

When my turn came to say something about what evil is, I apologized for not having a clear grasp of it and not liking to deal with it. The best I could say at that moment was my feeling that evil is more than just a matter of hurting others; it has something to do with *enjoying* hurting them, with feeling powerful and getting pleasure from knowing you're hurting them. I confessed that I had enjoyed hurting people at times in my life and was particularly disgusted by and afraid of that kind of feeling, even though I had to admit that I had the capacity for it. But I insisted, truly, that I tried to never indulge in that pleasure.

The next day I was driving in the fast lane on the freeway, trying to be mindful of the world around me and my internal state. This practice of mindfulness in the midst of daily activities and some formal sitting meditation are my fundamental spiritual practices at this stage of my life. I wasn't being very successful at it just then: a moment of mindfulness, ten minutes of mind wandering.

I noticed that a man was trying to pass me, but I was blocking the fast lane and there was too much traffic in the other lanes for him to go around me on the right. Well, I felt I was going fast enough and it was just too bad if he would have to wait a minute to get around me. Suddenly, I realized that, for all my claimed aversion, I was indulging in evil. I was enjoying another's suffering and feeling powerful and satisfied with what I was doing and feeling.

Admittedly, this was a pretty petty evil as evil goes in the world, but it was nonetheless evil by my own understanding. I had not been mindful of my own convictions. On a deeper level, I had not been mindful of my real, deeper nature, which is, I believe, something that is not totally separate from others. So the suffering I was causing the man in the other car was also suffering I was causing myself. I was mindless of our fundamental connectedness, of my own belief that in some real sense we are all one and that to hurt another is to hurt oneself.

So we can have levels of mindlessness, ranging from simple inattention to the immediate physical world through insensitivity to our interactions with others we care about to a deep and fundamental mindlessness about our most important values and real nature.

G. I. Gurdjieff, the Middle Eastern mystic and teacher, said repeatedly that "man is asleep." At our worst, we live in a tangled and neurotic fantasy world, a waking dream. Unfortunately, we still act, stupidly and mindlessly, in the physical world, creating enormous amounts of suffering for ourselves and others. There is no paralysis circuit, as there is in nighttime dreaming, to keep us from acting out mindless and harmful actions.

To the extent that we are mindless robots, stupidly creating suffering, there is only one question that really matters: How can we awaken?

Mindfulness. Ordinary levels of functioning can involve a reasonable amount of politeness and consideration for others, *habits* of functioning that make life better for all. But in too many cases they are simply habits, ways of being conditioned, like Pavlov's dogs were conditioned. A conditioned way of perceiving the world categorizes situations simplistically and evokes habitual responses, both inwardly and outwardly. Reality is constantly changing, though, and subtle shades of differences in situations are often undetected. Thus, our habits of perception, thought, feeling, and acting lead us into many mistakes.

Yet it is possible to learn to be mindful in our daily lives, to see more accurately and discriminatingly and so behave more appropriately toward others and toward our own inner selves, as well. The results cannot be fully described in mere words, but words and phrases like *freshness, attentiveness, beginner's mind, perceptual intelligence,* or *aliveness* point in the right direction. A stale, narrow life of habit and conditioned perceptions, feelings, and actions can slowly be transformed into a more vital, more caring, more effective, and more intelligent life.

Awakening. "Man is asleep." But what would life be like if we could really transcend our conditioning? See the world with eyes as fresh as a child's but with the intelligence and power of an adult? Free our vital energy from blocks erected by old traumas, defensiveness, and habit? Quiet the incessant racket in our minds and begin to perceive who we really are? Be mindful on the deepest levels?

For most of my life I have been trying to discover who I really am, who we really are. My journey has taken me through years of rigorous scientific work on the psychology of altered states of consciousness (ASCs), psychic phenomena, and human potential; to Buddhist retreat centers; to Christian churches; to growth training centers; to dojos where Aikido, a Japanese martial art, is taught; to circles of friends sharing Sufi stories; and to many other exotic gatherings, not to mention many apparently "dead-end" roads, many places and processes that were valuable to others but not suitable for me.

I have been lucky that my personal search has also stimulated my scientific career, so that my psychological researches have sometimes been useful to others in their personal growth searches. It's also lucky that the scientific training I have had, which can be considered a specialized kind of "mindfulness" training, taught me to be clear in my thinking and to watch out for biases that could distort my understanding. In a very real way, increasingly, I have tried to put the desire for truth, as best as I could perceive it, above the desire for happiness. Yet there is a very satisfying kind of happiness that comes from looking for the truth above all.

Don't misunderstand. I am not someone who has the "truth," or who is "awake" in any absolute sense. My ignorance and limitations are all too apparent to me. But I have learned some useful things about being less deluded, less mindless, more in touch with both inner and outer worlds, and being at least a little more awake.

In 1986 I shared some of the best results of my search in *Waking Up: Overcoming the Obstacles to Human Potential.* I was able to use my knowledge of modern psychology to expound (and I hope expand in some small ways) one of the great mindfulness training traditions, the teachings of G. I. Gurdjieff. That book has been the most important of my works.

Waking Up is a systematic, thorough presentation of the nature of waking sleep and a systematic technique for beginning to awaken. It was aimed at both the psychological audience of my peers in transpersonal psychology and at the general audience of anyone trying to become more mindful and awake. Judging from letters I received from readers, it has been very helpful to some people.

Since 1986 I have continued to try to understand and practice mindfulness in everyday life and have added a regular meditation practice that allows deeper moments of mindfulness and insight. I'm not sure I've learned anything drastically new since writing *Waking Up,* but I have become more flexible in life and practice and, perhaps, a little more sophisticated, yet simpler, about what I know.

For the last nine years, I have been studying the *Dzogchen* teachings of Tibetan Buddhism, with several Tibetan lamas, particularly the well-known Sogyal Rinpoche. For me, for now, it is the right extension of my earlier work. The emphasis on mindfulness that is basic to the Dzogchen teachings reinforces much that I knew previously about mindfulness and awakening, and the Dzogchen emphasis on developing compassion and devotion to the highest degree is giving me an education of the heart that I have always needed. The Dzogchen teachings go profoundly deeper than my own understandings, and I hope that they will lead me much deeper in my understanding and practice of life.

In the fall of 1991, Sogyal Rinpoche asked me if I would give a workshop on my psychological approach to mindfulness as a benefit to the Rigpa Fellowship, the organization that facilitates Rinpoche's teaching in the United States. The format that I developed for that workshop—beginning with an intense day of background and basic mindfulness techniques, followed by three evenings for students to get coaching on how to actually apply mindfulness in their everyday, personal lives—proved very useful. Participants came with a wide variety of previous experiences in formal meditation and psychological growth practices and with a variety of vocations, including engineer, physicist, nurse, social worker, carpenter, and school teacher. One had spent two years in an experimental training group of mine learning to increase her mindfulness in daily life. These students' questions on what to do in specific situations and their reports on what occurred as they tried to be mindful in real life, their "successes" and their "failures," were especially rich and stimulating. Fortunately, everything was tape recorded.

People tell me that my style of teaching at a workshop is fairly different from my normal writing style. It's less formally organized but richer, more dynamic, more alive. Thus this book. I have done a little editing and adding of material for better understanding, but I've kept quite close to the flavor of the workshop. In a workshop, the same material is sometimes covered from several angles as students actually work with it, but I almost never do this in formal writing, as I am compulsively efficient. Yet I know it is good for learning. Experiential exercises and basic mindfulness practices that were used in the workshop are described in enough detail to be useful to you readers, who weren't there. I still recommend my *Waking Up* for a systematic exposition of mindfulness techniques, but combining it with this one will make the whole presentation richer.

I have added two appendices, which were not part of the workshop. The first is an article of mine that originally appeared in the *Journal of Humanistic Psychology* dealing with specific exercises for extending into everyday life the mindfulness sometimes developed in formal meditation and with the general principles of such exercises. This more formal presentation should supplement many of the themes in the main part of this book. The second appendix is suggested readings on mindfulness in daily life and in formal meditation.

I cannot, however, stress strongly enough that, while reading about mindfulness is helpful, *ideas about mindfulness are not mindfulness*. Thinking about being present is not being present. The ultimate value of this book lies in the degree to which you try out the mindfulness practices and apply them in your life. Otherwise, the material herein, instead of starting to grow into a reality, will remain only pleasant fantasies about what could be. While I have tried in this book to keep the flavor and dynamics of the workshop setting as much as possible, writing cannot really capture the flavor of actually being there. Further, working with other people who are trying to become more mindful, preferably under the direction of a teacher who is more mindful than you, is extremely helpful. I will later discuss at some length this and some of the pitfalls associated with group work.

While the informality of this book makes it easily accessible to the general reader, I should note that it is also addressed particularly to my colleagues in transpersonal psychology. Accurate and deep observation of internal psychological processes is essential to the development of our field. The methods for self-observation and self-remembering in this volume can be used in a wide variety of transpersonal investigations and applications.

I hope that all readers who want to help improve the sad condition of our world and to live more mindful lives will find the following material useful.

Pine Aerie, Mendocino County, California
4 July 1993

ONE

WE ARE MINDLESS ROBOTS
. . . WHO CAN CHANGE

OUR WORKSHOP TODAY and the three Monday night sessions following this are a benefit for the Rigpa Fellowship. The Rigpa Fellowship is the group that built this shrine room we are meeting in. The word *rigpa* is a term used in the Dzogchen tradition of Tibetan Buddhism to point toward what the mind cannot "define," our original Buddha nature, the ultimate clarity, purity, perceptiveness, and compassion that could be ours.

I am a member of the Rigpa Fellowship, the American branch of an international organization that supports the teaching and work of Sogyal Rinpoche, the well-known Tibetan lama.[1] I am not going to speak as a Buddhist in our workshop, however. I am a beginning Buddhist and not much of an authority on Buddhism. I am somewhat expert on the Gurdjieff work, which is a tradition of becoming more mindful in the midst of everyday life. That will be the primary tradition I draw from. What I say will be influenced by the Dzogchen I've been studying, though, as well as my background in modern psychology and other growth disciplines.

I happen to like everyday life very much. I really have no desire to live in a monastery, and so I find being more present and mindful in everyday life extremely valuable for the style of life I live. I am also, like everybody else, lost in my thoughts a good deal of the time or carried away by my emotions or a little crazy, but I have found that the kind of mindfulness practice that comes primarily from the Gurdjieff tradition—I bring a lot of modern psychology in, too—can be very helpful to escape at least partially from that tyranny of overactive thought and feeling that makes us lose contact with reality.

GOOD NEWS AND BAD NEWS

Remember when good news / bad news jokes were popular? I'll start by giving you the good news.

The good news is that because our deeper nature is really wonderful, there is hope! We can become less crazy. We can have more vividness and realness in our lives and can get in better and better contact with our own deeper nature. Part of the good news is that there are a lot of techniques for doing that, although they often require social support. They are hard to do solely on our own.

The bad news comes in two major formats. One is that we have been programmed and conditioned to have a miserable view of ourselves and life, a programming that gets us into trouble all the time. The second part of the bad news is that not only were we programmed once but the program has become automatic, runs all the time, and is constantly reinforced by the mindlessness of our society. *We do not need the slightest bit of mindfulness to get through everyday life; we can run totally on automatic.*

Gurdjieff, who had a very no-nonsense, don't-bother-me-with-bullshit approach to things, put it very simply: *most of the people you see on the street are dead.* They are walking and talking, they have careers, they can get elected to high political office, but they are dead. Their real inner essence, their soul, their spirit, whatever you want to call it, has become so buried under the mass of automatic programming that, for all practical purposes, they are *machines,* and there is no hope for them.

I do not like statements about there being no hope for somebody—they are contrary to my hopes and temperament—but practically, a lot of people are very deeply immersed in their conditioning, and there is not much chance they will do anything about it. They will live and die as programmed automatons. And we are all like automatons to far too high a degree.

In our time together today, I am going to switch back and forth between, on the one hand, sharing some ideas that help make some sense out of why we want to be mindful and what inhibits and what promotes mindfulness and, on the other, giving you some experiential tools for being more mindful as part of your everyday life. This will mean that you will get some fundamental kinds of practices for using mindfulness, which, if you do not practice them, will become totally useless. But *they* work if *you* work.

MINDFULNESS

The first thing to note about mindfulness is that it is not particularly hard at all to be mindful. It does not take a really strenuous effort to make yourself become mindful and more present. The effort is very small. The problem is remembering to do it! We forget it all the time. It is not hard, but we just do not remember to do it.

The ideal way to become more mindful is simply to make the slight effort to be more mindful at all times. Indeed, this is what we *must* practice. Since we are, unfortunately, a long way from being able to do that very well, a good way would be to have an enlightened, perceptive teacher with you at all times, someone who notices when you have slid back into the fantasy that passes for ordinary consciousness and who reminds you at that point, Wake up! This would be especially helpful at moments when observing your mechanicalness would yield great insights. It is hard, though, to come across enlightened teachers, especially those who can follow you around through your day-to-day activity, where you most need this mindfulness. So that is not a very practical method. We have to do this work on our own, but we can use techniques to help remind us.

If we cannot notice when the optimal moments occur to remind someone to be mindful, such as when a person is in deep fantasy and distortion and about to do something very stupid, we could at least tell people to remind themselves to be mindful as often as possible. But chances are they would not remember/choose to be mindful at times when they would become mindful of something that might deeply bother them or really shake up their lives. We have unconscious psychological defenses that bias us to avoid disturbing ourselves. That is, we tend to practice at low leverage times instead of high leverage, psychologically rich times, when we would learn more and accomplish more.

Lacking an enlightened teacher around all the time, we can have a *random* teacher, a teacher who reminds us at purely random times to be mindful—with no waiting because we are not in what we think is the right mood at that moment. Some of those random moments might be quite bland—though they will not be bland anymore if we actually make ourselves a little mindful—and some of those moments might be particularly interesting in terms of getting some insight into our psychological habits, our defended material, that keep us from being mindful.

RANDOMLY TIMED WAKEUP BELL

Our random teacher for these sessions is in a tape recorder. What this random teacher does is ring a bell at totally unpredictable intervals. At the moment the bell rings, whether we are just listening, talking, or whatever we may be doing, each of us will freeze for a moment. If we are moving physically, we will just stop for a few seconds and, most importantly, we will mentally stop. Let that wonderful train of thought go. Do not worry about losing the wonderful thought; there will be more. I promise there will be more! That is the one thing I can guarantee.

So whenever the bell rings, take a few seconds to just come to your senses right then and there. Particularly, *feel your body* during these stops. We are going to talk a lot about using your body for mindfulness, because your body has a wonderful quality that your mind does not have: your body lives only in the here and now. It does not know anything about the past or the future, but in the past or the future is where your mind usually is. You can use your body as a tool to ground yourself in the present moment.[2] (Read this note now, on page 189.)

After I'd been using this random teacher technique in workshops for several years, a friend told me that the Vietnamese Buddhist monk Thich Nhat Hanh once said that in some Vietnamese villages they used to have a custom—I do not know whether they still have it—that every once in a while, unexpectedly, a special bell in the village is rung, and everybody stops for a moment. It's a beautiful picture, all these people within a mile or two of the bell, working at various tasks, stopping for a moment and contemplating the here and now, reminding themselves, in the midst of daily business, of their inner nature. We have a less elaborate version of it for our time together.[3]

A BELIEF EXPERIMENT

To begin our work on an experiential note, before I present a lot of heavy conceptual material, I want to propose a thought experiment—or better yet, call it a belief experiment. A belief experiment is where you decide that you will *deliberately* believe, as much as you can, a certain thing for a strictly limited period, say, ten minutes. This is quite different from the many things we believe for all our lives, never having made a decision in the first place about whether and for how long we were going to believe them. So many of them were just programmed in by our world as we were growing up. A belief *experiment* is an experiment: you adopt a belief, observe what happens during the time you adopt the belief, and then let it go, so that you can evaluate what the effect of that belief is.

I designed this belief experiment to bring out some important emotional themes of the culture we modern Westerners live in, although these beliefs have spread all over the world at this point. It also aims to bring out some things we *implicitly* believe, even if we would never want to express them verbally as our beliefs. We are going to read a statement of belief, which is deliberately in the form of a religious creed. It is in a form parallel to the Apostles' Creed, actually, but it reflects modern beliefs and is not intended to imply anything derogatory about Christianity. It is about what goes on in our culture, what we have been taught about the way the world really is and who we really are, and about some of the consequences flowing from that conditioning. We are going to believe it and notice our reactions.

We will do this because we do not come to learn about mindfulness from a neutral background. We are not objective observers, unbiased people able to take and examine things as they are. We bring a lot of cultural baggage as well as personal baggage, and it is important to experience that fact.

Before you begin, close your eyes and ask your deeper self if it is all right to participate in the experiment. See whether your mind says yes or no.

(Reader, pause a few moments now to do this.)

If you get no for an answer, bargain a little to see if it will allow you to do this experiment for just ten or fifteen minutes. Then you can go back to believing all the beliefs that were programmed into you, which you think of as "your" beliefs.

(Reader, do this if needed.)

If you still get a no, then fake going through this experiment, but do not really put your energy into it. That way you won't look conspicuous to others.

In order to make use of various cultural norms to increase the emotional intensity of this experiment, I want you to stand up at attention, with your right hand on your heart, as if you were going to pledge allegiance to the flag. Stand in neat, orderly rows. We will read the statement aloud together, slowly.

(Reader, stand up in this posture, and imagine a whole group of people around you going through this with you, doing as you do. Read it out loud, in a firm voice!)

THE WESTERN CREED

I BELIEVE in the material universe as the only and ultimate reality, a universe controlled by fixed physical laws and blind chance.

I AFFIRM that the universe has no creator, no objective purpose, and no objective meaning or destiny.

I MAINTAIN that all ideas about God or gods, enlightened beings, prophets and saviors, or nonphysical beings or forces are superstitions and delusions. Life and consciousness are totally identical to physical processes and arose from chance interactions of blind physical forces. Like the rest of life, *my* life and *my* consciousness have no objective purpose, meaning, or destiny.

I BELIEVE that all judgments, values, and moralities, whether my own or others', are subjective, arising solely from biological determinants, personal history, and chance. Free will is an illusion. Therefore, the most rational values I can personally live by must be based on the knowledge that for me what pleases me is good, what pains me is sad. Those who please me or help me avoid pain are my friends; those who pain me or keep me from my pleasure are my enemies. Rationality requires that friends and enemies be used in ways that maximize my pleasure and minimize my pain.

I AFFIRM that churches have no real use other than social support, that there are no objective sins to commit or be forgiven for, that there is no retribution for sin or reward for virtue other than that which I can arrange, directly or through others. Virtue for me is getting what I want without being caught and being punished by others.

I MAINTAIN that the death of the body is the death of the mind. There is no afterlife and all hope of such is nonsense.

Now sit down, close your eyes, and observe your body state and your feeling state. Continue to watch your feelings and bodily state while you continue to believe this statement. Do not worry about intellectual considerations and arguments, but watch your feelings and body state.

(Reader, take at least a couple of minutes to do this. You might find it helpful to take some notes on your reactions before reading on.)

OK. It would be very valuable to spend an hour sharing our reactions and observations with each other, but since we have many other things to cover, let me share some of the ways people usually react to this belief experiment.

Some people report feeling depressed, like they want to give up. Most feel sad. I can see from many of your faces that you understand that. Others report feeling small or closed in. On the physical level, some people report that they feel contracted or dizzy, that their neck hurts, or that their heart rate has increased. Others may report the experiment helps bring them into the here and now.

In fact, this experiment is not asking you to believe much of anything that is particularly different from what is usually believed by you and by most people around you in the intellectual circles most of you live in. This is what Western scientistic culture teaches all the time. It is seldom put in the form of a bald statement, a creed, an *explicit* set of beliefs, but these beliefs are what you get reinforced for; this is "rationality."

People usually report they discover that a part of them really believes much of this Western creed, even though consciously they may think of themselves as spiritual people, who wouldn't at all agree with statements of this kind. I think that no matter how different people would normally say their conscious belief systems are from the creed, the fact that we are Westerners means that some part of us, often a big part of us, believes it. It has been conditioned into us and reinforced in many, many ways over many years. Some people who believe they are spiritual people have cried when they discover that a part of them really does believe much of this creed.

I can show you every ostensibly factual statement in this creed, in some form or another, in basic science textbooks everywhere. Science (in a distorted form) is the religion of our times. It is what is officially taught in a variety of ways. You can externally rebel against this creed, you can have your religious belief systems, but you know what so-called scientific people think about your religion, the delusions that weak-willed people like you, unable to face harsh reality, need to get by.

If you do believe in God, in some kind of spiritual nature to the universe, in a higher purpose to life, do you ever have moments of conflict when you think maybe you are wrong? Maybe your belief is silly? Maybe it is immature? We are all taught that so-called primitives need to believe in God, but aren't we educated people supposed to rise above primitive superstition?

Actually, in the real sense of science, this put-down is a very *un*scientific attitude, but as a social system, this kind of creed has been taught to us, indoctrinated in us, conditioned in us, often in much the same way that Ivan Pavlov's dogs were conditioned to salivate at the sound of a bell. This Western creed exemplifies *scientism*, science distorted into an intolerant, fundamentalistic belief system.

WHEN BELIEFS BECOME AUTOMATIC HABITS

Many of us are on a spiritual quest. We hope that there is more to life than is summarized in this Western creed. And yet its view is supposed to be sophisticated, proven scientific knowledge. This attitude constantly affects people on the path.

One of the things I am convinced of is that the more beliefs you have that are relatively unconscious, that are implicit, that tend to operate automatically, the more enslaved you are. The more implicit beliefs, the more karma you have, to use a Buddhist term. If you consciously *know* you believe something, you could test that belief.

If you know you believe, for instance, that people will always betray you, you could, if you wanted to, actually test that belief. You could say, "I believe people are inherently untrustworthy, but I might be wrong, so why don't I try an experiment of trusting a few people and see if they all betray me?"

Unfortunately, beliefs simply become habits of thinking, habits of feeling, habits of perceiving. They literally twist the way we perceive the world, and they just seem natural. We think that is simply the way things are. We lose the opportunity to question them, to test them. One of the very important aspects of mindfulness training is that you learn more and more to see your own beliefs, to see them in operation, to test them, and to start seeing the consequences they have for your life. Then you will eventually have a chance to make decisions about whether you want to continue to believe them or to change them, rather than just assuming that they are true.

Well, the ten minutes devoted to the experiment are up, you can go back to your old set of beliefs.

Except, in a sense, you may not be able to go all the way back. I hope that you will always be more sensitive to these aspects of your belief system. One of the great "spiritual teachers" of the world was the early American patriot Patrick Henry, who said, "Eternal vigilance is the price of freedom." We usually think of his statement on a political level, but it is extremely important on a psychological and spiritual level. Like any statement, it can be twisted out of context, so that you start thinking paranoia is the way to go, but let's not go that far. We have to train ourselves to be vigilant, however, because so much of our mind is automatized; it just runs by itself, taking away our liberty.

WHO WAS G. I. GURDJIEFF?

To expand this theme of how our beliefs and habits of thought shape our perception of what we take to be "real," I want to tell a story about *kundabuffer,* but first I want to say a few words about who G. I. Gurdjieff was, since I will be referring to him frequently.

He was from Armenia, or at least that has been the name of the country from time to time. He was born in a very interesting part of Asia Minor that somebody new tended to conquer every fifty years or so, and everything would officially change. He lived at a crossroads of cultures. He could find Buddhists, exotic (to us Westerners) varieties of Christians, including Russian Orthodox Christians, Zoroastrians, Yezidis, and Sufis all in the marketplace at the same time. In a sense, he grew up realizing the relativity of beliefs. He could see how people could absolutely believe one particular view of the world, while all these other people who seemed to function about as well had different kinds of views. It also gave him a conviction that behind these various beliefs somebody must have the truth—or at least maybe somebody used to have the truth.

The young Gurdjieff could see how a lot of belief systems were clearly superstitious degenerations of older systems that people came to believe in by rote, as it were, by conditioning, and how there must have been some real knowledge behind them once upon a time. He spent his life searching for people who *really knew*. He got to Tibet; he spent time in India; he spent a lot of time in central Asian countries, time in Egypt, and time in other Middle Eastern areas at a period when travel was not easy. Later in life, he spent a lot of time erasing his trail. He wanted people to evaluate his ideas on the basis of their own merits, of the personal experience people had through working with them, not because he was to be regarded as an authority figure who had contacted mysterious Eastern authority figures. Of course, that made it all the more interesting for other people to try to dig up his trail.

It is clear that Gurdjieff spent time in Tibet, and it is also pretty clear that he got there by becoming an agent of the Russian Czar's secret service. People without money did not find it easy to travel in those days, especially to faraway, exotic lands. While he spied for the Czar, he learned a lot of Tibetan Buddhism. How useful his spying was for the Czar we may never know—unless, in these rapidly changing times, the old records surface from Russia. He was a very colorful character, to put it mildly.

He was an intense seeker after the truth. He wanted to *know*. He dug in old ruins, thinking that maybe there was ancient knowledge to be uncovered, and he studied with Sufis, Buddhists, yogis, Zoroastrians, and all sorts of exotic people. Eventually, somewhere toward the middle of his life, he found a secret brotherhood that had preserved in a living form the real, ancient knowledge he sought (this is the romance part) and supposedly he studied with this Sarmouni Brotherhood, a secret order in central Asia. The Sarmounis were supposedly the source that was behind all the other traditions that we see today. As I say, this is romance: you cannot write to the Registrar of Sarmoun University and inquire, "Did this man Gurdjieff really get a Master's degree back in the early 1900s or not?" This is mythology to us, whether true or not. It's great stuff, but like Gurdjieff, I believe we should evaluate ideas as a result of testing them ourselves, not because they come from some mythic, romantic source.

Gurdjieff eventually came to the West with what seemed to be a mission to teach, although he never fully clarified—at least not publicly—exactly what his mission was. He described it in some ways as a test to see if Westerners were ready to absorb some very profound spiritual ideas.

In many ways, it seems to me that he experimented on Westerners. That is, he had ideas and techniques that were designed for cultures that were very different from modern Western cultures. Could they be adapted so that they made sense for contemporary Westerners?

I think some of Gurdjieff's experiments failed. For instance, his primary written work is *All and Everything: Beelzebub's Tales to His Grandson,* which some Gurdjieff groups take as *the* gospel, to be read and minutely studied over and over again. It is incredibly difficult reading. I have heard that Gurdjieff was experimenting with the book, testing a theory that people will not appreciate an idea unless they have worked very, very hard to get it. So he would take some of his basic teachings, write a chapter about them, and make it hard reading. He would use stilted language, long sentences, invent new multi-multisyllabic technical terms, and then he would read it to his students. If a lot of them seemed to get it, he would rewrite it to make it more difficult. He would then try it out again, and if they still got it, he would rewrite it to make it more difficult. He succeeded admirably in making the final book difficult.

This story, whether literally true or not, appeals to my personal biases, as it justifies my not wanting to struggle with the book, so make your own judgment.

I am sure that there must be some people who, when they finally understood some teaching in the book, really appreciated it because of the immense amount of work they had put into it. But a lot of other people kept reading it religiously, over and over, felt they never really got it, and then felt bad about themselves because they could not understand it. It was an experiment with mixed results, or perhaps it was a failure.

THREE TYPES OF PEOPLE, FOUR PATHS

So Gurdjieff experimented a lot with Westerners, and his primary experiment was to develop techniques that would be applicable in and practical for everyday life. He said going off to a monastery is fine for certain kinds of people, but it is no good at all for other kinds of people. He categorized the *effective* spiritual traditions of the world as being of four major kinds, which corresponded to three fundamental types of people.

There are three basic types of human beings, and these three are all you ordinarily find, because it takes tremendous work to develop beyond the basic three. The first type is people who are centered in their body. It is how their body feels and "thinks" that is their main way of relating to the world. They use physical strength and analogs of physical strength to get somewhere. These people have certain kinds of advantages and certain kinds of disadvantages. The second major type is the emotionally centered person. Their primary way of reacting to the world is emotion, which can be very useful and also very detrimental. The third type of person is primarily intellectual. Their main way of relating to the world is to intellectually categorize it, to think about it, to analyze it, to relate it to other things they know, and to come up with intellectual concepts about it.

WAY OF THE FAKIR

There are spiritual paths developed for each of these types. The bodily type, for instance, is usually attracted to what Gurdjieff called the way of the *fakir*. He meant fakirs like he had seen in India, people who had developed such incredible physical will power that they had, for example, taken some physical posture and not moved for years. He had seen people who had adopted a religious posture of praying, for instance, and had literally not moved for twenty years. There are still some people in India like this today. I suspect they are rarer, but I do not really know. Fakirs start out by imitating some already accomplished fakir. At first they can only hold the pose for a while, then have to relax, and then do it again. And again and again and again, in spite of the heat, the flies, the other insects, the dust, and the glaring sun.

These fakirs all had disciples. They *must* have disciples by the time they become very advanced, because it reaches the point where they literally cannot move any more even if they wanted to: their connective tissue is frozen. Their disciples force feed them. When they get too dirty, their disciples pick them up like a statue and dump them in the Ganges to wash them off, or clean them up after they evacuate their bowels, and so on.

To become an advanced fakir is an incredible feat of will power: Gurdjieff also pointed out that it is an incredible spiritual dead end. While they have developed amazing will power, they have not applied it to anything other than standing still! Although this feat looks very impressive and people can make up religious theories about it, he thought it was particularly stupid. He said there is hope for these people, though, if someone with a more comprehensive kind of spiritual development can rescue them and show them how to apply this will power more productively. But otherwise they are, in a sense, just spiritual oddities.

WAY OF THE MONK

The second type of person, the emotionally centered person, usually follows a monastic path. This is a path involving tremendous focus on prayer, an intense emotional yearning for salvation, involvement, reaching out for help, and deep emotional experiences. It usually involves subjugating oneself to someone else's will as practice for subjugating oneself to the divine will.

According to Gurdjieff, people on this path who get very good at it frequently acquire psychic powers. They can produce what we call miracles. He also pointed out that when this path is pursued in extreme on its own the result can be what he called "stupid saints." These are people who can pull off miracles, but perhaps not very smart miracles. As an example I've created to illustrate this, imagine a person who, through prayer and longing, has developed the ability to cause a miracle, who can, in the poverty stricken country where he lives, a country ruined by overpopulation for two thousand years, earnestly pray and so cure couples of infertility. That is miraculous, but from a more comprehensive viewpoint, one might ask if this is the best thing to use miraculous power for.

WAY OF THE YOGI

The third kind of person, the intellectual person, pursues a path of an intellectual kind of yoga. I used *yoga* in a restricted sense here, as Gurdjieff did; there are obviously many kinds of traditional Indian yoga. The Gurdjieffian yogi is a person who has insights, who learns to understand things, and who can conceptually connect everything with everything. Pursued in isolation, however, Gurdjieff says that what results is the "weak yogi," the person who *knows* everything but who can *do* nothing.

I think excellent examples of what one might call weak yogis are college professors. They know many, many things; they are verbally brilliant, can put everything together, and explain everything. But when one looks at the quality of their personal lives, one sees that they are usually just as dumb and neurotic as all the rest of us, in spite of saying all these incredibly wonderful insightful things. I speak with authority from too much personal experience here!

THE FOURTH WAY

Gurdjieff talked about having learned and trying to teach a path that he called the Fourth Way. The way of the fakir was first; the monk, the emotional person, was second; and the intellectual yogi third.[4] The Fourth Way called for a balanced development of all three modes of functioning.

He put it another way. Remember, part of his experiment was putting his ideas and techniques in terms that Westerners could comprehend, and so he talked about our having three "brains." He used the word *brain* because, in a materialistic world, it was a term with much higher prestige than mind. We all "know" that the people who study the brain are the real scientists nowadays, and that was also the case when Gurdjieff was teaching in the early part of our century.

He said we are "three-brained" beings. In addition to our intellectual brain, which is usually the only one we think of as being a brain, we have an emotional brain and we have a bodily/instinctive brain.

All of them are brains in the sense that they (a) take in information about yourself and the world around you, (b) process it and compare it to past experience, (c) use their own kind of logic in making decisions about what to do, and (d) recommend acting in a way that seems sensible based on its own innate kind of logic.

The trouble is that practically everyone has only one brain that is reasonably well developed. Some people are primarily intellectual, some people bodily/instinctive, and some people emotional. The other two brains are not only undeveloped but are often at the level of idiots—and not only idiots, but typically neurotic idiots, because of unbalanced development.

Intellectuals try to solve almost all problems in life in terms of thought. But there are times in life when you have to use your body and *push,* and there are times in life when you have to listen to feelings. Emotional types try to solve all problems in terms of making things feel right, but there are times in life when you have to abstract yourself from feelings and intellectually analyze, and times when you need to tap your body's intelligence. Bodily types try to use will power to push their way through everything, but there are times when you need to listen to feelings or to think about problems. Gurdjieff's attempts to develop mindfulness, therefore, also centered around developing all three aspects of oneself, so that one comes up to a relatively normal level intellectually, emotionally, and bodily/ instinctively. That kind of balanced development is central to the Fourth Way.

All right, I've been talking for a long time, giving you an introductory overview. Let's have some discussion now, so you can be clearer about things and I can see how well I've gotten these ideas across.

MINDFULNESS IS BASIC

STUDENT: *I've read a little about Gurdjieff and he seemed to be trying to get people to wake up. When you talk about mindfulness are you talking about the same idea? Is this important in other spiritual traditions?*

To oversimplify, I can summarize the essence of the higher spiritual paths simply by saying, Be openly aware of everything, all the time. As a result of this constant and deepening mindfulness, everything else will follow. It is the filling in the details of *how to do this* that constitutes the meat of the enterprise.

The easiest way to illustrate the vital importance of mindfulness is to consider nonmindfulness.

Have any of you ever done something stupid because you have missed out on some important cue in your environment through being involved in fantasy?

[*Everybody's hand goes up.*]

Without getting into unconscious motivation yet, that kind of stupidity is the essence of nonmindfulness. I can go into that in infinite detail, unfortunately. Now, I am really interested in enlightenment, not mindlessness, but I do not "know" what it is. On the other hand, I consider myself an authority on *endarkenment*. I have not only professionally studied endarkenment, but I have also personally practiced it with tremendous determination for more than fifty years, and I know a lot about how endarkenment works!

To some extent, knowing how endarkenment works helps you to be more mindful. In an ideal world you might directly develop a sort of pure mindfulness, an enlightenment that allows you to totally bypass all the details of how we get lost in fantasy and how our perceptions are distorted and so forth. You could bypass all our human problems. But in practice, it helps to get a good idea as to how endarkenment works. It is easier, for example, to put gas in your car if you know where the gas cap is and understand that when the gauge reads low you really must put some in if you want to get anywhere.

To define mindfulness as a complex, open, honest awareness of everything all the time is technically correct, but it is so abstract as to be of almost no usefulness to people. If I am really absorbed in my fantasies, for example, my experience may be vivid and exciting, but my fantasies block out so much else. So we are going to talk about very basic mindfulness, namely, an accurate perception of what is happening right here, right now.

We are usually not very aware of the world around us, in spite of being well equipped to know it. We have, for instance, an extraordinary set of physical senses. When you really investigate our physical senses, you realize that they are incredible feats of engineering. If you have normal hearing—if you have not listened to too much loud rock music, which too many have now, unfortunately—and you go into a room that is absolutely soundproof you do not hear *nothing*. You hear a slight hissing noise. What you hear is the noise of the air molecules bumping against each other! This is an incredibly faint noise. That is also the maximum sensitivity you would want an ear to have. There is no point in making an ear more sensitive, because there would be a hiss overlaying everything. All our senses are incredibly good, and yet most of us miss all sorts of things, because we live in a waking dream.

Gurdjieff said, "Man is asleep." He said that over and over and over again and then elaborated it in a way that I actually think is a more accurate metaphor: we are walking around in a *waking dream*, a dangerous dream. The dreams we have at night are quite safe, actually, because we just lie there in bed. We do not do anything in the physical world that could get us into trouble. The dreams we have while we are awake, however, get us into a lot of trouble, because we are not in clear, accurate touch with what is going on around us, yet we act, and we reap the consequences of our actions. The bell has just rung.

Our random teacher has just spoken! To be more mindful right then, when the bell just rang, to come to the present means, for me, among other things, that I got much more into my body. I am trying to be mindful while I talk, including right now, but it is difficult. So when the bell rang, I became much more aware of my body in quite specific sorts of ways. There was a different quality of the sensations in my feet and the lower part of my legs than there was in the rest of the body, for example. I could feel my pulse in my chest. Of course, I am talking about the past now, trying to freeze a moment. To really be mindful on a bodily level would be to keep track of bodily sensations moment by moment by moment, as they come, as they stay, as they transform, as they go.

LIVING IN ABSTRACTIONS

If you are in a situation where you are receiving sensory stimulation, to be mindful is to be aware of that sensory stimulation in a relatively raw, unabstracted form. By that I mean that in our ordinary state of consciousness, we almost never stay in simple, direct contact with what is actually happening around us.

We see a rose, for example, and there is a moment of sensory contact. The light rays from that rose reach our eyes, turn into neural impulses in the retina that then reach our brain, and then get transformed into consciousness somewhere. We all know that roses are beautiful things. What usually happens when we see the rose, though, is that almost instantaneously an automated abstraction process takes over that gives us a symbol, a semi-arbitrary construction about a rose. We throw away most of the actual physical appearance of that rose, and in our consciousness, it is replaced by a standardized symbol of roses.

The symbol is almost completely verbal for a lot of people. It is as if we went blind a tenth of a second after we saw the actual rose and then heard the word "rose" in our heads. A bunch of stored memory associations (including pictures, touches, smells, and so forth) about roses immediately pop into our head. What we then experience is very much of our past history of roses, as it has been shaped in our personal experiences and in the cultural programming that gave us our attitudes about roses. We may see, smell, and feel very little of the actual rose that is right in front of us this moment.

ATTENTIONAL DEFICIENCY DISEASE

Gurdjieff had a fascinating idea about this normal process of living in abstractions about sensations, an idea that I think is quite true. Gurdjieff said that sensation, perception, is a kind of mental *food*, essential for mental nutrition, and if we do not get enough of this kind of nutriment of sensation, we suffer from mental deficiency diseases. We all know, for instance, that if we do not get enough vitamin C, we get scurvy, a vitamin deficiency disease. If the body does not get enough of certain basic chemicals, metabolic compensations are made that are forms of illnesses and that have various symptoms. Gurdjieff said we suffer from the parallel to vitamin deficiency diseases; these are perceptual deficiency diseases.

Because we do not actually pay much attention to our sensations themselves, certain processes do not happen in our body and nervous system that could nourish us, and consequently we develop deficiency diseases that we try to compensate for. Some people get a nutritional deficiency disease that causes them to eat unnatural things like chalk or dirt, a behavior called pica, because there is some nutrient in the dirt that can help the disease. Unfortunately, the needed nutrients are very diluted in the dirt, but it is better than nothing.

If you see a rose and actually stop your wandering, abstracting mental processes and come into the present for a moment, really look at the rose and really smell it, something happens that is nourishing. Gurdjieff speculated that there were literal chemical transformations in the nervous system, and I suspect he will eventually be shown to have been right. If, on the other hand, you see the rose but do not make the effort to come into the present, you are hardly nourished at all by the experience.

The *food of impressions* is another phrase he used. Really paying attention creates a kind of food that nourishes. As you learn to become more present, more mindful in everyday life, you get a rich diet of this kind of nourishment. This process is, in my personal experience, subtle, not necessarily a special thrill. It produces a gradual shift in you, one of the results of which is that you feel happier and you start to function in a more healthy way.

ATTENTIONAL DEFICIENCY AND RELATIONSHIPS

We need attention. We need rich sensory impressions as much as we need vitamin C. If we do not get them, we develop various kinds of psychopathology. A classic example is when children who do not get enough attention from their parents are deliberately bad. The attention you get when you are being punished is much better than starving for attention.

We think acting bad just to get attention is a weird thing that happens with some children, but actually, as adults, we do it all the time. A lot of the quarrels we get into, the situations that go bad and cause stress, especially interpersonal situations, are actually implicit, subconscious maneuvering on our part to force attention. It is better to have somebody yell at me than to be ignored. A lot of the karma we create, a lot of the obligations we get into, a lot of the interpersonal relations we set up, are ways of forcing attention from other people, but they are not psychologically clean. They have hidden motivations, they involve psychopathology, and they generate a lot of negative side effects.

Gurdjieff talked about not getting the full nourishment of impressions, not the full food, but watered down food. Consequently, we become more voracious, driven, we eat "junk food" of impressions, we eat anything—we've got to have it! But if we become more present in everyday life to what we are actually experiencing in a sensory way, right *now,* moment by moment, we start to nourish ourselves. Then a very interesting thing happens: we start to get into cleaner relationships with other people, because we do not need them so desperately to fill our attention needs. We do not need people to shout at us or to seem intensely in love with us and then break up with us by having a wonderful quarrel that seems to give us a lot of attention, because we are more self-sufficient.

ESCAPISM IS NOT THE WAY

Learning to nourish yourself with the food of impressions by living in the here and now does not mean that the goal of life, as some people interpret it, is to be so self-sufficient that we do not need anybody. This is one of the pathologies of the spiritual path. If one is soured on people, then one is attracted to a spiritual path that lets one quit: "I'm going to hide out in *nirvana* forever. So much for you, you unenlightened jerks!"[5] That's not the real goal, but the spiritual path is often misinterpreted in a way that reflects some people's psychological defenses.

I recently read an interesting interview with the noted Buddhist scholar Robert Thurman in the *Inquiring Mind,* the vipassana meditators' newspaper, where he talks about how the Buddha was aware of this tendency.[6] Indian culture at the time of Shakyamuni Buddha had a lot of escapist tendencies. I can understand that. My first visit to India was shocking because of the grinding poverty, the heat, dust, flies. I felt that if I lived there, I would want out!

I have noticed this theme, with varying degrees of emphasis, in some forms of yoga and in some aspects of Buddhism, too. The basic goal is the feeling that it is so rotten here that I want out!

The Buddha did not deny this desire. Thurman argues that the Buddha was smart: he could not say that there is no real personal escape because we are all interrelated, part of a cosmic unity. That would have turned people off right away, and they would not have listened to the rest of his message. He let that idea of nirvana as an escape persist, but then he amplified it by making it clear that personal escape is not the highest form of attainment, not real enlightenment. The highest form involves deeply realizing that the ordinary self that we protect so desperately is an illusion. If you have no vulnerable self, there is no need to escape it.

Another Buddhist factor added to this, in my limited understanding, is the vital importance of developing compassion. This leads to the bodhisattva ideal, a goal and commitment that you do not want to leave this existence by permanently escaping into some altered state of bliss while anybody else is suffering. This ties in with a realization that if you reach the highest realization of emptiness, you naturally develop bodhisattva motivation, because you realize that you are not separate from everybody else and so you cannot be enlightened all by yourself.

If you're confused by the idea that there is no real, personal self, yet this self seeks enlightenment, don't worry: it is confusing and probably inherently incomprehensible to ordinary consciousness. Yet it's dealing with a reality that we will touch lightly later.

To sum up these last few minutes, the practice of mindfulness is nourishing at a deep level, and because it nourishes you, you can grow and you can have cleaner relationships with other people: you do not routinely create complex undercurrents and psychological conflicts. Cleaner relationships and a deeply nourished inner essence form a solid foundation for the development of compassion and enlightenment.

Now, I've talked a long time, giving you an overview of consciousness, mindfulness, and so forth. Let's have some comments and questions from you, so I can see what I have and haven't gotten across and to give you a chance to go deeper on areas of special interest to you.

[*A minute passes with no one in the group saying a thing.*]

STRESS, EMBARRASSMENT, AND FANTASY

Now we are experiencing what is considered a socially awkward moment, which is excellent for mindfulness! If you really want to understand your own mind, all kinds of things that are normally considered suffering, stress, embarrassment, and awkwardness become wonderful opportunities to observe yourself, because the intensity of your mental energy goes up for a moment as a result of the stress.

I practiced self-observation intensely this last minute: I asked for questions and nobody said anything. Within a few seconds my fantasy generator kicked in: I must have bored everybody to death! How embarrassing! I also thought I must have confused everybody so much that they do not know what to say or—horror of horrors—everybody dislikes me! Because I was being mindful, however, none of those ideas caught me, and I could observe them and note that these are old programs in my mind that tend to get activated in moments of stress. Because I am trying to be mindful, they do not automatically suck me in.

Sometimes automatized reactions like these do suck me in part way, and sometimes they suck me in all the way. But because I've been intermittently practicing mindfulness for years, even when I get partly sucked in, there is more spaciousness in my mind, more room to maneuver. I'm not able to be *fully* mindful and here-and-now, but I've still got more psychological space than I used to have. Having some space, I can remember to deliberately become more mindful, to get into the here and now. By paying more attention to the here and now as it comes in through your senses and through your body, you create a kind of psychological spaciousness, which means you do not get sucked in so easily by your automatized thoughts and emotional reactions, and if anything, you can then experience them in a clearer kind of way, a less identified kind of way, and a cleaner way.

STUDENT: *When I try to be more present I can't be aware of everything, too much is happening in each moment for me, I fail.*

COPING WITH OVERLOAD

You have to be selective. You cannot go around being mindful of everything all at once. It would be paralyzing.

When Gurdjieff explained what enlightenment was, he used the term "being fully awake." That is a wonderful idea, being fully awake.

In their excellent introduction to the art of meditation, *Seeking the Heart of Wisdom,* Joseph Goldstein and Jack Kornfield write:

> It is said that soon after his enlightenment, the Buddha passed a man on the road who was struck by the extraordinary radiance and peacefulness of his presence. The man stopped and asked, "My friend, what are you? Are you a celestial being or a god?"
> "No," said the Buddha.
> "Well then, are you some kind of magician or wizard?"
> Again the Buddha answered, "No."
> "Are you a man?"
> "No."
> "Well, my friend, what then are you?"
> The Buddha replied, "I am awake."

Gurdjieff said that being awake meant *knowing everything you know all at once and feeling everything you feel all at once.* He did not mean, however, that all the data, everything you know and feel, is dumped into ordinary consciousness simultaneously. You would be totally paralyzed if that happened. He meant being in touch with the moment and having all of your *relevant* knowledge (intellectual, emotional, and body/intuitive) immediately accessible to help you deal with the situation. He meant being present and flexible, with no blocks to retrieving relevant information. How many times in life have we screwed up in a situation and afterwards we saw there was a simple thing we could have done that would have saved the whole thing? But it did not come to us at the time. The bell sounds. Stop: come to the moment.

We do not have ready access to much of our knowledge and skills a good deal of the time, partly because we become identified with our specialized, limited concepts about the current situation and get caught up in them, as well as for deeper psychological reasons. I will be teaching you to use your body sensations as an anchor, an anchor in the present that is a source of stability in the midst of the whirlwind of life.

STUDENT: *If I try to be really mindful and aware of everything, I worry that I will lose my motivation to accomplish anything! It doesn't sound very practical, like I'll just be passive.*

BEING PRACTICAL ON THE PATH

We have to be practical. There are formal meditation practices in which you try to be totally passive during the meditation, passive in the sense of not taking any action whatsoever, but simply being attentive to whatever arises in experience. The Buddhist term for this kind of meditation practice is *vipassana*. That's fine as a meditation practice.

Now, if you are trying to find your wallet and car keys because you are going out of the house, you do not want to be attentive to *every* single thing no matter what, because (if you could really do it) you would probably lose track of the fact that you are looking for your wallet and car keys and would never get out of the house. On the other hand, you do not want to be so attentive, so focused on looking for your wallet, that you do not notice, as you go through the kitchen, that you have left the flame on under an empty pot that is going to burn up in a moment.

Meditation is, in one sense, a luxury practice. Formal meditation is what you do when you have technically simplified your physical world situation so you are not on call. You are not responsible for driving the car and being certain you do not crash, or watching the pot so it doesn't burn, or answering the telephone. You have the luxury of just sitting, being quite passive as to what is going to come into or arise in your mind, and just being clearly attentive to what does come in. Or there is the luxury practice of concentrative meditation, in which you try to put all attention on a single thing. This can produce trancelike states that give you temporary bliss. These states are great accomplishments, but they also make you blind to the world. You wouldn't do concentrative meditation as part of walking around in the world, either.

MARTIAL ARTS AND AWARENESS TRAINING

Let's look at this issue of being practical in applying mindfulness in the real world in a little more depth.

Aikido is a good example of being able to function in a more attentive, yet unextreme, way. Aikido is a Japanese martial art, a self-defense art. It is classed as an *inner* martial art in that a lot of attention is paid to perceiving what is going on both inside and outside, moment by moment, rather than mainly emphasizing specific, external techniques. In the highest form of Aikido, there are no particular techniques, everything you do is original and appropriate to your clear perception of the exact, particular situation at that particular moment.

Aikido is also an example of not becoming *identified*. If I become so terrified that I am going to be hit by my attacker the bell has just sounded that most or all of my attention goes into this fear, I am in a very dangerous situation. In the worst case, I am dead. I have to be aware that I am being attacked, that this is real, that energy, in the form of a blow or a grab, is moving toward a vulnerable part of me. I cannot go blind to this supremely important reality. But if I am being sensitive, here-and-now in the way that Aikido and other mindfulness practices train you to be, I see *exactly* where the attacker is, I see *exactly* the trajectory of the attack and where it will contact my body, and I can meet that energy *without getting aggressive and excited*. I can pick the energy up, blend with it, lead it in a certain kind of way, and redirect it to a point where the attack doesn't harm me and the attacker is immobilized.

In life, different amounts of attention to immediate reality are required. In some situations you can get by without paying much attention. You can daydream in most classes, for example, because the instructor does not call on you. Some instructors try to prevent this by maintaining a climate of fear, where they might call on you and ask a question at any moment, but that is creating a mechanical kind of mindfulness by brute emotional force. In a lot of classes, however, you can daydream if you just remember not to actually fall asleep, close your eyes, or snore, because that draws attention. At other times, you have to give a situation more attention, and then in special situations, like formal meditation, you deliberately remove the press of the world and learn to maintain mindfulness voluntarily, without the support of externals. Situations vary, and you have to be practical.

EMPHASIS ON MINDFULNESS IN EVERYDAY LIFE

I have said that Gurdjieff's path is primarily a matter of mindfulness in everyday life. He taught, to the best of my knowledge, almost nothing in the way of formal, sitting meditation practices as we would ordinarily categorize them—although they were introduced to some extent by some of his students later. His theory was that the place in which you create all your trouble is ordinary life, and so that is both the place you need mindfulness the most and the best possible place to learn it.

I personally find Gurdjieff's techniques for creating mindfulness in daily life much more practical and successful than Buddhist ones. In my (hopefully, too limited) acquaintance with several Buddhist systems, they always stress that you *should* be mindful in ordinary life, not just in meditation, but in practice, almost all the emphasis is on formal meditation, and there are very few, if any, practical techniques given for bringing this mindfulness to everyday life.

Gurdjieff said one of the best ways to become mindful in everyday life is to use your body. For instance, feel the sensations in your right hand now. Are they in the future?

(Reader, try this.)

No, they are *now*.

Where are they?

(Reader, try this.)

They are *here*.

Buddhists do talk about how being incarnated in a human body is actually the best of all the six realms of existence for practicing enlightenment. We have tremendous advantages here. One of the advantages is that we have these physical bodies that are anchored in the here and now. Our bodily sensations and sensory perceptions exist in a specific place and time, the present moment and place, so we can use them to stabilize our minds. Gurdjieff's technique for creating mindfulness in everyday life is to deliberately split your attention, so that a small part of your attention is always monitoring what is happening in your physical body. This deliberate split of attention acts like an anchor in the here and now, so that you are not swept completely away into thoughts, emotions, fantasies, reactions to thoughts and fantasies, reactions to reactions, and on and on that are evoked by both external events and previous thoughts, feelings, and fantasies.

INTO YOUR BODY: MUSICAL BODY EXERCISE

To bring us more into our bodies, I am going to have us do an experiential exercise that runs for roughly half an hour, an exercise called the *musical body*. I have a special tape prepared for doing this exercise, but you can do it at home with almost any kind of smooth, flowing instrumental music—not music accompanied by words, though.[7]

It is a multilevel exercise. At one level, this is a way of being nice to yourself, because you pay attention to your physical body, and your physical body likes having attention paid to it. On another level, it is a way of training your ability to focus. On a third level, it is a way of nourishing yourself. And on a fourth level, it is a way of preparing yourself for other, more formal, day-in-and-day-out mindfulness exercises. Basically, it's about living *in* your body in the here and now, where life actually exists, instead of beside it or ahead of it or behind it.

[*Workshop participants do the exercise and discuss their positive reactions to it afterwards. I have not included the discussion here.*]

Readers wanting to do this at home should follow these basic directions. They are simplified since you have to guide your own attention, rather than having someone else do that part for you. Pick some smooth, soothing, flowing instrumental music that lasts for about half an hour. Arrange the situation so you won't be disturbed. Start the music and lie or sit comfortably. After relaxing for a couple of minutes, listen to the music *in your feet*. That is, focus your attention to feel whatever actual sensations are in your feet and "imagine" that you hear the music there. It's easier than it sounds. After about a minute, feel the sensations and hear the music in your ankles. Then, at roughly one minute intervals, progress to your calves, your knees, your thighs, your genitals, your buttocks, your hips and abdomen, your chest, your shoulders, your upper arms, your elbows, your forearms, your wrists, your hands, your fingers, then back up to your shoulders, your neck, your face, and the rest of your head. Then sense and feel the music in your whole body until it ends. Get up slowly afterwards, retaining a sense of your body.

FIRST HOMEWORK ASSIGNMENT: BODY SENSING

Your homework assignment for lunchtime is to use this little musical body boost you have gotten for getting more into your body and maintaining contact with your body while you are getting to lunch, through lunch, getting back from lunch, and driving or being a passenger. What I want you to try to do now is to keep a part of your attention always monitoring what is happening in your body. I emphasize what *is* happening in your body, naturally. That is, there is no special way you are supposed to feel. I am not going to tell you that you should feel comfortable or uncomfortable, hot or cold, good or bad, or tense or relaxed. I am inviting you to keep some part of your mind, 10 or 15 percent, in touch with what your body is feeling at any moment, while you also pay clear attention to whatever else you are doing.

Do not take it to extremes the bell is ringing, however. I do not want any reports of zombies in local restaurants!

You may find it helpful to move slightly slower than normal to maintain the body contact, but just slightly. And look both ways when you cross the streets.

Now, if you are human, you're probably going to forget many times to do this mindfulness exercise during lunch. All of you who have made any attempts at this kind of practice before know that you are going to forget to do it. What then?

When you discover that you have forgotten to do it, you have two options. Option one is that you spend a minute or two feeling guilty and berating yourself for being so bad that you forgot it and then come back to actually paying some attention to your body and the rest of what you are doing. Option two is going directly to doing it again, coming directly back to sensing your body and surroundings.

If you find option one is forcing itself on you, then try to be fully aware of the way in which you are berating yourself *and sense your body at the same time.*

This does not mean that you should have a horrible time at lunch! The Gurdjieff work often gets misinterpreted in terms of people's strange ideas. Gurdjieff said that we are asleep and so the human situation is terrible. I have seen a lot of people who somehow seem to interpret that to mean that if you are serious about waking up you have to look and feel miserable most of the time, because that means you are doing the work.

Do not get hysterical and fanatic about this. It is very hard to be present when you are hysterical. Just try to keep a little bit of your attention, 10 to 15 percent, monitoring what is happening moment to moment in your body. Do not try to fix these sensations into something solid, do not try to keep them from changing, and do not try to make them be anything in particular. Just notice whatever they *are*, moment by moment.

If you find it hard to keep track of your body in general, if that seems to be too tiring or you cannot pull it off, reduce your focus. Just keep track, say, of your arms and the rest of what you are doing and perceiving externally. If that is too hard, you can bring your internal focus down more, say, to one hand. So if worse comes to worst, just keep some awareness of what one hand is doing while you are ordering lunch or talking with companions at the table or driving to a restaurant.

Keep a general openness to whatever the feelings are in your body. When your compulsively interpretive mind comes in and has to figure all this out, when it is taking you away from actually keeping track of your body and perceptions, you might try the trick of saying to yourself, I know you are the best thinker in the world and can really think and analyze wonderfully, and I will get to you later, but meanwhile I am going to notice what is actually happening now.

TWO

MINDFULNESS EXERCISES

MINDFULNESS AND RELAXATION

We get up in the morning and, too typically, within a few minutes we have worked up tensions. Tensions here, tensions there, and by the middle or end of the day, tensions everywhere. Tensions we often do not consciously know we have. Yet we carry them all day, and they feed on each other, increase one another. It is incredibly fatiguing and wearing on the body and on our selves.

Mindfulness practice, in its purest sense, is simply this: be aware of what *is*, what is here in this moment. In formal mindfulness meditation practice, such as vipassana meditation, you do not attempt to change or improve what is, you try to refrain from judging it. When you are aware, however, of tension that is, in a sense, being voluntarily (even if unconsciously) held, there is usually a natural reaction to relax it. This is not always true, but generally mindfulness tends to bring about relaxation. It is hard to keep on doing something stupid, like being unnecessarily tense, when you consciously know you are doing it. It is easy to be stupid, to be uselessly tense, when you have forgotten you are doing it or never knew you started doing it in the first place.

STUDENT: *I've found that for long periods of time I was really insensitive to my body and the world around me.*

Unfortunately, that's normal.

STUDENT: *Then I really got interested in doing this sensing. So I'm walking around, and I could notice that my body is cold, I could feel my foot, but it doesn't really grab me as that interesting. And I think that's maybe why I don't really pay attention.*

BOREDOM, SUFFERING AND SPACING OUT

The trouble with ordinary reality is that a lot of it is dull, so we long ago decided to leave for somewhere better.

STUDENT: *Yes, fantasy is much more interesting!*

We leave reality for at least two reasons. One of them is that sometimes it is just so-so; other times it is painful. In both cases we leave: we go into a fantasy world in our heads, which provides a certain amount of immediate relief. The problem is that it then becomes automatic to leave all the time, to go off to fantasy places. Then, when we try to be in reality, we are fighting against years of accumulated habit.

To learn how to live in the here and now, you must learn to stay there even when it is not very interesting by your ordinary self's standards. Actually, if you really get there, deeply sense the here and now, it is very rare that here and now reality is not interesting. It is a matter of depth.

Sometimes it is a matter of accepting: "I am fully present, my body is uncomfortable, I am bored, and that is how it is." Learning to be present and attentive to the moment under these conditions is a necessary skill for deeper development.

If you *know* how to get into reality, if you know how to be mindful of it, and you then consciously choose to send your mind somewhere else, that is a very different matter than if your mind always gets automatically sent somewhere else the moment things get dull or threatening.

STUDENT: *I keep thinking there must be something wrong with me because I'm not noticing something interesting, that I should be having these in-depth "Aha!" experiences. So if that's not happening, I must be failing.*

RESULTS: SO WONDERFUL, NOTHING SPECIAL

I've done exactly that many times when I have been sitting in formal meditation. I sit there, I get quiet, I get clear, and it is nothing special. I think, Well, look, God, I am doing what you said, I am doing meditation, how come this is not fantastic? I complain that my experience is not up to what I think are my standards. In terms of real growth, though, I have to note that the bell is ringing now realize that this judging is more internal material to look at: Why am I so demanding? Why does the universe have to be so special for me, on *my* terms, every instant?

When Lama Sogyal Rinpoche teaches about realization in Dzog-chen, about the enlightened state of mind, he talks about it in two quite different ways, which drives me a little crazy. One is when he talks about this wonderful, incredible state of rigpa, of enlightened mind and all that. There are hymns written about this state and long poems in praise of it and ceremonies celebrating it, so it must be very special. Then, every once in a while, he mentions rigpa as being perfectly ordinary. What? The part of my mind that wants something special says, What do you mean, perfectly ordinary? I'm not here for the perfectly ordinary! Where's the thunder and lightning? Where's the psychedelic vividness, the fantastic insights, the mystical something or other? I want more!

And yet when I have suffered a lot from my mind going off on endless jags of delusion and craziness, which is its common mode, and I get a moment of just being present, what a relief it is! How natural, how simple just to be present and not be creating dramatic, delusory scenarios moment after moment. How wonderfully ordinary!

Now I'm not saying that if you don't sense the world and your body every instant that you're a failure. When I read science fiction, for example, I do not try to keep good track of my surroundings. I take the trip. I do my reading, of course, in situations where nothing external is required of me. If there is, like if the telephone is ringing, I am not so immersed in fantasy that I will miss it. There is a skill we need to develop, however, of being present when you are walking around in a world where things happen. There is a skill in being able to be present when you cannot really act adequately just by dealing with the surface level of things as they are manifesting to our ordinary, consensus consciousness, when you have to get deeper into them in some way. Many situations in our lives require more depth, but unless we've developed the capacity to be more present, more mindful, we won't recognize these situations.

And don't forget, there is the important skill of accepting being bored sometimes.

DEALING WITH PHYSICAL PAIN

STUDENT: *I have been unable, for quite a while, to not be out of my body. There's pain in my body: I don't want to be there!*

I don't blame you for wanting out.

STUDENT: *It feels frustrating and ironic to be learning exercises to go into my body, when all I want to do is be out of it. How does this state of enlightenment really help?*

Wait, I am not talking about a state of enlightenment just now. I do not know what enlightenment is. I am talking about being more present, which is more accessible to us.

Now, the method I have been suggesting for being more present is to use the body. But if you have been sick or injured and your body has been a place of pain for a long time, obviously that is not a very attractive course.

Some people who are purists about method, who are devoted to this method, might say that you have to be there in your body anyway, no matter what. There is, actually, an interesting thing about pain: if you get more and more mindfully present to it, it stops being *pain* and becomes something very interesting—it becomes *sensation*.

But that, in my experience and the experience of the people I have talked to, generally happens only when you have the luxury of being able to make the pain the object of formal mindfulness meditation. If you have other things to do in the world, going deeper and more mindfully into the pain does not work. When you are in that state, where you are certainly in your body enough to feel the pain but you do not have the luxury to make it a formal meditation *and* the advanced meditative skill to break the pain up into its vibratory components, that middle ground is awful.

Personally, I hate it. When I am in good health and feeling good, I can speak about how you should always focus on the body the bell is ringing, sense your body sensations, but when I am sick and feeling bad, I certainly like to leave unless, as I say, I have the luxury of making it a formal meditation.

STABILIZING, ANCHORING IN THE HERE AND NOW

Now, as to the deeper-level answer to the issue you're raising—I'm trying to think, do I know a deeper-level answer thoroughly enough to discuss it?—one deeper-level approach to this issue is that there are other methods. Using your body as a tool to be more present is not the only way to be more present or more mindful, nor is it the only way to stabilize.

For example, there are two major consequences of focusing in your body. One is to be more present, more here and now. Because you have more of your attention directed to sensory input, you can more accurately perceive the world around you, which is a great advantage. There are times when you have to do that, even in spite of pain. There are external things you have to be very careful about, whether you are suffering or not. The other major consequence of using part of your attention to focus on the body is the development of the stabilization that I mentioned this morning. Instead of every thought carrying you away, you have an anchor in the here and now through your body.

There are other kinds of anchors available. For example, some people follow a discipline where they subvocally repeat a mantra all the time. A way you can think about this practice is that the mind has got only so much attention available. Let us pretend that you could measure how much attention you have and that there are only a maximum of ten units available at any given moment. If you have nine units of it deliberately focused on something, then the one unit available for other stimuli to catch cannot do much to create mischief in your psychological system. If somebody tells you you are an idiot, but you are so busy saying your mantra internally, it is like water off a duck's back. You don't have enough spare attention available to feel really offended.

So constant use of mantra is another way of stabilizing your mind, with a consequence of reducing suffering. It is an extremely useful technique at times. But I am suspicious of it as a general way to live your life, because there are times when it is really important to know exactly what is happening *now*, because, for example, that truck is going to be around the corner in a second and, if you are not listening to external sounds and seeing external sights but are in a state of great pleasure induced by your mantra repetition, you may get run down! Even if you normally want to stay away from the body because of painful sensations, you do need the skill to get precisely here when you think it is critical.

IMAGINATION, PAIN, KUNDABUFFER

Besides deliberate mantra practice, it is certainly true that spacing out reduces pain. This issue reminds me of a story.

We have heard about the mysterious *kundalini* of yoga, the force that is supposed to be at the base of the spine, which goes up and activates *chakras* and, we hope, brings enlightenment. Gurdjieff said that Westerners actually seriously misunderstand kundalini.[1] According to the understanding that he got from his teachers, the proper name for this energy was kunda*buffer,* not kundalini. Kundabuffer was an "organ" that the higher forces of the universe installed in human beings at a time when life on earth was much worse than it is now (Gurdjieff had a whole seemingly mythical cosmology, which said that our planet had been in the wrong place and had received bad radiation, or something like that) and pain was far, far more common. It was so severe that people were routinely becoming discouraged and dying, which was not very good for the race. Kundabuffer was implanted essentially as a powerful kind of imagination creator, so that people could all the time escape into mental constructions and images, which automatically isolated them in part from their bodies, took them away from the pain, and allowed them to imagine all sorts of things that made them more hopeful. It was first aid, palliative treatment that covered up the pain, because nothing could be done at the time about the real cause.

According to Gurdjieff, the planet is no longer in that bad sector of the galaxy, so we do not need kundabuffer any more. But they forgot to take it out! In fact, it is right now the major hindrance to our genuine growth.

To share my more psychological understanding of this story, we have a power to imagine vividly. That power is a two-edged sword. That power can make things far worse than they are now or it can be the source of our greatest creativity. The kundabuffer process can be used to create unhappiness as well as happiness.

If you are walking down the street and somebody looks at you funny, your imagination picks that up, usually in an automated way. It is not that you *choose* to react to the situation badly. It's machine-like: situation A occurs and reaction B is automatically run. Your imagination then reminds you of your boyfriend or girlfriend rejecting you, which reminds you of all the times you were rejected in childhood, which reminds you of the world situation where nothing is any good, and on and on. From one moment's funny look, that you do not actually know was intended as a rejection of you—the person might have had a moment's pang of indigestion as his head happened to be turned in your direction—your whole day has been spoiled because your imagination tremendously elaborated that look.

Learning to keep checking in with reality can stop that imagination from running wild and inhibit this process of psychological projection. That is the purpose of the basic meditation instructions in vipassana meditation, for instance. You are sitting there, trying to come to your senses, paying attention to your body. You can suddenly discover that your imagination is off and running, that you are mentally off in another galaxy. When you discover it, you try to let imagination go and come back to the body, to your senses, to what is actually happening at this moment in your real physical body and the immediate physical world. It is a process of *dis*identification with the power of the imagination. Using your body to be more mindful in everyday life, as we shall discuss more, has the same effect of keeping you from being carried away.

If you're having physical pain, it might be useful for you to be very present for, say, five seconds at a time, several times each hour, and to be able to do it whenever you want to, but because there is a lot of physical pain, you might choose not to do it all the time. When one has genuine choice, it is really useful.

What else did people notice as you attempted to keep track of your body over the lunch break?

STUDENT: *Quite a bit. Following the directions was not that hard, as I was already in a receptive place. But it's hard to do right now, when I'm talking.*

It is like the mouth is a big hole and consciousness flies right out when it is open. [*General laughter as others recognize the problem from their own experience*]

STUDENT: *The other is . . .*

But you can practice doing it right now. Keep track of your body right now as you talk.

STUDENT: *Oh, yes, I wasn't doing it, was I? The other is that I'm not that sure when I was embodied whether I was really physically embodied or . . .*

Right now, have you noticed a change in the way you're embodied when I reminded you to do it?

STUDENT: *Yes.*

How would you describe it?

STUDENT: *More awareness right back here* [touches parts of body], *and I'm sure my voice has dropped down into my body.*

Yes, I spotted it immediately as your voice changed. Your voice took up much more of your body, whereas before it was kind of isolated up in your head. There was a little, subtle postural change, too. So go on.

STUDENT: *I'm not sure when I was embodied that it was very full. It was kind of a way of being "mentally embodied." I'm not sure I can make this distinction very well.*

BEWARE MY DELUSIONS!

Now I'm a little worried that I've inadvertently confused you. See, I can give you these concepts about being present, but they cannot substitute for what you learn on a deeper level from actually practicing. I should warn you, though: I am slick. I am too much of a *weak yogi,* in Gurdjieff's terms, someone who has got the right words without enough real depth behind them. And I am very persuasive. I can be quite charming and, worse yet, I *believe* what I am saying, so I have some power to mislead you all too easily.

I know I have that power, so I try not to mislead you. I make a concerted effort, for instance, to speak from what I know experientially is most true and not let theories and ideas creep in that I really do not have any feeling for on a deeper level.

Of course, while I recognize that it is good that I try to be careful,

47

I do not know when I slip. I do not know when some charming ideas come out that, in passing, have hypnotized me into believing them. They might not be true. This is a warning: everything I say to you should be taken not as Truth but as stimulation, stimulation to try out in your own investigation of your own reality, if it interests you. Just because I have said something does not mean it is true.

ETERNAL VIGILANCE IS THE PRICE OF FREEDOM

Returning to your observations, your sense of your body will change if you do this body sensing practice that we tried over lunch. But I must warn you of a tricky part.

If you have a particularly good experience one time when you do this, if you feel you are really in your body and really present, your mind will, unfortunately, tend to take that as a standard. It is going to say, Oh, this is what doing it *right* is like, and then start rejecting future experience because it does not feel exactly like standard.

Things are changing in reality, however, all the time. If you move into a mode where you unknowingly want to repeat a former pleasant experience, instead of doing the practice of sensing what is happening now, you are in trouble. As we noted earlier, eternal vigilance is the price of freedom.

While we are touching on that line associated with the American Revolution, you know we have the constitutional right to pursue happiness, but the *pursuit* of happiness is what leads to suffering. We all pursue happiness. You try to arrange the real events in your life—the kind of food you eat, the kind of people you talk to, and so on—so that they are enjoyable. This is a sensible thing to do in certain ways. We get attached to happiness.

But we inevitably run into situations where we cannot arrange the external reality to be just what we want. Then our automatized mind "helps" us. It alters, edits, transforms our perception a little bit here, a little bit there, so that things *seem* better than they are, and that is the beginning of the Fall. So I want to emphasize the difference between staying in touch with reality (and making *reasonable* efforts to arrange things the way you prefer them) versus getting so attached to happiness as conditional on getting desired things and events that your mind starts to trick you. Then it tricks you more and more, and you end up in the state called *samsara*.

SAMSARA: LIVING IN ILLUSION

To most Americans, the concept of samsara, if they've heard of it at all, is a strange, Eastern idea. What do those Easterners mean when they say samsara is living in illusion? Do they mean the world is not real or something like that? That question is not the main point. Whether or not the world is seen as ultimately "real" depends on which Hindu or Buddhist school of philosophy is doing the talking. But what they all emphasize practically is that we reconstruct our world so much and distort our perceptions so much that the *experienced* world we live in is an illusion—a dangerous illusion. Meanwhile, the actual world is whatever it is. But we are often way out of that actual world, and that is the problem, that is what creates useless suffering.

It is funny. Samsara, living in illusion, is an Eastern concept, but curiously, I now think that Western psychology knows more about the details of living in illusion than the East does. For close to a hundred years now we have had work in the fields of experimental psychology, psychiatry, psychotherapy, and the general study of psychopathology that has laid out in exquisite detail quite specific ways in which you can live in illusion. But, on the other hand, these Western disciplines have never put their knowledge together under the concept of living in illusion the way the East has. Our whole Western framework is caught in the belief that there is *normal,* sane consciousness, which all we psychologists possess, of course, and there are these funny, *ab*normal deviations that "patients," people quite different from us, have. So even though we know the mechanisms, the nuts and bolts, as it were, of precisely how samsara is created in many ways, we do not have the concept of samsara connecting them. That is why one of my interests is in creating cooperation and rapprochement between Eastern and Western points of view: they have a lot to teach each other.

What else happened at lunch? Let's have one or two other reports.

WHEN SOMEONE LOOKS AT YOU FUNNY

STUDENT: *I noticed the connection between certain neurotic thoughts, like how I respond to the stray glance . . .*

Well, they *were* looking at you, weren't they? [*General laughter*]

STUDENT: *But then there's the process of how that gets taken from the realm of my thinking it into a feeling about it. It's the feeling that really carries me off. I found that I was able to hold the thought more and notice the thought without being swept away so much into the paranoia, or whatever.*

Again, it is as if we have ten units of attention available. You may be devoting a little bit of attention to sensing the world and some of your thoughts, but when somebody looks at you funny, suddenly 95 percent of your attention is gobbled up by this mental machine that generates paranoid feelings. We do, in a sense, have to do something forceful at times to break the hold of that machine.

Training yourself to be present will do a lot of breaking up of the operation of this automated mental machinery. Just training yourself to keep a little attention in the body and trying to be as accurate about the rest of your external perception as possible will help a lot.

MORALITY IS THE BASIS OF MINDFULNESS

Also, although we do not emphasize it anywhere near enough in the West, this process of spiritual growth that this workshop is all about is based on the premise that you are living a basically decent and moral life. If you are hurting people in a variety of ways, you are creating situations where you are *never* going to get the kind of mental peace that can grow from mindfulness practice. As a Buddhist teacher and friend of mine, Shinzen Young, put it, you can see this as a moral issue or you can see it as a real technical issue: when you have been out stealing and killing all day long, it is hard to settle your mind for meditation at the end of the day.

But never forget that this really is a basic moral issue: we are all vitally interconnected at some spiritual level. To hurt others, consciously or unconsciously, is to hurt your deeper self and block future growth. Your deeper self knows that harming others is wrong.

Your consciousness does not really want to be mindful of itself when it is hurting others, and so it blocks the growth of mindfulness.

STUDENT: *I was feeling a great deal of tension while walking a few blocks at lunchtime. It was in most of my body. The fact that I was fighting it, and wasn't doing any good in my fighting it, just heightened the body effect, the pain I was getting.*

BODILY SENSATION FOR GETTING INTO THE PRESENT

It sounds like your pain was helping you, helping you be more aware.

STUDENT: *Oh, it does, it does make me more aware! But it hurts to pay attention. My neck and shoulders are usually in great pain.*

Let's try something. Close your eyes and focus on experiencing that neck and shoulder pain as fully as possible . . . what happens as you do that? What are your neck and shoulders feeling like right *now?*

STUDENT: *Feeling taut, but not in pain.*

Good! Pay even more attention to that tautness. Close your eyes and focus on it. Experience it as fully as possible.

STUDENT: *I feel a jerkiness in my muscles . . . and . . . [Voice quality changes, volume goes down, voice becomes higher pitched]*

Have you stopped sensing yourself?

STUDENT: *Yes.*

I want you to continue feeling what's going on in your neck and shoulders.

STUDENT: *Umm, quite warm and tingling . . . vibrating . . .*

Yeah, that's it, go on. What's happening at *this* moment?

STUDENT: *The vibration is slowing down.*

Do you feel any tension from my questioning you?

STUDENT: *My hands feel very warm when you talk. As I keep sensing my body I get more relaxed.*

That's good. I'm not going to take time right now to go on working with this—although this kind of personal work is a valuable part of group mindfulness work—but it is an illustration of what we were talking about earlier: sometimes if you go in more deeply into pain there is a certain kind of natural relaxation that takes place. Sensations become more articulated and rich in a useful sort of way, they are not just "pain." It is something to experiment with.

Generally, you can use your body as a way of getting more into the here and now any time by just starting to sense it, but it can often be helpful to have more specialized practices, practices to get you in the mood to do it, to help you overcome mental inertia, to remind you that this is the sort of thing you need to do, as well as having special practices for focusing on body sensations. The musical body exercise that we did earlier is a special technique for getting you fairly deeply into your body, but it is a lengthy technique. It is the sort of thing that you can do perhaps once a week, when you have a half an hour to spare. If you are at work and are tense and frazzled and have only one minute to relax, you cannot take a half hour to play a tape. We need special techniques that do not take such a long period of preparation. We really do not need them in some ultimate sense, but we need them on a practical level.

STARTING YOUR DAY: THE MORNING EXERCISE

The technique I am going to describe now is one Gurdjieff taught. In the formal sense, it is intended to be used in the morning, the first thing after waking. It takes about ten or fifteen minutes to do when you first learn it, but you can get it down to two or three minutes with practice—although it's more satisfying to do it for a longer period when you can. When you are particularly stressed during the day or are finding it really hard to get into *any* kind of contact with your body or the here and now, you can sometimes just close your eyes for a minute and then rapidly do this morning exercise. It refreshes your ability to focus and, of course, it serves as a reminder that you have a more important aim in life than just hurrying along. The *morning exercise,* as it's traditionally called, isn't hard to do, but like most mindfulness techniques, remembering to do it is really the most difficult thing.

Ideally, this is done first thing when you wake up. Most of us, when we wake up, the first thing we focus on is our troubles. What do I have to do? What are my problems? What should I really have done yesterday? Last month? Is it any wonder that we have lots of troubles all day? We get into that trouble mind-set immediately. I do not know if it solves anything to automatically think of your problems first thing in the morning, but it certainly increases your worries.

This exercise isn't only for the first thing in the morning, of course. You can do it at any time to settle yourself and increase your contact with the present moment. I've often called it the *priming exercise,* an analogy with priming the pump to get it going. Here, you are priming your purpose and sense of contact.

The first step in the morning exercise, as I teach it, varies for people. If you are the kind of person who can hardly remain conscious until you have had your first cup of coffee, you might have to have that first cup of coffee before doing the exercise. On the other hand, if you are a person who is in a full worry fit within three seconds of opening your eyes, you have to do this before you start your worry fit. The point is to do this before you put on your ordinary personality, before you start your ordinary set of worries, preoccupations, plans, and concerns.

This practice is like the musical body in some ways. You systematically go through your body, but the pattern is somewhat different and is slightly simplified. It is a way of sensitizing yourself to the facts that (1) you have a body; (2) you have a body not only in the sense of some kind of *concept* about having a body but also in the sense of actually feeling your body, getting real, direct contact with it; and (3) it is also psychologically very symbolic, because to do this it means that you consider your deeper self important enough to take ten quiet minutes with yourself at the start of the day.

I find that a lot of people resist doing the morning exercise for that last reason. Their self concept is so poor that they think it is not right to take ten minutes just for themselves. Well, a little hedonism is all right—take ten minutes to be with yourself.

You can do this exercise sitting up. You can do it in some formal meditation posture. If you are the type who is quite sleepy and is going to fall asleep again, certainly do not do it lying down. You can do it sitting up in bed if you are reasonably awake so that you do not just drift off.

GUIDANCE FOR THE MORNING EXERCISE

Now let's do it. You take a moment to settle into your position, close your eyes, and take a moment to relax. I'll guide you through the morning exercise now.[2]

(Reader, you can get a lot out of reading this exercise *slowly* and doing it, even though your eyes are open.)

Focus your attention into your right foot. I want you to open your mind to whatever sensations there are in your right foot at *this* moment . . . and *this* moment . . . and this *moment*.

There is no sensation in particular that you should look for or try to make happen. Whatever is there is what you focus on. It might be numb, as if nothing is there. It might tingle. It might be warm or cold. It could be painful or neutral or pleasant. Whatever you experience in your right foot moment by moment is fine. Just open your mind to sense as openly and clearly as possible whatever is there.

I want you to *savor* the sensations in your right foot. It is as if a dear friend gave you a glass of wine or something special he or she had cooked and said, "Really taste this, it's special and subtle." You would just want to suspend your thinking and expectations, open up your senses and *grok*—to use a seventies word from Robert Heinlein's novel *Stranger in a Strange Land* many of you probably remember— the sensation. So just grok your right foot, just be open to whatever sensation is there.[3]

Now move your attention to the lower half of your right leg. You can let your deliberate focus on the foot go. You do not have to reject the foot, but just focus on sensing whatever is in the lower half of your right leg now. If you drift off into thinking about things, just come back to sensing whatever the sensation is there now.

(When you are doing this on your own, the guiding principle is to spend a few seconds on each of these body parts just sensing them, a few seconds after you have gotten good contact, then move on to the next part.)

Now move up into the knee and the upper half of your right leg and sense whatever sensations are there.

Now move your focus up to your right hand and open your mind to sensing whatever is happening in your right hand.

Now sense your right forearm and whatever sensation or pattern of sensations is happening there. Whatever is there, just sense it.

Now sense, grok, savor whatever you experience in the upper half of your right arm. Remember there are no right or wrong sensations, just sense whatever is happening moment by moment. Sense, don't think about, sense.

Move your attention across your body now to the upper half of your left arm and sense whatever is there.

Now down through your elbow to the lower half of your left arm.

Now sense whatever is happening in your left hand. While you are focusing on these various parts, it does not matter if sensations from other parts of your body come in. Neither grasp them nor reject them nor get totally lost in them. Just focus on the designated part.

Now the left hand and fingers.

Now move your attention down to the upper half of your left leg. Sense whatever is happening there.

Now move your attention down to the lower half of your left leg.

Now move your attention down into your left foot.

Now I want you to widen your focus of attention to sense both feet and both halves of your lower legs . . . and both halves of your upper legs, simultaneously. Sense your legs, including the feet.

Now I want you to widen your focus even more, and while still continuing to sense your legs and feet, sense your arms and hands at the same time, so you are sensing your arms and legs, hands and feet all at once.

Now while continuing to sense your arms and legs, I want you to add in *actively* listening to whatever sounds there are.

Hearing is a more dominant sense than feeling, and so more of your attention may go to hearing than sensing, but I want you to listen and sense your arms and legs simultaneously. *Really* listen in the sense that you are open to hear whatever sounds are actually audible at each moment. There is nothing special you need to hear or any special way of hearing it, just listen and sense your arms and legs.

This listening while sensing your arms and legs (or your whole body) can be a valuable formal meditation in and of itself, but we'll just do it for half a minute or so as part of the morning exercise.

Now, in a moment I am going to ask you to expand your field of attention a little wider and slowly open your eyes, while simultaneously continuing to listen actively to whatever sounds there are, and to feel your arms and legs.

Vision is our dominant sense, so looking will take most of your attention. It is like putting 50 or 60 percent of your attention in vision, maybe 30 percent in hearing, and 10 percent or so in sensing the sensations in your arms and legs.

Slowly open your eyes now, while continuing to sense your arms and legs and to listen actively to whatever sounds there are.

Now, with your eyes open, I want you to look *actively* at things. That is, I want no blank-eyed stares at anything, because looking fixedly at something is quite hypnotic. I want you to actively, curiously look at something for a few seconds and then shift your eyes to something else for a few seconds.

I like to humorously call this the "shifty-eyed technique." It is necessary when you are beginning to practice. There is something that fogs over your mind when you look too long at any one thing. Actually *look,* don't just park your eyes in a certain direction. Actually look at something, and then move on to something else in a few seconds.

BEING PRESENT: SENSING, LOOKING, AND LISTENING

[*Workshop participants are now quietly and attentively looking about the Rigpa Fellowship shrine room. There is a subtle quality in the room, which must be experienced to be understood.*]

You are in your bodies now, you are sensing the pattern of sensations in your arms and legs. And you are also hearing, actively listening to whatever sounds are happening from moment to moment, including my voice. You are actively looking at various objects, taking them in, like a curious child, looking with *beginner's mind,* like seeing some things for the first time.

All of you are practicing a quiet, yet powerful, mindfulness technique, one descriptively called *sensing, looking, and listening.* It is a technique that Gurdjieff spoke about as *self-remembering.* It is a way of being consciously present to the moment by (1) using your kinesthetic senses, (2) actually listening to things, (3) looking at things, and also by (4) simultaneously making the *small effort of will it takes to keep your attention deliberately divided.* This fourth point is very important. You never let all your attention go into listening or just into seeing, but keep it divided, just a little bit in touch with your body sensations, the arms and legs, looking actively, listening actively. Sensing, looking, and listening is a way of being *present*.

Just as in sitting meditation, if you suddenly find you have gotten caught up in some chain of thought and you have effectively left this world behind, just come back. Skip the guilt part and just come back to looking, listening, and keeping track of your arms and legs.

You have gone through the morning exercise, the priming exercise, and you are now doing the main practice in Gurdjieff work, sensing, looking, and listening. You are actively, although not strenuously, being present to the immediate world around you. The particulars of the immediate world will, of course, usually change from moment to moment to moment. At other times it will seem to just sit there in an apparently boringly still way, until you look more closely, until you become more attentive and present.

Would anyone care to share what effects on your consciousness that doing this is having?

INITIAL EXPERIENCES WITH SENSING, LOOKING, AND LISTENING

STUDENT: *I was very tense and anxious before we started doing this. I'm often that way. But now I can't seem to find my anxiety!*

You lost your anxiety? I'm sorry. Maybe you will find it again somewhere else. It is hard to be anxious and pay attention to the real world around you at the same time. That's good.

STUDENT: *It makes me aware of how, in some way, I like being carried away by thoughts and emotions.*

That's a good insight.

STUDENT: *I like it, being carried away by strong emotions. But doing this practice, it's like it will be in a really altered state of consciousness, very strongly at times.*

Will be?

STUDENT: *Is.*

Good. I like descriptions in the present. If we spoke more while being in the present, about what we are experiencing in the present, it would be quite amazing how much more we would stay in it.

In what way is doing this exercise an altered state?

STUDENT: *It is like being balanced, balanced between things. Which is a very rare way of being for me.*

Yes, that can be one of its qualities.

I am trying to encourage you to discover the qualities arising from this practice for yourself. I do not want to program in artificial experiences, nor do I want this sensing, looking, and listening to degenerate into some kind of quasihypnotic technique to try to shape people up. This is a *discovery* technique, as well as a staying-present technique.

What else are people noticing?

STUDENT: *I feel a kind of, uh, I want to say edginess, kind of like moving from each of these three realms. Not edginess—there's no room for thinking, because tension is just taken and it's kind of peaceful, the bell is sounding now, maybe it's alertness, some kind of alertness, and there's something a little bit exciting about it.*

Yes, it is exciting to be alive.

STUDENT: *Calmer.*

Calmly exciting, yes. Doing this practice is not conducive to hysteria, but it has its own emotional quality.

What else are people noticing?

STUDENT: *When you started doing the exercise and I started focusing on the different body parts, I became aware of being thirsty. Instead of, uh, I had an* urgent *thought that I had to quench my thirst, that I had to make myself comfortable.*

And then I thought that maybe that's just an idea that I had, that I needed water or something, so I focused on the sensations that I had in my throat and my mouth. And so I alternated between focusing on these sensations and focusing on the body parts that we were going through. It got clear that I didn't have to do something about this thirst, I could just observe it.

THE POWER OF IDENTIFICATION

This is a good time to give you another exercise. I do not usually piggyback these two on top of one another, but this will be a little experiment to see how it works.

I want you to keep up this sensing, looking, and listening all through this. Sit or stand somewhere so that you can see this cup. [*Puts paper coffee cup down in middle of floor.*] It should be in your visual field.

One of the most important psychological processes is *identification,* that is, giving our essence, our energy, our power to something. To show you how readily this can be done, I want you to identify with this cup. I want you to look at it and feel that the cup is a part of you. Just let go of the barriers between you and the cup, just let your energy flow into the cup, just be one with the cup. Allow your mind to flow into it.

[*CTT suddenly stamps on the cup, smashing it.*]

Did anyone feel any pain? [*Many people raise their hands.*] Yes, good, you've learned something for the very small cost of a moment's pain.

It is incredibly easy for us to give psychological power away. I have had people gasp loudly and jump when I have done this exercise with them. Think about it for a moment.

It is really a silly little exercise. This cup was not something precious like, say, the gift your loved one had given you on your anniversary. We did not go through a prolonged hypnotic induction or meditative exercise. I hardly spent thirty seconds asking you to just identify with the cup, and yet many of you felt pain when I suddenly stepped on it. You suffered. You identified.

This process of psychological identification is something that can get turned on and off almost instantly, a process that gives great power to whatever you identify with. Identification can be applied to *anything.* If this contrived exercise was powerful, suppose that we were standing beside your car, I had a hammer in my hand, and I hit *your* car? Or your precious whatever?

The worst thing about identification is that it is usually an involuntary, unconscious process. Our life histories and our cultural programming have set up all these automatic connections to things that we identify with automatically. Some people identify with their clothes, for example. If someone says, "Oh, I saw one just like that at the secondhand shop the other day," you can really be hurt by what is basically a purely mythological construction. You identify with something that is not really you, and when something happens to it, you are hurt.

When someone in our group reported being thirsty, it sounded as if, at first, he instantly identified with it: *I am thirsty. I really have to have a drink.* When he said that, it resonated in me and I felt a sudden thirst. I was really thirsty! Then I began to think about how that could lead into the cup identification exercise and I forgot all about being thirsty. Identification can go, as well as come, almost instantly if the situation changes, but while it is there, identification sucks up your energy, makes you psychologically vulnerable, and makes you crazy, in a sense. You will suffer over purely symbolic kinds of actions. *My* country, *my* flag, *my* religion, *my* this, that, and the other thing.

(Reader, are you remembering to sense, look, and listen as you read on? For most of us it's hard, but see if you can keep at least a little *voluntary* awareness of at least some parts of your body as we go on.)

SITTING MEDITATION AS DISIDENTIFICATION

One way you can view the process of formal meditation, one way it can be understood psychologically, is as trying to practice *disidentification*. When you do formal vipassana meditation, for example, you are told to just watch whatever comes up—sensations, thoughts, and emotions—with equanimity, without following after them, without analyzing them, without craving after some and rejecting others. You are practicing disidentification.

If you are meditating, for example, and thirst comes up, and if you are good at vipassana-type meditation, then it is seen for what it is, a particular pattern of sensations, with the label *thirst* being secondary to the basic experience. The varying sensations come and go. And that's that. That's the reality. That's all. The label *thirsty* may come up, and it is observed for what it is, a thought, and it too passes. The label *I* may come up, and it is observed for what it is, a thought, a concept, and it too passes.

In our ordinary state of mind, multitudes of things come up, and things we are conditioned to identify with automatically grab all or most of our attention and energy, so we live mainly in a mental/

emotional world. These things we identify with often have very strong emotions connected with them, and so we suffer a great deal over things that are not genuinely painful, don't actually involve the neural firing of a pain nerve, but that are artificial, like the smashing of the paper cup.

The self-remembering practice of sensing, looking, and listening is also a process of training in disidentification. Instead of letting yourself be captured by whatever situation happens to come along and grabs your attention, by resolving to keep a little of your attention in your body, to look attentively at things as they come, and to listen attentively to the quality of sounds as they come, it is not so easy for things to grab you up. It is not so easy for samsara to be activated. I do not know that samsara has anything to do with the external world: samsara has to do with our constructions and projections and delusions and identifications about the world. When those things run unchecked, samsara is the reality you live in.

I want to hear what else people are noticing from doing this exercise. I also want you to continue doing this exercise for the rest of the day. That is important. Do it forever, actually, but I know I can't yet require that of you.

STUDENT: *When I did the exercise I felt more like a little child, which I haven't felt in a long time. I mean like more innocent, looking at things, filled with the ecstasy that a child looks at things with. Looking at things like they are, looking without judging and without analyzing it. So it feels like a lot of freedom.*

BEFORE THE FALL: THE VIVIDNESS OF CHILDHOOD

Yes, that's a very good observation.

Do some of you know William Wordsworth's poem, "Intimations of Immortality"?

> There was a time when meadow, grove, and stream
> The earth and every common sight
> To me did seem
> Appareled in celestial light,
> The glory and the freshness of a dream.

Then he switches to adult perspective.

> It is not now as it hath been of yore.
> Turn whereso'ere I may,
> By night or day,
> The light which I have seen
> I now can see no more.

Part of the process of growing up, of becoming "normal," is that the light is squeezed out. The freshness of perception, the "nutrition value" of sensation is eroded away. After all, it is childish to enjoy walking around outside, actually pausing to really look at and smell the roses: We adults have *important* things to do! There is a systematic denial as you get older of those simple sensory pleasures. You are a career woman, aren't you? You don't have time to stop and look at the roses. You have your briefcase and you have to get to the office so you can be as involved as men are in the artificial world.

THE LOSS OF OUR DEEP SELF

It is not only that we get less and less reinforcement for really enjoying our perceptions, being present to the here and now, but also that we are expected to deliberately stop being sensual creatures who really enjoy sensations. So-called normal development frequently involves many processes whereby we get further and further confused about what is real and important and, on top of confusion, we are frequently made to feel guilty about enjoying simple pleasures. We are all neurotics, to some degree, because we have been confused about what it is we actually feel.

We grow up in a very strange and tragic situation. We come into this world with the heritage of our true *buddha-nature,* our primordial purity. This heritage gets buried very fast. As infants, we don't know much of anything and we can't do anything. Along come a "god" and a "goddess." I think that is the only appropriate way to describe the relationship between infants and their parents. The difference in their powers and knowledge compared to ours as infants is so enormous that they seem to know everything. They have incredible powers.

You, the infant, naturally love them. I think that is part of our biological makeup, our basic nature as human beings. You love your parents. It does not matter if they are the worst people in the world, not worthy to be alive, much less be parents. You are preprogrammed to love them. They are your model for gods and goddesses, for what normal adults are like. Your very survival, your life, depends on pleasing them.

We start modeling ourselves on them, and they tell us what reality is. You may say, for example, "I don't like Uncle Jack. He does nasty things to me." Your parent says, "Oh, that's just your imagination. My brother Jack is a very nice man. He loves you." Your experience with Uncle Jack, however, is that he is not a nice man. There's something scary and strange about what he does with you when you're alone with him, something you don't really want to talk about. But one or both of your parents, who know so much and are all-powerful, say that he is a nice man. You start getting confused.

There are an enormous number of these contradictions, not all so dramatic, occurring in the growing-up processes. Our experienced realities, which are indeed based on more limited knowledge than our parents have but which are a lot of times quite instinctually accurate, are denied. They are often denied in quite psychopathological kinds of ways, so we have conspiracies of silence in the family, areas that are taboo, and things like that. We grow up unsure about whether or not we can trust our own feelings. We grow up having suppressed a lot of feelings, because "good girls don't feel that," or "good boys don't think like that." Often this process is combined with conditioning that undermines our sense of self-worth, and so we feel unworthy or guilty all the time. We feel we are only existing conditionally. We have no inherent right to exist, we have to be earning approval all the time: we have got to be good. And maybe nothing we do is ever good enough.

ESSENCE AND FALSE PERSONALITY

Gurdjieff talked about this situation very specifically, and modern psychology has added a lot to our understanding of the details of this enculturation process. He said the way we are when we are born could be called our *essence*. It is what is essentially ours, our personal as well as our transpersonal inheritance. But as we grow up, essence is suppressed more and more and its energy is stolen to nourish and grow *false personality*. What we ordinarily call *personality* he called false personality, because by and large, it is not of our choosing. It was forced on us by people and circumstances far more powerful than we were. It is ours in some sense, because we struggle and compromise with the forces trying to shape us, trying to preserve some of our essence, but a lot of what we think of as our personality as adults is not at all our natural essence. It is what we were forced into.

There is an unorthodox form of psychotherapy that I went through years ago in one of Claudio Naranjo's groups. It was still in an experimental phase and was then called Fisher-Hoffman Therapy.[4] It has changed a lot, but originally you started out in it by making long lists about what you did not like about yourself, all your shortcomings, your negative traits and characteristics. You put these lists away for a while. Later on, when you were working on your parents, you made lists of all your mother's shortcomings and your father's shortcomings. Later in the therapy came a very shocking session where you compared these parent lists with your own lists and discovered that something like 95 percent of what you did not like about yourself was either a direct incorporation of parental traits, of being just like your parents, or a direct reaction formation, being just the exact opposition of a parent. If you're being the exact opposite to a parental trait, you are still being controlled by it, as much as if you adopted it outright. When you see this, your sense of originality receives a real shock.

We are shaped tremendously as infants and children. Essence gradually loses its natural energy, shrinks, and goes underground, and false personality grows, dominates, and gets almost all the energy. Most people do not know about the falseness of their ordinary personality, except as a sense of unease, a sense that *something* is not right or authentic. They may experience this unease later in life as the popular midlife crisis: you are a successful lawyer and, when you turn fifty, you suddenly realize, I don't like being a lawyer! I never liked being a lawyer! I did this for my parents—it's not me! There are many variations of this midlife crisis scenario, unpleasant enough that many people turn to the bottle or get a lifetime tranquilizer prescription or become workaholics—anything to avoid facing the thought that they have lived a terribly inauthentic life.

Part of the purpose of trying to awaken, of becoming more mindful, is to start to see yourself more clearly and understand your psychological machinery—all the automatic reactions that are running your life. Then, as you start to be able to disidentify with the machinery, you start to see its parts even more clearly. Eventually you start to discriminate more finely, noticing, say, Yes, this part is a very deep part of me; this other part is false; it was grafted onto me by force of circumstances and psychological pressure. Or you realize, This sounds like my mother's voice speaking in my head, not mine! The bell has sounded. If you become really successful at this practice, false personality gradually weakens and "dies," loses its automatic grip, and essence grows.

That is a tricky process. After you start making discriminations between your essence, or deeper self, versus your false personality, you then have to reparent yourself. You have to take these parts that were suppressed while you were still a child, that are often very tender—they are down there somewhere, even now, deeply protected—and you have to draw them out gradually, nourish them, encourage them. Then you can become what *you* really want to be, which may be (but is not always) very different from what you have been most of your life.

DON'T KILL YOUR EGO!

A dramatic way of saying it is that false personality dies. Saying it this way has drawbacks, though, because it sounds too destructive. We have too much conditioned hostility toward ourselves already without adding to it. In the seventies, most people on a spiritual path were trying to kill their egos. It is not as if you kill false personality, but rather that (1) you get enough sense of who your deeper, inner self is and (2) you develop enough mindfulness and focus to put the energy back into your essential self. Then all the parts that made up your false personality do not automatically take you over any more. If you are an attorney and you discover this is not your essence, you may go and do what you really like to do. But if you ever have to function as an attorney, you will be able to function very well. All the skill and knowledge is still there, but it no longer automatically sucks you in.

Let's move back to being more experiential now. We've been rather heady and conceptual for too long.

FIRST INTERPERSONAL EXERCISE: SHOWING YOUR HAND

For the next exercise, pick a partner, preferably someone you do not know well, and sit beside her or him.

You are going to play a role in this exercise, a role that is quite artificial, of course, but it is going to make you more genuine: it is going to be used as a tool to increase your mindfulness.

Continue to sense your arms and legs, continue to listen to the quality of sounds, and remember not to stare fixedly at something so that you trance out, but look around every few seconds.

Choose who the A partner is and who the B partner is. OK. The job of the B partner for the next few minutes is to remain completely present, looking, listening, sensing your body, and sitting completely still. You, B, are not to give any kind of feedback, make any kind of comment, or make any body movements or facial expressions in working with A. Your job is to sit still and be very aware of what your partner is doing. Don't stare fixedly into your partner's eyes, but rather, look around a little bit.

The A partner's job is to show the B partner your hand, to show it in various ways. And, of course, you have to sense, look, and listen, too, being very aware of what you are doing. Stay with your senses.

Thoughts and emotional feelings will come. Be aware of them when they do, but do not encourage them or get carried away with them. Nor should you fight them. Just keep coming back to your sensing. Stay in the present.

[*People do this for five minutes, A showing B his or her hand in various ways, with occasional reminders from CTT to stay present by sensing their arms and legs, actively listening, and actively looking. After five minutes A and B switch roles.*]

(Reader, I recommend finding a partner or partners interested in learning the sensing, looking, and listening procedure and then doing these exercises.)

Now stay present while I give you some new instructions.

The A partner is now going to become the witness, as it were, and stay present and fully aware without reacting, and the B partner is going to talk. The topic of the monologue is going to be somewhat specialized. What you are to do *continuously,* with no long pauses, is describe what you are experiencing *in that very instant.* That is sometimes a little scary to some people: Suppose I experience something unacceptable or embarrassing? If what you are experiencing is so socially embarrassing that you would die to say it, then say you are censoring. As long as you continue to censor, just say, "I am censoring." Otherwise, talk about what happens in the now. If it's not that embarrassing, say it anyway.

I'll do this for you to illustrate what I mean.

Now I feel my right shoulder blade lifting up from the tension in my arm. Now I feel like that is a stupid thing I just said. Now I notice tension at the back of my neck. Now I notice I am swaying on my feet.

I made a point of saying "now" at the beginning of each sentence to emphasize that you stay in the present, but you don't have to say "now" as long as you remain in the now.

The B partner has to stay in the present in order to describe what he or she is experiencing in the present. Do not go off on associations. Do not say, for example, "Now I feel the tension in my shoulder blade and that reminds me of the time I hurt my shoulder back in '82 in a gray Chevy." Keep your monologue in the present.

Remember, the witnessing partner is to give no feedback of any sort. No nods, no smiles, no words. This inhibition of feedback is very important.

Go ahead, do it.

[*People do this for five minutes, B continuously describing her or his experience moment by moment, with occasional reminders from CTT to stay present by sensing their arms and legs, actively listening, actively looking. After five minutes A and B switch roles.*]

ANOTHER INTERPERSONAL EXERCISE: DESCRIBING AND LYING

Here are some new instructions. If this is an embarrassing or awful exercise for you, I want you to sense and fully appreciate its embarrassment and awfulness as sharply as possible.

For the next part of these exercises, the A partner does a running monologue on what he or she is sensing here and now, while remaining present to the body, except that I want approximately one third of your statements about what you are experiencing to be lies. I want you to say, for example, that you are itching when you do not itch.

I want them to be good lies. I want you to be present; I want you to lie; I want you to be convincing in your lying and to be very aware of what you are doing. Of course, the witness, B, is also very present, taking it all in but not giving any feedback whatsoever.

[*This exercise goes on for about five minutes with occasional reminders from CTT, as before, to sense, look and listen. Then the partners switch roles.*]

Now end the exercise with your partner in a way that seems appropriate, and be present while you do so.

[*Some pairs explain things to each other. Some hug. Much tension is released, with accompanying mindfulness, we hope.*]

Let's take a break now.

THREE

DEEPENING PRACTICE

LET'S REFLECT on this series of exercises.
I noticed that during the break a lot of excited contact and socializing resulted from these little exercises. That was the short form of these exercises. I've sometimes had people get married as a result of the deep contact that can result from the long form of them!

These simple exercises can actually be very powerful, because our implicit social contract is, by and large, to never pay real attention to each other. When we do, even in the course of a simple exercise, it is very interesting. Also, it is very good to get genuine attention from somebody, especially if you are not so needy and asleep that you have to drum up a better-to-beat-me-than-ignore-me sort of attention. We've discussed that earlier under the idea of the food of attention.

I would like to suggest that you continue to sense, look, and listen through the rest of the day. Do it while you ask questions, while you listen to others ask questions, while you listen to me. And remember this "shifty-eyed" trick. I don't know what the mechanism is exactly, but it's very hard to stay present when your vision is fixed—it spaces you out real easily.

SECURITY FROM DISCOVERING WHO YOU REALLY ARE

STUDENT: *When you talked about attachment to someone's looks and gestures, their reactions to you, and going off in the drama of what that means, I realized that most feelings of approval that I've experienced in my life have come exactly from that, from my attachment to someone's reactions to me. I live in a drama of getting approval. Therefore I am OK, I'm somehow being successful in the social sense when I am getting a certain kind of reaction. What I feel is that if I'm not getting or giving approval, the exercise creates a vacuum, it's very unpleasant. I'm trapped in needing that approval.*

Samsara is really awful. The enculturation process for most of us knocks out our natural, essential sense of self-worth, so that we desperately need approval from other people. Although we do have certain natural instincts of wanting to be liked and approved of, the more our essential self-worth tends to be buried and diminished, the more desperate we are for approval from other people at any cost. Our social instinct is enslaved, its natural functioning becomes distorted and pathological.

You can learn to disidentify with those needs, as in formal meditation—and sensing, looking, and listening will also do that to a large extent.

Meditation is an excellent practice, but it is not the whole story. There is a way in which meditation can be misused to become a sort of nonchemical tranquilizer. A lot of people implicitly see it that way: "I've been hurt, so I'm going to learn this meditation stuff, which is my way of numbing myself out." It is Buddha as that mythical American folk idol, Joe Cool: "Nothing will make me feel any suffering or show any reaction, I'm above it all, I won't even feel anything. I'm cool!"

The other side of formal meditation practice and of sensing, looking, and listening, this form of self-remembering practice, is that as you discover your own essence and begin to bring it out there is a basic security that develops. There is a basic liking of yourself that slowly grows, a basic, essential confidence.

I almost said *self*-confidence, but I deliberately did not. It is not a confidence in your ordinary self so much but rather a confidence in something much greater than your ordinary self. All these elements we have spoken of so far—disidentification, greater ability to focus, self-remembering—can combine to put you on a much more secure footing, so that you do not have to desperately get approval from people. Then you can be genuinely nice to people—or firm when it's needed—without getting so caught up in the need for approval.

Now I am interested in getting technical questions about how to do this self-remembering practice. I want to be sure you have a good understanding of what to do before our initial day ends. You do have a homework assignment to keep doing this. Your experience with sensing, looking, and listening in your ordinary life will be the main material we work with Monday night.

PRACTICAL ADAPTATION OF MINDFULNESS TO LIFE

STUDENT: *Could you say something about whether it would be more helpful to concentrate on doing this at certain times of the day or all day long? For instance, I'm a nurse. Once I get into the mode of being a nurse at work and the work becomes intense, sometimes it's pretty hard to sense myself.*[1]

That's a good observation. Ideally, one should do this practice all the time. In practice, we accommodate to our real situations.

There are some situations that simply require too much of you. If you are busy getting out of the way of a truck, don't stop to wonder, Am I sensing my arms and legs properly before I jump, so I can do this really mindfully? If you are in situations that are so stressful that you are failing repeatedly at being mindful, it is all right to say, It is too hard for me to do it in this situation right now, so I am not going to try now. I emphasize *now* in that kind of statement, as there's no point in programming yourself to reinforce your current limits.

I do not want my injunction to sense, look, and listen all the time to go to your superego. If you have a harsh superego, and many of us do, it says that you should be able to do this perfectly all the time, and if you don't, you are a total shit. We get enough of that kind of thing from our superegos already.

A note on the meaning of the term superego: it's a term so widely used that we tend to lose track of its exact meaning. The concept of the superego was introduced by Freud to refer to that automatized part of our mind that incorporated parental and social ideas of what was right and what was wrong, and which, in a mechanical kind of way, watches and judges our thoughts, feelings, and actions. When we do, or even think about doing, something that isn't up to its standards, the superego mechanism make us feel guilty. In extreme cases, it can create so much guilt over such a long period of time that people will commit suicide. It's policeman, judge, jury, and executioner all in one automatic mechanism. It's conditioned morality.

You may, in doing this practice, see aspects of yourself that you do not like, but you will also have a lot of very nice things happen, and I want those to happen in some balance. The practice should not become so difficult that we have constant failure experiences and so give up on it. So yes, you can make this realistic adjustment.

SPECIAL DIFFICULTIES FOR INTELLECTUALS

STUDENT: *Do you have some tricks of the trade to help those of us who are always caught in heavy-duty intellectual stuff or who work at a very intellectual job all day long?*

Ouch! I understand the problem all too well! I once wrote an article on the phenomenology of my meditation experiences while sitting in front of my computer, typing it out, which I thought was quite something, but I the bell rings now—Wow! This random bell has certainly caught me in some weird and embarrassing facial expressions! [*Laughter*] May it be the worst of my suffering! Anyway, as I was saying, I had to switch back and forth between being caught up in doing the typing on the computer and meditation. It is hard to practice any kind of mindfulness of your world and body and psychological state when engaged in intellectual activity, especially when you are first trying to learn it.

I would say to do the sensing practice at least intermittently. Work for ten minutes and try to remember to then come up for air for thirty seconds, to be present to your real world and real body.

It is quite hard to do this practice continuously. Talking is generally the most difficult situation of all for doing it. That is what most people find. It is very hard to talk and do this practice at the same time, but it can be done. This whole workshop, for example, is intense practice for me to try to maintain some degree of presence when I'm up here talking almost all the time.

SOCIAL SUPPORT OR INVALIDATION FOR MINDFULNESS

It also helps a lot to have social support. Many of you will probably find that you can do sensing better—it will feel more vivid and you will do it more often—when we are meeting together than when you are out in ordinary life. There are no reminders out there and no social approval for it. The stream of ordinary life is biased toward mind*lessness*. You do not need any mindfulness to be a good consumer, and there is no reward for it. Mindful consumers are probably dangerous to the gross national product.

There is also the social contract we implicitly live under. Most of us are asleep, are relatively mindless, are living in our waking dreams because that was the best we could do to protect against suffering, against the mindless assault on our essence when we were children. Someone who begins to show some signs of awakening can be very disturbing to people who are still heavily defended and deeply asleep.

Remember the story of the emperor's new clothes? There are some people who are very disturbed, they are suffering a lot living in their personal version of samsara, their waking dreams, but when they see someone who appears to be more present, more alert, and actually noticing things, they are threatened. Your mindfulness might be contagious, might threaten to lift the repression and the deadening that keeps their particular form of samsara going.

So don't run around to your friends telling them, "Hey! You're asleep! Wake up! I'm going to shape you up!"

If you do it that blatantly, you'll be little or no threat to them at all, of course. They just put you in the nut category and no longer pay any attention. But there are some people who are disturbed when they see someone who seems to be really present and noticing things.

In our temporary group now you have other people around who you know are trying like you to become more mindful. They remind you of your purpose. I am frequently reminding you. This is a special situation. Ultimately you want to be able to do it as part of everyday life, because that is where we live. Do not be surprised, however, if it is harder to do when you are at work or at home.

SEEK TRUTH, NOT PLEASURE

STUDENT: *I'm not sure if the kind of thing we've done today will help with the kind of problem I have, with trying to be aware in daily life, which would be to . . .*

Remember to sense your arms and legs now, while you're talking—it doesn't sound like you're doing it.

STUDENT: *Yes. Thank you.* [Pauses a moment to recenter] *Anyway, a broader kind of awareness, when I try to teach this to myself what I have done is try to focus on one thing at a time . . .*

That's good, you're staying with the present now, keep it up.

STUDENT: *But it has been a real problem. I have a little system for myself for when I'm driving, using memory . . .*

Wait, let me stop you at this point before you reinforce this belief in your difficulties. We are all geniuses at convincing ourselves that we will *not* be able to do something, and therefore, we do not try it or only try it half-heartedly. Then, sure enough, we are right. It does not work. Try being aware in your daily life. Do not convince yourself ahead of time that it will not work.

STUDENT: *But what I want to know is whether there is something special that makes people lose the fulfillment, the joy of being present. Like when I would become mindful that I am driving this car, I have my hands on the wheel, sense where my back is, sense where my feet are, it's great. Then I put the car into the shop and the mechanic said, "Was there anything in particular wrong with it?" and I said, "Oh no, it's just a regular checkup." Then he called me and said, "Do you want me to fix this stuff, this shaking that the car does?" And I said, "What shaking?" I just space out in this kind of situation, I lose it. The thrill of being there, as when I'm driving and being mindful, gets lost. What can I do?*

Go for *truth*, not for pleasure. When you are driving your car and really into being mindful about it, so that it becomes pleasurable, there will be a temptation to think, This is the Zen of driving! I am always going to feel good as I sense my feet and turn the wheel! That is not trying to pay attention to what *is*, that is trying to prolong or re-induce a special, pleasurable state. If the state or pleasure comes by itself, that is fine, but if you try to induce it, you are no longer seeking the truth; you are seeking pleasure. If you are seeking pleasure more than truth, you are running the risk of distorting your perceptions.

WE WILL MAKE MISTAKES

Doing this process does not mean that we all become Superwoman or Superman, with X-ray vision and super hearing. We will still make mistakes, we are still human, but we will probably eventually notice that we make fewer mistakes.

As an example, just about every time I physically hurt myself, it is quite clear a second later—which is too late, of course—that I was not being present. There used to be a humorous sign they had in some factories that said, as nearly as I remember it, "Put brain in gear before engaging machinery." It applies to our physical bodies. When we move our physical bodies but are thinking about other things, we tend to hurt ourselves. I do not think I have ever hurt myself when I have been paying attention to what I am doing.

DAYDREAMING ABOUT BEING PRESENT IS NOT BEING PRESENT

A warning here. You can *daydream* about being present. I do it all the time. I first read about this sensing technique in a book by Gurdjieff's best-known student, P. D. Ouspensky, back in 1964. When I was about halfway through the book, I suddenly finally got the idea of coming to the present in my senses and *I did it*. In retrospect I can say I had a mini-awakening right then and there. Relatively speaking, I awakened!

I told people about it, I discussed it, and I continued reading the book, but three months later I realized that after my one second of mini-awakening I went right back to sleep and daydreamed about the process from that point on. You can easily daydream about what it is like to be more mindful or to awaken, about what you believe you should be feeling, and talk yourself into thinking you are. That is why in properly doing this process you keep coming back to sensing what are my arms and legs *actually* feeling *now*, what am I *actually* seeing with my eyes *now*, and what are the *actual* sounds I hear *now*. Those things are in the present, they are real. This technique interferes with the tendency to daydream about self and world instead of actually perceiving them. I have, unfortunately, had a lot of daydreams about being present and what it means. Understanding this and personally perceiving your tendency to substitute daydreaming for real perception is, of course, an important part of the learning process.

Boy, I've had so many wonderful daydreams about being present!

DEALING WITH INFURIATING IDIOTS

STUDENT: *Can you talk about being mindful at times when you find that you're emotionally reacting to someone or someone's emotional reactions are directed at you?*

Like, say, when you want to kill that idiot?

STUDENT: *Yes! Those are the ones I really have trouble with.*

It's not at all uncommon. I wanted to kill several people on the way back to our workshop after lunch. I used to want to kill people who tailgated me on the highway. I knew, in principle, that mindfulness would cure that, except that it took about three years of repeated mindfulness practice before I lost the urge to kill those tailgaters. I was embarassed for years that this feeling wouldn't go away just because I was mindful of it. I wanted instant results.

Now I automatically feel anger, although usually not the full desire to kill, when drivers ahead of me do not signal their turns until they are actually turning. I get stuck behind them—I, precious *me*—I could have saved several seconds, maybe even a minute, if they had signaled their intentions. I could have gotten into the right lane and gone around them. How can they be so inconsiderate of and hostile to *me*!

All I can say is, hang in there, keep practicing mindfulness. These little emotions—little from a more awakened perspective, big from our usual ego, consensus-trance-state perspective—are triggered and seize your attention, and you have to struggle to regain some mindfulness. Maybe, because you are trying, you can become mindful five minutes later.

STUDENT: *I'd like to be able to get to the present right then, right when somebody is throwing emotions at me.*

Right! Maybe with more practice it only takes two minutes to regain mindfulness, maybe eventually only a few seconds, maybe eventually you learn to be mindful during these emotional reactions. As you know, such immediate mindfulness is really something.

Again, do not be too hard on yourself. We have all had twenty, thirty, forty, or more years of practice at spacing out; we have been socially reinforced for it and had all our needs and emotions tied in to it. You cannot change this overnight. The nice thing about self-remembering—about sensing, looking, and listening—is that it is not only good for you but it will provide a lot of moments when it is clearly very rewarding to do this practice. There is a subtle kind of happiness about being present that is very nice. You are just more alive. And the contrast with being carried away in some kind of emotional fit is especially good for helping you realize the value of being present.

Especially with emotional situations, sometimes you just cannot remember to try to be mindful, or you may only vaguely remember and struggle to sense your arms and legs. You (more properly, your conditioned mind) may decide, What are my arms and legs worth, what is mindfulness worth, compared to my feelings about this bastard in front of me? Sometimes the best you can do is finally come to the present five minutes after the argument is over. You can at least take a deep breath then and relax slightly.

If you are not trying at all, however, it may be days before you ever come back to the present. If you come back to the present five minutes later, there still may be time to apologize before the relationship is soured forever. Maybe with more practice, you may actually come back to the present three minutes later. With more practice, even in the midst of an emotion, occasionally you can touch into the present right then and there and at least think, Slow down, keep my mouth shut! before the next emotional/cognitive fit comes on.

PARADOX: "OUTSIGHT" LEADS TO INSIGHT

There is an apparent paradox in self-remembering through sensing, looking, and listening that I have not talked about yet. If you do an intellectual analysis of this process, it seems as if it is all designed to make you more aware of the external world. There is 60 or 70 percent of your attention going to vision, 30 or 40 percent going to hearing, and only 10 percent or so going to the body. It can make you much more acutely aware of the world and your physical body. You get nourishment from that conditions and you become more accurate in perceiving the world.

At the same time, however, the process actually makes you more aware of your own inner life. Why? Because you do not get so caught up in psychological reactions, fantasies, hopes and fears, and so forth that you lose track of what is actually going on. As a result, you become more sensitive to your thoughts, feelings, and intuitions. You do not have to be enraged before you notice that something is irritating you, for example. Also, your emotions are liable to be smaller because they are not gobbling up all your energy if you are sensing, looking, and listening, and a smaller emotion is usually easier to perceive accurately.

THE WATCHER AT THE GATE

Robert de Ropp created an analogy that you can use to describe the ordinary state of our minds. De Ropp was a very interesting writer on Gurdjieff's thought, although I found that he seemed a rather embittered person. So if you read him, you have to filter out his own personal nihilism and bitterness. He had a *very* difficult childhood, so it is understandable.

De Ropp said that we can imagine our minds to be like a medieval walled city, and access to the town is controlled through one main gate. Like any town, there are different sections. There are art galleries, museums, and theaters in one part, markets in another, a manufacturing district, universities in another part, and there are also slums. Note that the bell has just rung.

The things that happen to us in life are like travelers coming to the open gate of the town. Ordinarily, travelers wander in and out as they will. Life happens to us. Some of those travelers come in and give a useful lecture at the university, and we are richer for it. Some bring supplies we need to exist. Some are a pleasure to talk with. Some of them go down into the slums and start riots, and you pay for it. Some of them are, so to speak, emotional provocateurs who come in and agitate.

Doing this sensing, looking, and listening is analogous to having a *watcher at the gate,* who sees travelers coming and makes some discriminating judgments about them. For certain travelers he opens the gates wide, but for other travelers he closes them. In order to intelligently select which "travelers" are allowed to enter, you have to be present. These people can come up to the gate very suddenly, and if you are looking away for even a second, they may slip inside.

I have noticed in my own practice that this analogy is quite useful.

If I am being reasonably present—not perfectly present, but at least checking in once in a while—and if, say, a car horn blows loudly beside me, I jump, because my body is programmed to jump. But I am instantly aware that I jumped because of a sudden sound, what the sound was, and that the car is not bearing down on me, so I calm down very quickly.

If I am not present, that jump sets off alarm systems in my body and I am agitated for about half an hour afterward. If certain stimuli occur and you are not present right away, and so you don't understand whether this sudden occurrence is a real threat or not, it sets off an adrenalin reaction. Once that adrenalin pumps into your body, it will usually take a long time for you to calm down. Mindfulness is still helpful in coping even if it is late, but if it's more than half a second or so late, the adrenalin reaction has started and all that extra energy in the body makes mindfulness harder to practice.

I am not saying that you should live an emotionally suppressed life, where you are on guard never to encounter anything unpleasant, or that you should keep yourself from ever reacting to anything unpleasant. Eventually self-remembering creates a whole new relationship with your emotions, one that is quieter yet more intense and psychologically cleaner. But through self-observation and study, you may understand that realistically you cannot handle certain kinds of situations yet. They may set off emotional riots, and then your energy is lost for an hour, a day, or more.

TRAINING EMOTIONAL INTELLIGENCE

STUDENT: *Are you saying that we're not supposed to listen to our feelings? That if something is upsetting me I should focus on my arms and legs instead and so get rid of my feelings?*

The analogy I just gave you is primarily about extremes; it is about stopping emotional riots. Ordinary levels of emotions provide wonderful opportunities to experience and to learn. By continuing to sense, look, and listen, by staying grounded in your body, you can see the emotions more clearly and more subtly, more discriminatingly than you usually see them, although at first it may seem overwhelming because you see more of them than you usually do. This process is also part of the training of emotional intelligence. *Our emotions need training,* just as our intellect and body do. They are usually left at an undeveloped, neurotic level. Two of our three brains usually are.

Remember, an essential part of mindfulness training is to become clearer about what is actually happening moment by moment. The emotion of anxiety, for example, is usually a global, undifferentiated feeling. To be more mindful is to know, for instance, that you are specifically fearful about A, B, and C, and to be able, on a bodily level, to sense the moment-to-moment variations and qualities in what fear feels like.

When you can do this, you have a more intelligent, a more discriminative and articulated, perception of the situation. You may learn in some instances to simply accept the situation, or if there is something in reality you can do about the situation, then you can act more clearly and effectively to change it. The point is not to confuse the emergency procedure—closing the gates—with day-to-day living. But we should learn to create the *watcher at the gate,* the observing part of the mind, as much as possible in order to learn.

IRRITATING IDIOTS CAN BE USEFUL

Gurdjieff used to go out of his way to stimulate his students' emotions. He had a training center in France for some years, an old chateau, the Château de Prieuré. Students came to live there regularly and would end up working in the gardens, painting the walls, cleaning out the gutters, and so on as well as attending classes and otherwise getting instructions. Gurdjieff also had some Russian immigrants living there, this being shortly after the Bolshevik Revolution. One of these immigrants, a man who we shall call Bekterev, though this is not his real name, was particularly annoying to those who had come as spiritual seekers. He was not a student of Gurdjieff. Indeed, Bekterev thought everything spiritual was total nonsense. His personal habits drove everybody up the wall. He seemed the most inconsiderable, egotistical, irritable man alive.

Gurdjieff's students hated Bekterev: they were there for serious spiritual work, and this idiot was constantly irritating and distracting them. They started playing practical jokes on him, and they eventually played such nasty practical jokes that he was driven to leave. I can't recall precisely, but they finally did something like steal his false teeth and roll them in cow shit—something like that. He left in a rage.

As soon as Gurdjieff heard, he immediately got in his car, went to Paris, where Bekterev had gone, and begged him to come back, offering to pay him a magnificent salary just to live at the Prieuré. He later explained this to his students, saying something along the lines of, "This man is one of the most valuable teaching instruments I have. You are here for self-study, and this man steps on your emotional corns every day, giving you marvelous opportunities to see how your psychological machinery is constructed. His absence would be a great loss to the gaining of real self-knowledge—real as opposed to the fantasies you have about yourself and your lofty spiritual aims."

I am not suggesting that you go out and deliberately find somebody like that. Life will probably provide, actually.

It is the shift in attitude that you can make that is most valuable. You begin to recognize that you do not know your own psychology; that you are caught up in automatized, unconscious reactions that you do not understand and that cause you trouble. You come to realize that you *must* understand what is going on in you before you can effectively do something about it, and that you need to engage in self-study, self-remembering, and self-observation. Then the stresses and strains of life become gifts. They give you opportunities to see things that it might take you years to see otherwise.

This is another reason why Gurdjieff was not enthusiastic about monasticism and spiritual retreats. Retreats are arranged to be very calm and peaceful, and so all your nasty problems go dormant. No one steps on your corns. You do not really solve your problems. You are in an artificial situation that is advantageous in some ways, but which can allow you to get lost in what amounts to fantasies about your level of spiritual development. Get out and work on yourself in life, where these annoying things keep happening, providing rich material for study.

Again, you should not misinterpret this statement to mean that you should try to make your life more miserable. Life will provide sufficient misery. You do not need the hair shirts.

STUDENT: *I work in the same building as a person like that, some-one who stamps on my emotional corns. She's one of my colleagues at work. I frequently stop by her office on business and engage her, but she pushes all my buttons. She's a demon incarnate! Sometimes when I leave her office I am literally homicidal. She drives everybody nuts. But one day I know I'm going to be able to interact with her and observe myself at the same time, see her as an actual person.*

She's a special tutor for you.

STUDENT: *Yes! Exactly. She's valuable to me. But it's nice not to have to work for her.*

In fact, you may actually be doing something nice for her, whether she knows it or not, because you seek out her company. If she does this to everybody, she may be a very lonely woman. That someone actually seems to want her company once in a while may be nourishing to her on some level.

STUDENT: *I wouldn't want to be forced to spend a lot of time with her though. [General laughter]*

ANOTHER STUDENT: *It's nice to be able to work like that on your own timing, not the other person's.*

Yes, controlling the timing is nice, but you can do a lot by deliberately setting up situations that push you. It's tricky, though. In some ways you may also minimize your possibilities for understanding and change because you unconsciously select an uncomfortable situation so that it will not really be *too* uncomfortable. When life throws them at you unexpectedly, you generally have more material to work with.

STICK WITH IT

I do not want to overwhelm you with the thought of the difficulties of becoming more mindful. True, we have been actively engaged in the practice of illusion and waking sleep for many, many years. Becoming more mindful, striving toward enlightenment, is difficult, but there is a real reward.

I do not really know what enlightenment is, but I do know that it is possible to become more present to what really goes on and to find a subtle, but very important, kind of pleasure in living more in the present. It is an aspect of what Shinzen Young calls the dimension of *unconditional happiness.*

Most of our happiness is based on "success": If I get what I want, then I am happy. If I don't get it, then I am unhappy. That's conditional happiness. There is something about learning to be present and mindful, however, that produces a kind of happiness that is beyond this conditionality. Reality, life, just *is*. By being present and accepting, we usually do not create more bad karma, we do not blindly and desperately strive for pleasure, acting in unrealistic, thoughtless ways that create negative consequences in the long run.

Learning to be more present, more mindful, more attentive, can lead to a lot of moments of vividness, of beauty, of satisfaction, and of insight, as well as times when you have to stick in there and put up with awful realizations about yourself, embarrassing things, and clear perception of your own and others' cruelty and suffering. Gradually you develop a wider psychological space to live in and greater satisfaction in all areas of life.

EXTREMES OF EFFORT

STUDENT: *I wonder if you have any thoughts on the amount of effort to exert when we engage in practice? Obviously, if you don't exert enough effort, you're not going to get anything, but it seems to me that if you exert too much the bell has just rung, freeze external motion, be silent and observe yourself for half a minute, you're going to bite off more than you can chew and fail. Is there any sense one might get of an optimal amount of effort?*

Yes. I'd say be reasonable most of the time and occasionally be unreasonable.

Gurdjieff was not "reasonable" on this topic. He said efforts do not count; only *super* efforts count—the efforts you make when you have driven yourself past the point of exhaustion. That attitude was partly truth, partly Gurdjieff's personal style. He was that kind of person, a certain personality type, a type 8 on the Enneagram of personality, a type that, when confronted by obstacles, automatically pushes harder.[2]

You're right: at times too much effort is clearly counterproductive, but at other times you should make super efforts. For instance, in a Gurdjieff group I was in once, we occasionally had special events, miniretreats that would last several days. And several nights, for you did not spend any time sleeping on that kind of retreat. There was continual activity as well as the injunction to self-remember, to sense, look, and listen, all the time.

It is not too bad the first night, but by the second night it gets pretty bad, and you see something about sleep in more than a metaphorical sense: you get a lot of direct observation of clearly clouded consciousness. You also see something real about making efforts.

Those retreats were extreme, but they were limited in duration. Some people partially kept them up afterwards, saying they would cut their hours of sleep down to, say, four hours per night for the next two months to see what would happen. I personally think that action reached the point of craziness, because some of those people nearly ran their cars into telephone poles and the like. There is too much real danger in keeping up that level of sleep deprivation.

For me and many others—there are individual differences—a couple of nights of total sleep deprivation can be as powerful as a dose of LSD in some ways. The fatigue and sleepiness begins to destructure all your ordinary, automatic habits. When you have some basis already in knowing how to focus, observe, and have insights, to a certain extent, a brief period of sleep deprivation *in the right context of a working group* can be useful. As a way of life, it is stupid—unless you like to live on the brink of danger all the time, which some people do.

SEEKING DANGER TO KNOW YOU ARE ALIVE

One response to the deadness of ordinary life, to the shallowness of living in samsara, in consensus trance, is to seek out danger. To paraphrase Descartes, I can be killed any second, therefore I really am. In certain dangerous sports, for example, like skiing to the limit or auto racing, you *must* be present to the physical world. If your attention lapses for two-tenths of a second, you may maim or kill yourself. You are forced to be present. As another example, a lot of World War II veterans, when interviewed later, said that being in combat was the most alive, most real time in their lives.

If you want to wake up and be more present, having somebody trying to kill you can be a very effective training routine. It is effective in terms of really pressuring you to be sensorially here. This can generate that food of impressions and so nourish you in some ways. Of course, there is the major disadvantage that you can get killed and another disadvantage that you probably have to shoot back, not to mention the moral problems.

The fact that this kind of danger can force us to be more present, and so feel more vital and alive, is one of the problems with trying to stop war. Among sleeping people, as Gurdjieff would describe us, war is one of the few things that makes people feel alive, and so it is not going to be gotten rid of on some purely rational basis. That is why I think it is vitally important to teach people techniques like sensing, looking, and listening, like formal sitting meditation, like Aikido, where you can become more alive without having to put yourself and everybody else in mortal danger and cause great destruction in the process.

So be reasonable about the super efforts, but occasionally push yourself. Be practical, however, so that it is not a situation of real danger. Don't do sleep deprivation if you have to drive.

DELIBERATE REMINDERS, ALARM CLOCKS

STUDENT: *Would it be OK if we put signs up? Like reminders?*

For now, yes.

STUDENT: *I just had the feeling that I could come tomorrow night and find I had just completely forgotten to continue doing this.*

Yes, put signs up reminding you to be present. These are what Gurdjieff called *alarm clocks.* If you want to use the analogy for so-called normal consciousness that we are asleep, then how do we normally wake up? An alarm clock goes off, we're startled, we awaken.

Eventually, though, we get used to the alarm clock, and we learn either to sleep through the alarm or to work the alarm into our dreams and so sleep on. The signs we put up initially remind us to be more present, but we start adapting to them and having automatized fantasies about being awake, instead of making that little effort it takes to actually be mindful. The alarm clock eventually ceases to serve its purpose. At that point you can change to different kinds of alarm clocks that you are not used to. You will eventually adapt to them, too, but they are helpful at the beginning to remind you.

STUDENT: *The random bell sound: can we use that to wake up? Could we get a copy of the tape? Or would we eventually adapt to that, too?*

I occasionally use a variation on this tape—a calculator I've programmed to sound chimes at random intervals—for a few days at a time, and then I put it away for a while. I get too used to it. See, this is the problem. Part of our mind learns things rapidly and puts our experience and behavior on automatic. In many ways that is a very useful skill and in other ways it is a curse. *Everything* can go on automatic, and so real consciousness is not needed. On the other hand, after you have learned how to drive a car, you would not want to have to relearn the skill every single time you got in it. You want those lower level, automatic habits to know how to steer the car. That's OK, but then we get higher and higher levels of habits.

Sadly, I must emphasize that consciousness, real attentiveness and mindfulness, is not needed for most of ordinary life. You can become a robot and live your life that way: a happy robot or a suffering robot, but a robot.

STUDENT: *That's what I've found in the context of working with computers. A few times I've tried to set up alarm clocks. Like one way to put a task on automatic pilot is to have another task that's really important going on at the same time. And I've never had an alarm clock last for more than a third of a day.*

You could use the computer to remind you to be present by setting up "bombs" in the computer that, once in a while, suddenly print out, "I'm locked up for five minutes, you have to pay attention to your arms and legs!" For a while that might work. The computer will need to give you a specific message like this, or otherwise you may just think it is a malfunction requiring all your attention to repair.

Generally, it is easier to be present with simpler sorts of tasks. In formal Gurdjieff work, for instance, there is a lot of plain and simple physical work done, such as sweeping the floor, washing the dishes, repairing the roof, or putting insecticide on the roses one petal at a time with a cotton swab. I have done that.

It is easier to sense, look, and listen with simple physical tasks than when you are talking. Interacting with people, especially sleeping people, almost always makes it harder. In contrast, I was able to help you achieve some present consciousness in these interaction exercises earlier, partly because I deliberately added a certain element of stress *after* you had first gotten in some sensing practice, and partly because the social atmosphere here is right. Ordinarily, we are so desperate for approval and so locked into our social habits that we forget even the possibility of being more present in interacting with others. We go totally into automatic, usually into a pattern we know pleases the other person.

There are rare occasions when you can be relatively awake and present and talk with someone else who is relatively awake and present. These occasions are quite wonderful, but they are far too rare. There are far too few people practicing this technique in the first place for there to be much of a chance of it happening, statistically speaking. A workshop like this may be the only occasion in some people's lives. If you do get into an interaction with someone else who is being present, even imperfectly, it starts to potentiate your own process. And, of course, as you train your own ability to be attentive and present, your chances for this fulfilling kind of interaction go up.

It's quite wonderful to mindfully interact with a mindful person.

THINKING ABOUT BEING PRESENT IS NOT DOING IT

STUDENT: *I have a tendency to think that everything is very compli-cated and that the techniques you've introduced now the bell has rung, sense yourself, sounded very simple, maybe too simple. So I start thinking, Maybe I haven't gotten it right.*

Would you like a more complex version? [*General laughter*] I can design one for you.

STUDENT: *But somehow I'm compelled to think I'm missing some piece, and my natural tendency is to ask if this is written somewhere, so I can go back and review.*

Yes, it's written out in my book *Waking Up*. But if it's not complex enough for you, I can add more. You can visualize a green letter *z* in the center of your head while sensing your arms and legs, while keeping track of the mantra—which mantra should we use?—*Sa la me, sa la me, bah low knee.* [*Laughter*] It's a traditional American childhood mantra about spiritual practices.

But seriously, your intellectual mind may indeed analyze these exercises and say they are too simple. But actually being present is not the same thing as describing it or thinking about it. I use the global word *sensing,* for example, to describe feeling your arms and legs, but it is not as if there is *a* simple sensation in your arms and legs. There is a whole complex, changing pattern of things. What you see also changes all the time, and what you hear changes all the time.

Also, the other senses come in. If you are eating something, you can *taste,* look, listen, and sense. If you are smelling something, you can smell while keeping track of your body sensations. I focus on looking and listening because they constitute the vast majority of sensory input that we have.

DON'T BE TOO HARD ON YOURSELF

I do not want to leave you with an implicit suggestion, given what I've said, that will make it harder for you. Let me say that it will be quite rich enough if you actually *practice* it, but thinking about it is not doing it. Just remember that we are human beings, and if we could do anything perfectly, we would probably not be here. You are going to do it, and you are going to do it "wrong." You are going to do it again, and again you will do it wrong.

I must emphasize this. We are people. If we could do things perfectly, we would not be here learning about mindfulness. So you are going to do the practice and you are going to do it wrong. And you are going to do it again and you are going to do it wrong, over and over and over, but you gradually learn something.

Too, my words describe it poorly. Much as I intended for them to make it clear, they probably describe it all wrong for you. But I hope they start you in a certain direction. Then, through your own direct experience, you start to refine the process and pick out what is important in it and what works for you.

Just accept that you will sometimes obsessively think *about* it, instead of doing it. I know—I am a compulsive thinker. When somebody tells me something, I have done half a dozen analyses on it before they have finished talking, because it has taken them so long (by my standards) to get to the point. It has taken me a long, long time to learn that obsessive analysis is often not the reality.

When I took up Aikido many years ago, for example, I had an instructor, Alan Grow, who was very good, but he was the strong, silent type. He did not say much. I found that within two weeks I believed I could explain Aikido much better than he could. I could relate it to different philosophies, religious traditions, and modern psychological ideas. But I kept noticing something: I could not actually *do* anything. Yet he could throw me across the room with what seemed like hardly a flick of his wrist.

It kept being brought home to me that these clever words about Aikido did not constitute the important knowledge at all. It took me more than two years before I could learn to stop getting caught up in the endless stream of words my mind generated and simply pay attention with my body to what he was teaching and to what was actually happening. I discovered a new style of learning that way. That was a very important part of my education in beginning to educate my body/instinctive brain out of the idiocy of its usual state.

I have not said much about emotional education. Educating your emotional brain comes in part from practicing mindfulness. It enables you to get a clearer understanding of what it is you actually feel, both physically and emotionally, moment by moment. I am not convinced, however, that mindfulness training alone is enough in most cases.

I think this is an area where the West has a great deal to offer in facilitating spiritual growth. We now know a lot about emotional problems, subconscious processes, and defenses that take experiential processes and data out of consciousness and make them extremely difficult to observe. I am convinced that the best progress in emotional growth, enlightenment, and maturity will eventually come from skillful combinations of psychotherapy-like counseling with formal meditation, mindfulness in everyday life practice, and mindful devotional practice. They really need to complement each other, because we know that some emotional processes hide their roots from consciousness, so it is very hard to discover them with just meditation and / or self-remembering techniques. You might eventually succeed, but there are probably times when a week with a therapist or facilitator would enable you to discover them now instead of after five years on the meditation cushion.

STUDENT: *Charley, you spoke about emotional and devotional practice. What do you see as to how devotional practice would help devotional practice?*[3]

This is tricky. If you are thinking of the kind of devotional practice we do here at the Rigpa Fellowship, which stresses devotion to the teacher and the teacher's lineage, for instance, or the similar sort that happens in a lot of spiritual groups, I think it's both quite necessary and quite dangerous.

There is what we could call intelligent devotion, a feeling of respect and gratitude that naturally arises toward someone who has taught you something quite valuable. Such intelligent devotion can further motivate you to practice and learn. But devotion is dangerous in the sense that we tend to project unresolved conflicts with and expectations about our parents onto the teacher. That projection is unrealistic and can badly distort the reality of the situation. Projection is a primary creator of samsara. Projection gives the situation or teacher power to make rapid changes in us, because it puts emotional "juice" into the practice. But it is based on a foundation of unconscious and unresolved conflicts, so it can be very brittle and can change very rapidly.

There frequently occurs what is technically called a *transference* reaction onto the teacher, such that the teacher becomes the Magic Mommy or the Magic Daddy to the projector's unconscious mind. *Apparent* spiritual progress is then usually quite rapid: the student may have ecstatic states and unusual experiences and seem to be getting very far. Then one day the teacher does something or a personal life change for the student occurs that suddenly upsets the projection, and the student feels, That bastard has been exploiting me! It's all phony; he's a charlatan and an evil man. The student then loses the "progress" already made and goes into a negative transference. This is because transference involves powerful but infantile emotional feelings about parents, feelings of deep love for supposedly perfect parents *and* unresolved negative feelings of disillusionment and anger at the parents.

So any devotional situation is very high-powered, perhaps unconsciously involving the intensity of an infant's feelings, and so very tricky. I do not think Eastern teachers understand this situation very well. Some seem to think, for example, that Easterners are raised with so much love that there are no unresolved problems in the unconscious. I cannot really believe that child rearing was so much better in Tibet that there is no projection at all among Eastern students, that everybody has a perfectly clean unconscious. That is why I think that, as Westerners, part of our contribution to spiritual growth is to figure out—probably through making a lot of mistakes along the way—where the more specialized Western emotional growth techniques dovetail with meditation and devotional techniques, and so create a sounder basis for practice.

Personally, a part of me tends to envy people who get this transference reaction and have this marvelous emotional juice fueling their spiritual life—until I see the outcome when the transference becomes negative and all the apparent spiritual progress disappears.

Transference is also incredibly destructive to teachers. Look at the cults that end up with cyanide in their fruit-flavored punch or at scandals about sexual exploitation of students by the teacher. One can see, in retrospect, very strong transference reactions and projections, transferences that not only drive the students crazy, but also drive the teachers crazy. If a teacher is anything less than a perfectly realized being, is someone with any seed of neuroticism, transference reactions can feed that neuroticism and make it much worse. Everybody then goes crazy in a spectacular way. I don't think we have too much of a transference problem to Lama Sogyal Rinpoche here in the Rigpa Fellowship, for example, but transference reactions always have to be thought about and balanced.

I should add parenthetically that I suspect that my concerns about transference reactions might have something to do with my own limitations, so don't take what I've said as the final word.

STUDENT: *I find that I tend to put my feelings of that sort into more abstract places, like having strong feelings of devotion toward Padmasambhava [a historical figure credited with the founding of Tibetan Buddhism and seen as a second buddha] or Dilgo Khyentse [a recently deceased teacher of Sogyal Rinpoche and other lamas, who was highly esteemed in Tibetan Buddhism] rather than toward Sogyal Rinpoche personally.*

Yes. Sogyal Rinpoche shows sensitivity to this problem also. He encourages his students to direct their devotion toward his teachers rather than toward him personally, even though most of Tibetan Buddhism puts tremendous emphasis on devotion to one's teacher. There's some safety in this: the transference, to the degree it occurs, is toward someone dead or far away who is unlikely to be affected by your transference and then exhibit behavior that will activate your neuroses.

I've focused on the dangers of transference, which devotional practice can increase. At the same time, the emotional aspects of devotional practice give you power that can bring a lot more focus and energy into your practice, and so take you places you might not go alone. One of the reasons I am a student at this Tibetan Buddhist center, instead of just being in a Gurdjieff group, is that, while I think that the Gurdjieff groups are technically better at teaching mindfulness in everyday life, I find a certain coldness, a certain lack of heart in them that, for me, is a very serious lack. The tape now sounds the bell, be present.

I have a tendency to be somewhat withdrawn and cool, based on some childhood traumas. I have to be very careful about that tendency in myself. For people who get emotionally involved and overwrought all too easily, though, what might be really good for them is a much cooler approach. I find Gurdjieff's idea very sensible in this way. We have to develop the body/instinctive, the emotional, and the intellectual intelligence, balance them, and *then* a kind of transference can take place on a firm foundation. If the transference does not occur on a firm foundation, there can be a lot of trouble.

People differ, but personally, I need to worship sometimes. I need to get my heart involved in something much bigger than me, not just cool, meditative concepts about the changeability of things, the need not to get caught in negative emotions, and so on. So I find the combination of Gurdjieff work and Tibetan Buddhism works well for me.

STUDENT: *Are there techniques in the Gurdjieff work for developing and balancing these three brains?*

Oh yes, that's why people end up doing Gurdjieff work for years and years. There are powerful methods available that really promote growth. But I am not sure the Gurdjieff work is a complete system in itself. It seems to me that Gurdjieff died without teaching all that was needed. Or perhaps part of the experiment that was his teaching in the West was to leave it incomplete. So there are many specialized techniques in the Gurdjieff work, but I've taught you the central practice, as I know it, to which the others are adjuncts. This one practice of sensing, looking, and listening can take you a long, long way. Also, it's not really a simple practice. I have a "gift" for describing things clearly that probably makes it seem much simpler than it really is in practice. But the sensing, looking, and listening practice works on multiple levels. I'll let you folks discover that for yourselves.

STUDENT: *There's a lot of times when I'm tired. From my personal experience, when I'm tired, I don't function as well, I do destructive things, I don't think clearly. When my body is rested, I think much more clearly. I'm sharper.*

Me too. Which leads me into the error of semiconsciously thinking, Whenever I feel good and feel in the mood, I'll do some spiritual work, but I shouldn't be expected to do anything when I don't feel good.

The trouble is there are going to be lots of times in life when you do not feel good, but you need to be mindful and more spiritual, in some sense. You have to develop the capacity to work under difficult situations. If you have broken your leg, I am not going to say you must march ten miles while saying your mantra and sensing your arms and legs. Go get a cast on your leg and take it easy for a while. There might be a time, however, when you would have to walk ten miles on a broken leg in order to save your own or another's life: if you have had a little practice in working under stress, under difficult conditions, you are stronger, more likely to save your life.

There is an analogy here with lifting weights. If you just lift a one-pound weight every day because it is pleasant to watch your arms go up and down, you will have fun, but you will not get any stronger. You gradually have to increase the size of the weights. That does not mean that the goal of life is always to be struggling along under the heaviest possible load, but we want to develop our capacity to function in difficult situations, not just when it is fun.

MANTRA PRACTICE

STUDENT: *Charley, do you think that mantra practice, as we ordinarily see it, has a place here? Does it have a purpose of bringing you more into the present, more into mindfulness, or do you see it as a way to not be present?*

Well there are several ways to do mantras. I will say something, however, from the Gurdjieffian perspective, as I understand it. This will take a little background.

We are already devoted practitioners of *scientism,* a philosophy, a view of life, and a religion that is expressed in the Western creed exercise that we did together earlier. Sogyal Rinpoche kids us in Rigpa once in a while with a phrase I love to use ever since I heard it: *We are already dedicated, devoted practitioners, practitioners of samsara.* We expend enormous amounts of energy reinforcing our illusions, bolstering our defenses, and creating misery for ourselves. We think nothing of spending thousands of hours mentally repeating, in slightly varying form, mantras like, *I can't do it, I never could do it, I can't do it, I never could do it, it will turn out bad, it will turn out bad, it always turns out bad.* Things like this go on in our conscious and semiconscious thoughts all day. *I can't do it, I never could do it, I can't do it, I never could do it, it will turn out bad, it will turn out bad, it always turns out bad.* The automatized quality of our minds means that we have repetitious thoughts that reinforce the beliefs that we already have.

It is not that we are neutral, objective, uncommitted beings who ask the question, Should we go through the work of doing some kind of spiritual practice? We are already practicing. We are practicing a semiconscious religion that, by and large, is not of our choosing, but was indoctrinated or enculturated into us, a religion that makes our situation worse and increases our automatization and misery. And we are good at it. Most of us can effortlessly create unnecessary suffering at the drop of a hat.

Now, you can dull your misery by concentrating on almost anything. You can use a formal mantra, either chanted aloud or just done internally, as an anodyne to pain now the bell rings. I suppose for some people, under some circumstances, that is all a mantra does. It distracts you from your emotional or physical pain. If you are in pain and saying a mantra makes you feel better, and if that is the best you can do, more power to you!

You can also use mantra in a somewhat more skillful way to interfere with your automatized practice of samsara. If you are constantly chanting your formal spiritual mantra over and over again, it is hard to simultaneously repeat your mantra of *I can never succeed, things always go wrong, I can never succeed.* Formal mantra practice interferes with the practice of samsara. If you are constantly putting energy into making your mind and life worse, *anything* that takes energy away from that is a definite step forward. If you have at least a partial rest from the negative thoughts, then perhaps the negativity is weakened a bit. But saying a mantra is busywork. In that sense, a mantra could consist of nonsense syllables, meaningless sounds, because all it does is distract attention.

Mantra practice can get more sophisticated than that, however. The mantra can be used to induce a mood. Sogyal Rinpoche talks about this aspect, in which formal mantra practice can be a *preliminary* practice to put us in a good mood for directly practicing mindfulness. Ideally, we ought to be able to be mindful when we are in a bad mood too, but very few of us would choose to be in a bad mood and be mindful all the time. We would rather be mindful in a good mood. You can usually also pick up more power to practice in a good mood than in a bad one. So if the mantra practice inspires you, it can be quite helpful.

There are other levels of mantra practice, too. For instance, if you chant mantras aloud with your eyes closed and get involved in the practice, it can reduce your sense of separation from the world around you. Vision is a sense that has its own neurological processing mechanisms that emphasize separateness. Vision emphasizes discrete objects, boundaries, edges, spaces in between discrete objects, and foreground versus background. With sound, these distinctions are not so clear. The sound world is more one of dynamic processes flowing into one another than of separate, discrete things.

In terms of awakening practice, mindfulness practice of the sort we are emphasizing in this workshop, mantra is, by and large, useful mainly as an emergency control measure to stop your mind when it is in a crazy state, to stop automated, negative samsara practice, so that you can become mindful again. Or it can inspire you, and then you move on to practicing mindfulness.

Now, I don't want to present myself as an authority on Buddhism. I'm not. But this is my interpretation of the Dzogchen practice that Sogyal Rinpoche teaches, namely, that the essential Dzogchen practice is mindfulness. Chanting and mantras work well as preparation to put us in a more spacious kind of mood and so help us be mindful. But remember, mantra *per se* is not mindfulness, and it can certainly be used to increase mind*lessness,* to cut us off further from what is actually happening moment by moment.

STUDENT: *Sometimes when I notice my mind has a lot of crazy thoughts about someone or something, I try to replace it by repeatedly saying, "Blah blah blah blah!"*

That's a good replacement mantra.

The ideal, in a sense, the way it's traditionally talked about, is that you are *so* mindful all the time that you never get caught up in and identified with all this crazy, delusional stuff, that you are well in touch with your true nature all the time, coming from an enlightened space: that's the answer to everything. I guess that's great when you get there. Sometimes when we're even just a little bit on the way there, that's clearly the way to proceed. There are other times, though, when we need emergency procedures: your mind is freaking out and going nuts and you need to stop it *now.* The car is starting to roll down the hill, you've got to apply the brakes *now,* not think about the ultimate mindfulness technique to apply to it. But then, having calmed it, you come back to the mindfulness practice.

ACCEPTING HURT

STUDENT: *Is there any way . . . there are these false edges between our selves and others, between us and things, I know that, and yet we get hurt, like when you stepped on the cup. Can we drop these false edges but not get hurt?*

Yes, in some ways, but you have to accept the hurt.

One of the reasons we are not mindful, one of the reasons we live in a constant, ongoing flow of delusions, is that while living in illusion creates its own kind of suffering it also *seems* to defend us from real hurt, deep hurt. It turns out to be a poor defense, though, because it creates hurt of its own.

We were hurt a lot as children: we were squeezed, conditioned, pressured, shaped, denied, confused, and in some cases, even tortured and beaten. You can talk about and put down our neuroticism, our defenses, and our devotion to samsara, but we should not be too hard on ourselves: the "neurotic" defenses we erected were the best we could do. We were just little kids, trying to defend something alive in us. Unfortunately, those defenses got more and more rigid. We made a suit of armor that protected our tender inside against some of the blows. We still have the suit of armor on, but since we have grown, it is very stiff and cramped in there.

Becoming more mindful will mean suffering more intensely, in a more real way, at times. I have experienced this personally many times, and I do not like it one bit. There have been, for example, occasions when I am mindfully walking down the street and I see a mother being really cruel to a child. Seeing that cruelty hurts me terribly. I empathize with both the kid and the mother, but there is nothing I can do about it. Not being able to do anything about it is especially painful. I tell myself I should stay mindful, but my automatic defenses are usually activated, and I suddenly think about an article I have to write or some experiment I have to do.

We have to learn to be present to deeper pain sometimes. We are not little kids any more, however, and we can adequately handle a lot more stress and pain than we could then. And life is not all pain. But if you say, "I don't ever want to feel pain," as many of us did as kids and still do today, then you will never feel the good things, the joy in life. There has to be an acceptance somehow, and it is part of the opening up process. The general trend from practicing mindfulness is joyful, but if you say, "I'll take just the joyful," the mindfulness practice will not really work. You will substitute pleasant fantasies about reality instead of learning to be open to what actually is in each moment.

Now, it's five o'clock. I'm tired, and even though I'm being mindful about my tiredness, I want to quit. Most of you are tired, too.

Here's your homework assignment: continue sensing, looking, and listening as you leave this artificial situation of being in a workshop on mindfulness, as you go home to your families, to your significant others—what a weasel word, *significant others*—your boyfriends and girlfriends, as you go to work in the morning, and so forth.

If you like, you might carry a little notebook around and jot a few notes if you experience anything quite differently as a result of sensing, looking, and listening. But don't put the emphasis on taking notes: put the emphasis on being present, to experiencing things more clearly.

We meet here again tomorrow night.

FOUR

RESULTS OF MINDFULNESS PRACTICE
First Follow-up Session

WE EACH HAVE an opportunity this evening and the next two Monday evenings to do something that is all too rare in this world: to sit around and talk with a bunch of people who are working on being more conscious.

Being with people who are working on being more conscious can be a very rewarding experience, although you must not *try* to make it rewarding. If you try to make it feel good instead of simply devoting your efforts to being as present to this moment as possible, your mental activities begin to become distorted the bell rings and you create fantasies and daydreams about waking up, rather than actually becoming more awake.

So this evening you can report on things you've noticed while attempting to do this exercise since you left yesterday. We can also work with the process of what happens right now. After all, right now is what's most real.

So try to sense, look, and listen continuously while we're here. If you need to boost yourself, you can say, Gee, everybody else is managing to do it, I'll be real ashamed if I don't manage to do it continuously. This is the creative use of guilt. Better yet, just do it.

If we have periods of silence, it's just as important to sense your arms and legs and look and listen during those moments as at any other time. And remember, *don't stare fixedly*. I am not a hypnotic focus. This is about *de*hypnotism, not hypnotism. So, look around.

Who has something to report or bring up?

STUDENT: *When I try sensing, looking, and listening, I tend to feel as if I'm "behind" sensing, looking, and listening. For example, when*

I tried this technique while I was driving, the sights before me looked more three dimensional. And I don't feel I'm quite engaged, and my response time seems to slow up. Then sometimes I start to evaluate it and analyze my experiences. How am I doing?

Let's take one thing at a time. Has anyone else experienced anything similar, feeling your response times are a little slow, or something like that? [*Some people indicate that they have.*]

DISRUPTING ROUTINES

It is normal to find that your everyday responses in various situations are sometimes slower as you practice sensing, looking, and listening. It means that you are trying well. What you are doing is disrupting your routines. You have ten thousand slick, automated routines for getting through life. If all sensing, looking, and listening did was slow you down, that might not be good—well, it might actually be fine, given the frantic lives we lead. What can often happen, however, is that you have temporary disruptions of routines, because the energy is not flowing smoothly through the habits. Eventually, you can be mindful while moving at orthodox speeds while having the *internal* feeling of being unhurried.

Now tell me more about the second part of what you were describing.

STUDENT: *So the difference between my experience and my observing ego or awareness: I'm not quite participating in the experience; I'm behind my experience; there's a difference between seeing and somebody who notices these things or experiences.*

Let me make sure I understand this thoroughly. When you say "behind it," do you mean like literally physically behind your body, or is this just an analogy?

STUDENT: *Kind of an analogy. Like when I'm seeing something, if I don't pay attention, the sight is just there, but when I pay attention to seeing I'm behind seeing, something like that.*

You have some consciousness that you're seeing, instead of just being absorbed in the seeing?

STUDENT: *Yes, but then I feel kind of distanced. I'm not in it.*

That's good, it's working.

100

STUDENT: *But then I don't feel I'm involved, I don't feel I am in it. I'm not alienated, but I am distanced.*

Okay, there are two things to look at here.

What you are feeling as you first begin this mindfulness work will not always be what you feel. What you feel and observe in the self-remembering process can vary a great deal from time to time. Feeling that you are not so involved, not participating so much in ordinary life, is excellent to be feeling at the beginning, but it may change.

If you just want to feel that you are participating, that you are normal, just continue with the trance of everyday life, and many people will help you feel very involved. The television people set up programs to get you involved, for instance. Lots of people are willing to engage your intention, make you feel involved—and manipulate you in the process, because it is profitable. They do it also because that is the only thing they know. They are asleep, too. It is not a conscious conspiracy to keep people asleep; it is a conspiracy *un*consciously carried out by other sleeping people.

You may feel less involved, or that your experience is *less* vivid, or even that you are less alive at times. That is all right, because it means the process is working. But do not take that to mean that you are always going to feel less involved somehow. In fact, you may have some experiences in which you simultaneously feel less and more involved at the same time. An experience may become more vivid, more intense, more real, and at the same time, you are not totally in it, you are "behind it" somehow.

STAYING WITH THE NOW

STUDENT: *Yes, as we talk about it I'm gaining some understanding . . .* [CTT interrupts] Keep track of your arms and legs *now.* [*Questioner's demeanor changes as he comes back to the present.*]

Yes, that changes things, doesn't it?

STUDENT: *Yes . . . continuing, at the same time I think I was experiencing a certain aloneness, which wasn't that clear before I practiced.*

Now let's move this into the present moment. Right *now*, as you practice this mindfulness technique, you are in a world, stimuli are reaching you, you are having some kind of experience. You have some kind of contact with your arms and legs. Ask yourself what you are experiencing right now.

STUDENT: *More tension in my arms, and now a feeling of tension in my legs . . .*

That doesn't mean it has to stay that way, so don't freeze it. OK? Go ahead.

STUDENT: *Sort of a feeling of projected energy in front of me, affecting my visual perception. My vision is narrowed, its scope is less than 180 degrees, it's all focused more narrowly. My hearing is . . . just this moment my hearing was caught by the traffic noise outside. Then when I hear my voice it feels like the sounds are traveling through my skull. The bell sounds, come to the present.*

The sound of your voice really is traveling through your skull. That's part of the physics of reality.

Now how about the feeling of aloneness you were starting to describe from your past experience. Is there something like that you're experiencing now?

STUDENT: *Not identical, but yes, because I'm the only one who is experiencing my experience.*

DON'T CONFUSE THE CONCEPTUAL WITH THE EXPERIENTIAL

That sounds very conceptual, very intellectual somehow. Rather than describing your feelings in conceptual terms, try to describe them in simpler terms. Is it cold? Is it hot? Is it thick? Is it thin?

STUDENT: *Well, as I keep interacting with you, I feel with the heart, but then . . . now, when I talk, when I try to experience the aloneness, I feel the boundary of my body. It is very small, more acute, a sharp definition of what's inside and what's outside of my skin.*

Is it smaller than usual, or are you simply more aware of that boundary than usual?

STUDENT: *That's a good question. Maybe, normally I don't pay much attention. It might be the same size, I'm not sure.*

There is a cheap sort of form of union with other people in the world that comes with being rather blandly unaware of where one's boundaries are. I do not think that is the kind of union we are really looking for. Maybe the road to real union and contact starts with being aware of the actual feelings of being alone. I am venturing a guess. Stick with it, we'll see how it develops.

STUDENT: [New questioner] *This is very difficult. As soon as I left here I was involved in it. The whole night I couldn't stop practicing this awareness of my legs and arms and body. I had a lot of unusual sensations. I don't know if I'm doing it correctly. It was a very difficult night!*

And right now?

STUDENT: *Right now I'm feeling all right, a little conscious of my body. But sometimes during the day I've felt strange, it's been hard to blend in with what's been going on.*

I think you're experiencing some good transitional symptoms, like this gentleman I've just been talking with. You are interfering with your usual habits of forgetfulness and automatic behavior. When we have been used to being carried along by these habits year after year after year and then we actually begin paying attention, sometimes it is strange or uncomfortable or awkward. The temptation is to go back deeply to sleep, and the automatic habits will carry one on through life.

You're sticking with it, though. Or perhaps the process is sticking with you. Most people complain they can't remember to do it instead of being unable to stop! So you're having an especially fortunate reaction in some ways.

But suppose some part of you says, It's too much, can't I ever go back to sleep? Don't worry, it's all too easy to go back to sleep. I use *sleep* now to mean ordinary consciousness, consensus consciousness, *waking sleep.*

BE CAREFUL OF THE SUPEREGO TAKING OVER

I don't know if this is happening to you, but I'm sure it's starting to happen to some people, so I must warn you: be very careful not to let this process go to your superego. Your superego loves the idea of self-remembering; it sees it as a more sensitive way of catching all your faults, defects, and sins, to catch all those it has been missing. It will then punish you for being so awful. This mindfulness process, this self-remembering process of sensing, looking, and listening, is not intended to help the superego. Your superego is probably already quite good enough at finding fault, and you do not need to reinforce that. [*General laughter*]

What do you do, then, if your superego does get involved?

Perhaps you observe something about yourself and your superego nags, Yes, you never do it right, or perhaps, You've sinned again and you're going to go to hell! Continue to sense, look, and listen: this gives you a little grounding in your body and the here and now. Simply observe that your superego is now telling you how awful you are. Treat the superego as one more phenomenon to observe.

You probably should not try to make it go away, saying, as it were, Stop that, superego! That will give it more force and you will get into a longer argument with the superego. Simply note, for example, My superego says I am a sinner and I am going to go to hell. Got it. And now I notice that there's a feeling of flushing in my right foot. Keep that grounding in the body. Keep actively sensing, looking and listening, and superego attacks will eventually come and go, without becoming obsessions and taking over the mindfulness process.

Once in a while, too, give yourself a break. One of the ways that your superego can subvert this mindfulness process is by thinking, Aha! I've been introduced to a genuine spiritual technique. I have a chance and I *must* do it right *every moment*! That makes it hard to go to sleep at night. Once in a while you have to say to your mind, I've been good; I've been doing a good job today, and now I'm on a break. The bell sounds, again, and you become more mindful, again. Ooops, my own superego is slipping in there, saying I'm allowed a break if I've *earned* it, if I've been good. Hell, just give yourself a break sometimes, whether you "deserve" it or not!

STUDENT: *Sometimes as I was doing this during the day there were two of me, a "me" that was experiencing, and a "me" that was experiencing that I was experiencing. There was a gap or a void in between.*

Tell me more about this gap or void. Can you sense it now and describe it in the present tense?

STUDENT: *It was a void, and it was a very quiet thing. It is complete . . .*

You're going to make a lot of Buddhists jealous. [*General laughter*]

STUDENT: *I hope not!*

Wow, she's got the void, where it's quiet and empty!

STUDENT: *No, I don't think it's anything like that! I can't really say, though, I can't really name it, but it's like a void; I feel it. Because I was experiencing this witness in the back of my head, at least sometimes I was able to place it there, like somebody in the back of my head who was doing all this sensing of my hands and being aware of my talking, of my voice. So I can't say more about this gap, it was something . . .*

Are you experiencing it now?

STUDENT: *Not as strong as it was earlier.*

Keep up the process tonight, and if you start experiencing it strongly again, say something. We'll work with it then.

STUDENT: *I don't know if my experience is as good as the one we just heard, I had an experience in . . .*

Hey, your experience is your experience. You can say it. May I put to rest the delusion that there are standards about this and I'm judging you all to see whether you come up to standards? That's an illusion, that's a trap. I fall into it too often, but when I do, I try to get out of it.

STUDENT: *I had things that I wanted to get done, to get done on time, like cleaning up my home office. I did it very well, and I slept well. I was surprised by how well I did it and how great I felt. I didn't worry about it like I usually do, I just did it. That's unusual for me. Was it due to doing this sensing?*

Maybe it's attributable to this, maybe it's a coincidence. But it seems related. Now tell me if I'm putting words in your mouth that aren't accurate, but it sounds like what I mentioned earlier, that simultaneously you're being more detached and yet experiencing things more vividly? That's a very interesting experience.

STUDENT: *Yes, absolutely. This is what I've been wanting to experience, but I didn't have the tools before, I didn't know how. Today I did things that are hard for me, but I just got them done. Sensing my arms and legs really helped.*

105

One of the things the process of sensing, looking, and listening can do, to describe it a different way, is that it *embodies* us. Since the reality is that on this world, in this incarnation, we do have bodies, it is generally pretty healthy to be aware of that fact. That way we use the body much more effectively.

STUDENT: *One other thing that I have to mention. I usually get a massage once a month. Today I did go for a massage, since I thought that as long as I was so much in my body it would really help me.*

Did it?

STUDENT: *Yes, it really did. Usually I go there and I talk, I'm not very aware. But today I was quiet and practiced this sensing exercise, and I really felt it.*

I can strongly recommend that when you get a massage, make it a mindfulness meditation experience, try to stay in your body. I have always been amazed by how we usually drift away from the actual, sensual pleasure. Conventional Western psychology says that we are driven by the pleasure principle, that we try to maximize our pleasure and minimize our pain. Yet I used to notice that many times when I would get a massage, it would be wonderful, but within minutes, I would drift off into pleasant fantasies, where I was not feeling my body any more. I would think, Where is the pleasure principle? The pleasure is most strongly there if you stay focused in the body, but it is so easy to drift off, especially by talking. The pleasure of a massage is special and nourishing. The pleasure of fantasy is much smaller by contrast, and certainly doesn't provide what Gurdjieff called the food of impressions, that nourishment that comes through clear sensing.

I have nothing against pleasure. I rather like pleasure and definitely prefer it to pain, as long as one does not get too attached to it. A good massage is also excellent for your body and spirit.

In the Rigpa Fellowship, we often end various meditative and devotional practices with a dedication of the merit of the practice to help all sentient beings. Part of the formal prayer that goes with that is that all beings may live without *too* much attachment and *too* much aversion.[1] There is nothing wrong with having preferences. There is nothing wrong with preferring to have a good meal rather than go to the dentist, as long as it does not get so excessive that you will kill to have a good meal and you will put off going to the dentist when you really need to go, because you want to avoid the anxiety or pain so much.

Well, we're side tracking a little into pleasure here, but it's enjoyable to side track into pleasure. Thank you for your observation.

BLOWING IT

STUDENT: *I had a very nice day today and I felt very much in tune with nature and truth and all of that. But in the afternoon I went into this office where somebody had a cold. I felt the immediate presence of congestion and started feeling congested. I had anxiety. Usually in situations like this I can take a deep breath and get centered, but I became very anxious and concerned that I was catching a cold. I didn't know how to get out of that state.*

So you blew it. When did you know you blew it?

STUDENT: *When I couldn't breathe anymore. When I felt like I couldn't take a deep breath and relax. I didn't have the ability to get unstuck from this anxious state.*

Most of life consists of blowing it all the time and so catching things—not just colds, but other people's emotional states and other people's attacks, both overt and covert—and not knowing that we are blowing it, not knowing that we are catching these things. Life is very hypnotic, mesmerizing. People and situations suck you in all the time.

Knowing that this happens to you is unpleasant knowledge, but knowing it is the beginning of being able to do something effective about it. One of the reasons that we stay asleep is that starting to become more awake, more mindful, shows us over and over again how we keep blowing it, how we keep losing it. A lot of times that is very hard to face, and so we would rather go back to sleep and dream our daydreams and remain in ignorance. Part of mindfulness work is gritting your teeth and hanging in there sometimes, and seeing that automatic reactions carried you away.

The first time—I mentioned this yesterday afternoon—I ever really got the idea of being mindful and present in this way was in reading one of Ouspensky's books on the Gurdjieff work, years ago. I had a mini-awakening. After half a second, I lost it and did not know that

I had lost it for months. Now it usually does not take months. That is progress. This process intensifies our awareness of how little control we have over our minds, how easily we forget to make this slight effort that makes us more present. Keep hanging in there.

Did you catch the cold?

STUDENT: *No. But I really wanted to get out of there. I was able to come back to sensing much better once I was out of there.*

Of course, there was a realistic element to the situation. You can catch a cold from someone else. But the way you described the situation, things were blown way up out of proportion in your mental reaction. You caught the cold psychically long before a single germ could ever have crossed the space. Good. Thank you for the observation.

STUDENT: *I was very affected by the exercise we did yesterday, where we had to do a monologue in which one partner verbalized only what they were experiencing at that very moment.*

I think it might be worth our while to take ten minutes to do it again. [See p. 67 for a description of the experience.]

[*Ten minutes pass.*] OK let's come back together as a group now.

After a social interaction, even of the strange, artificial sort that we do in our exercises, there is a tendency to lapse back into a kind of happy unconsciousness. Try to stay with using your arms and legs as a way of being present. In addition, as one Gurdjieffian teacher of mine once said, you can get very, very conscious during a meeting or an experience, build up a certain amount of inertia, and "piss it all away" in one minute of hysterical conversation at the end. I've done that many times so I know it's true.

Let's continue with reports on what happened just now or during the day.

STUDENT: *I find, as I have before, that it's much easier to sense myself more thoroughly when I'm with other people who are doing it. The energy just builds up in a big way.*[2]

Yes.

STUDENT: *I also notice that I have a tendency to go in and out of practicing sensing. As I speed up, as I move fast, it simply conks out,*

I lose it. At work there's usually pressure to speed up, so this happens all the time. When I slow down, I can do it again.

Modern life is a tough place to do this work, because modern life is a kind of barely controlled hysteria in many ways. Everybody is hurrying to the future, which is going to bring happiness. The trouble is that you never arrive at the future. That does not stop people from hurrying, though, because they think if they just run a little *faster* maybe they would finally catch it. [*Laughter*] Yes, you all know what I'm talking about.

This illustrates that, while we may *intellectually* understand the need for spaciousness and mindfulness, this understanding alone does not give us bodily and emotional understanding, and so we hurry on.

One of the great things that the spiritual traditions teach us is that *there is no happiness anywhere but in the present:* the constant pursuit of happiness in the future is just perpetuating illusions.

The kind of mindfulness training I have been giving you comes from a tradition of a way, a path, *in life.* It is not a monastic tradition, but as you practice it, you will find that you will naturally want to find some time when you can slow down and just do some work in your garden, for example, at your own pace, or have a leisurely cup of tea, take a walk, or wash the dishes at your own pace—things like that.

We are all stuck in many circumstances in our lives where we have to move at a pretty fast pace, but we can always get at least momentary breaks, and we can still cultivate a little *inner* slowing down. It is harder when the outside pace is fast and the demands are greater, but remember our analogy: you build bigger and bigger muscles by gradually lifting bigger and bigger weights. You may find that a lot of situations you face now seem so difficult that you think it would be impossible to maintain any contact with your arms and legs, with the present, when you are coping with them. Yet a month later, after doing this practice more often, you might find that what was impossible is now possible, at least to some degree. You can take at least a moment to check in, to say, metaphorically speaking, Ah, I'm here! I'm embodied, I'm breathing, my heart is beating, the sun is shining. I am alive! And then forget it right away, because there's something you have to hurry to! And off you go to fantasy land. But again you can come back: Gee, I went far away there, but I'm back now. It's nice to be here.

WHO HAS BEEN MINDING THE STORE?

STUDENT: *I found I forgot about doing it for a few hours the bell is ringing now, be here. When I do the sensing exercise, part of me is doing it and part of me is wandering off all the time and part of me is . . . Today, for example, when I had determined to sense myself and be present, I found I had put the money in a parking meter but I hadn't been present at all. Now I'm wondering who is doing what? I'm wondering who is in charge of "me"?*

I've often had that kind of experience. When I remember to come to the present, I often wonder, Where have I been? Who has been minding the store? I can access the memory that there is a guy named Charley who is doing all these things, but I realize that this Charley is a very shallow fellow. I do not think he is very real, like I am real when I take a moment to come to the present. I can think about his psychological makeup. I know he is very handy, has skills, and knows the ropes, so I guess I'm glad he's minding the store when I'm "gone," when I'm asleep, but I'd rather be awake.

A good exercise if you often have to deal with parking meters is to intentionally set them up temporarily as special reminders, making a resolution to be especially present and sensing, looking, and listening whenever you are dealing with one. You can generalize this technique by thinking of something you do a number of times a day and then making a resolution that in those moments you are going to come to yourself, to the present. Even if you forget a lot during the rest of the day, during those moments you will remember. Use the constants in your life as alarm clocks.

Do not make any "eternal vows," however, because these alarm clocks work only temporarily. Using parking meters as an example, if you normally have to feed the meter half a dozen times a day, this technique will work for a week or so. When you are fumbling for the change, you will remember to come to your senses and come to your arms and legs, to *re-member* yourself in a literal sense. You will be present and wake up a little more for a moment. After a while, though, any particular technique like that will usually start to get taken over by habit. The habit may be that whenever you see the parking meter you will have a little fantasy about being present. It will run very smoothly and be a very pleasant fantasy, but you will no longer actually become present. When you notice that happening, it is time to change to a different alarm clock, to a different reminder.

Visiting the Zen Center in Green Gulch recently, I noticed that they had set up this kind of mindfulness alarm clock. If I remember correctly, what the people there were supposed to do was always go through a doorway by stepping the left foot through first. I tried it for the day I was there. It was a good way of reminding me to be present. But, technically speaking, it also seemed foolish to me to have such a fixed rule, because within a week most people would probably get in the habit of stepping through doorways with their left foot first, and perhaps form the *habit* of feeling good about practicing "mindfulness" instead of actually becoming mindful. Maybe they should change that rule every week. The bell is ringing now, stop, be here.

EYE CONTACT

STUDENT: *I have a hard time with eye contact in this practice and in the exercise we did. You told us to look around a lot, even when you're speaking to someone. I'm embarrassed by doing that. I feel I should look in the other person's eyes, yet there's a relief in not doing it.*

We are a very funny culture when it comes to eye contact. We want it and we do not want it. We can learn to fake it, too. We can learn to look into somebody's eyes without actually doing any looking—you learn to point your eyeballs at theirs while you are mostly off somewhere in fantasy.

Actually looking into someone's eyes can be part of paying real attention to someone else, though. In the pair exercises we have done, you may have noticed that there are times when you are really aware of the attention you are getting from your partner. Is it nice, or is it scary? [*General affirmations that it is nice, but definitely scary*]

That's OK, we can handle a little scariness.

STUDENT: *I kept spacing out looking at my partner. When I was aware, I didn't feel anything in my arms and legs, but my attention was drawn to the question, How could my body get hurt? I was aware of my shoulder blades and how tense I was and how cowardly.*

And what happened then?

STUDENT: *I don't think anything happened.*

You didn't relax a little? Wait, you look like you've just spaced out now.

BREAKING THE DAILY TENSION CYCLE

STUDENT: *I don't know. But every time I came back to my body in the exercise, I felt pain.*

And that, of course, can condition you to not do it, to not live in your body, so that you can stay away from the pain. Sometimes we may feel pain when we remember to be present in our bodies. As an experiment, when you remember to come back to your body, try hanging in there a few seconds and actually going a little more deeply into the pain. See if you can relax it, or see if there is a specific message hidden in the pain.

I think the way life works for a lot of us is that we wake up at seven o'clock and think about our worries and problems: we get a little tense. We get lost in our fantasies about our problems and forget to fully relax, and so we are already carrying, let us say, one unit of tension. At eight o'clock, we hear an item on the radio that bothers us, and we get a little more tense. At nine o'clock, somebody gives us a funny look, and we get a little more tense. Since we are not really being aware, we are carrying this accumulating tension without relaxing, and by the end of the day we may be carrying around a hundred units of tension. I say a hundred because after a while tension does not increase linearly by one unit each time, but it goes up by five or ten. When you are already tense, the same amount of stress can cause an even bigger reaction than it did before.

If you come back to your body, sense it at, say, 8:30 in the morning, you may realize that you are carrying your shoulders hunched up a little. Perhaps if you take a deep breath, you can let them down a little bit. Now, when the next bit of tension comes on, you may not be very present to it, but it does not build on as high a level of tension that is already there. Instead of tension gradually accumulating and accumulating and accumulating during the day, if you can remember to drop down into your body, to sense, look, and listen once in a while, at the end of the day, you end up with much less tension than before.

Remember, though, our primary goal here is not tension reduction. The primary goal is mindfulness. Sometimes that includes mindfulness of tensions that do not go away just because you are mindful or just because you try to relax; perhaps there is some deeper reason for them. A lot of your ordinary tensions, however, will eventually fade away if you regularly practice sensing, looking, and listening. Sadly, much of our ordinary suffering is stupid suffering. It is stupid because we are not really paying very clear attention to it and dealing with it right away, but we are trying to avoid it because it is a little painful. We would rather "trip out" somehow. The consequence is that the suffering accumulates and interacts with other suffering. It is stupid because if you stayed present to it you could drop it.

That does not mean that all suffering is stupid. Some spiritual traditions say that some suffering comes from more important reasons and, taken with the proper attitude, may become karmic cleansings. I do not know if this is true, but I hope so. I like to think that there are reasons for some of our suffering, more than just our own stupidity. Certainly by being more present you can undercut a lot of the suffering caused by tension.

But you have to watch the tendency to forget the goal of mindfulness, because as we discussed, many times when you come to your senses you feel pain, and almost by reflex, you suddenly become absorbed by something else again. That doesn't mean not to take some aspirin if you have a headache, but learn how to and practice hanging in there for a while.

OBSERVING SUPEREGO ATTACKS

STUDENT: *Perhaps this is an example of stupid suffering. I guess each one of us has a different kind of Achilles' heel, but mine is that when I receive undue or unfair criticism I get so caught, compulsively analyzing the problem: Why has this happened, it's unfair! Other people might not be so bothered by this. But even when I have enough presence to say to myself, Come back to my senses!, still that internal dialogue has compelling force to draw me in. I cannot get back to just sensing, looking, and listening, so isn't there some way I can do this right?*

How come you haven't mastered this already? You've had twenty four hours to practice it! [*Laughter*]

Please, we must remember to be kind to ourselves. We have had so many years of practicing the wrong thing that we cannot change it overnight. Some things can change relatively rapidly by becoming more mindful; a lot of things are stubborn, persistent, and deeply embedded. It is going to take a long time to the bell is ringing change them.

I'm going to give you at least two weeks, maybe three, to reach perfection. And there will be a quiz then. But meanwhile, relax.

I find it's getting to be more and more fun in life to speak for people's superegos: we all know how far we've come by being driven by guilt. [*Much laughter*]

STUDENT: *You've succeeded: my superego now speaks in the voice of Charles Tart!*

Ah, my dream come true at last: to be part of someone's superego. No, really, you don't have to let me into your superego.

You really do have to observe your superego. Observing it is much tougher than just coming to your senses in the here and now, but as you get better at just remembering your arms and legs, that process will give you the grounding so that superego attacks will become clearer for what they are, namely, a voice in your head criticizing you for something, a voice that is partially foreign to your own psychological processes and essential self.

As things are, too much of our experience is seen as and is identified with "ME"! *I* feel this way; these are *my* values; these are *my* standards. As we've discussed earlier, we tend to be totally caught up in and identified with whatever is happening internally. But there is no superego inherent in our arms and legs. They are completely in the here and now, so keeping just a little bit of attention on them grounds you, giving you more spaciousness to realize that this is a *part* of me, which is attacking me, and this is another *part* of me accepting the attack and feeling guilty.

There is a kind of spaciousness that comes from the observation of the superego, because then you are not quite so serious, not quite so fully identified with it. Then, with more of this kind of mindfulness practice, superego attacks could become even clearer, more distinguishable from the rest of you. Superego attacks for most people have a mental *flavor,* and you begin to *taste* the flavor that is attached to certain of your thoughts and feelings. You are thereby alerted to be careful about uncritically identifying with those thoughts and feelings, to keep sensing your arms and legs, and to look at the thoughts and feelings associated with that superego flavor a little more closely. It may not be you. It may be superego, your false personality, rather than essence.

STUDENT: *Normally, part of my mind is attacking me most of the time. But when I do the sensing exercise, it fills my consciousness, it keeps me busy, and there isn't much room for my superego to attack me.*

At the same time as we increasingly become aware of superego as not our real self, I think there is a sense in which we need to be kind to our superego. The superego was generally put there by our parents out of a desire to help us. We were kids and we were stupid about a lot of things, stupid in a way that could get us killed. There were prohibitions and do's and don'ts conditioned into us, which were intended to protect us.

Unfortunately, the process usually got out of hand. Some of what was conditioned into us was just neurotic crap from our parents, craziness that they had gotten from their parents, which they had gotten in turn from their parents, general cultural craziness, and on and on. They may have thought they were operating purely from love and goodwill, but it really passed on the bad karma of the family, as it were.

Some of it was for protection: "Don't walk out into the street because the cars will get you." Kids are forgetful, and maybe they need to be neurotically afraid of going out into the street. Better a neurotic child than a dead child. But we are grown-ups now and do not need such a compulsive, unintelligent, guilt-inducing control mechanism. The superego was in the first place put there out of love, at least in some ways, but you still have to learn its flavor, learn to distinguish it from the more essential you. Do not mindlessly attack

115

it back, because although there are some times when that is a necessary way of defending yourself from its attacks, as a general rule, attacking parts of yourself has its own negative consequences. So you might say, Hi, superego. I heard you. Now you can relax, and I'll do the intelligent thing here that comes from being a grown-up who is actually paying attention to the realities of the situation.

STUDENT: *I know we have to observe the superego and eventually come to terms with it. But I'm discouraged from my own experience with how persistent it is and from your story of having to observe your urge to kill drivers who tailgated you for years.*

When superegos are built into us they are not put in with time limits. They are given to us as absolutes, and as children, we tend to have very absolutistic minds anyway: This is *the* rule for *all* eternity! We are not taught to think, This is the way I have to shape myself for a few years until I get smarter, then I can make up my own mind. In addition, we often do not have direct access to these superego rules in our ordinary consciousness, because our adult consciousness is very different from our child consciousness, into which it was built. We have incorporated the superego as part of ourselves, as part of our false personalities, but it's a childhood part that's hard to get into as an adult.

SECONDARY GAINS

There is a concept in psychology that I do not think I have ever seen in Eastern thought, the interesting concept of *secondary gains*. It says that I may suffer in some obvious and conscious way as a primary effect, but actually I get something out of that suffering, a secondary gain. As an example, consider some kid who does not get enough attention. Remember what we talked about earlier, that we have a vital need for attention? So he has to be *bad:* then he gets punished, getting the attention that is so badly needed. It's much better to get low quality attention than none at all, much better to eat junk food than to starve to death.

Of course, this situation does not apply just to kids. There are some of us walking around who still have a habit, a psychological mechanism, that unconsciously says that when I yell at myself in my head, it is like getting attention from Mommy, and I really need that.

If we could make such a clear, conscious statement to ourselves, describing this kind of process, its ridiculousness would become apparent, and it would be hard for the process to run. It is not clear, however; the patterns are murky. It does not come up in a mindful way. With the practice of mindfulness, however, things are articulated more. To use the example of anger, you could say, I feel angry, but that is a vague, general feeling. Being more mindful, you might say, I have a burning sensation in my stomach, my muscles are clenched, and I'm thinking about so-and-so. By starting to articulate the emotion and differentiate it more, you can see it more clearly and, at the same time, be a little less identified with it by seeing it more clearly.

There are also individual reasons for any particular person's habitual suffering. For each person, your particular life history sets up particular secondary gains, tied in with particular psychodynamics that fuel these processes. I am sure that someone has invented this exercise in psychotherapy, but you might try having a dialogue with your superego in your head. Ask it, Okay, I get the guilt, I feel bad about myself. Now, what am I supposed to learn from this? See if you get an answer. Ask for clarification if you get a fuzzy answer. This tyrant, your superego, has been pushing you around for years; you are owed an explanation!

This is an exercise to play with. I just invented it. Maybe it will work, maybe it won't, but I think it's worth a try.

YOUR EXPERIENCES WILL BE UNIQUE TO YOU

STUDENT: *I was trying to do the exercise in the world, trying to keep track of my arms and legs, and I find that my left side is easier to sense than my right side. Is it normal? Can you say anything about this?*

Only you really know the answer to that. I never heard anybody report that particular experience before, but then I've heard a lot of people report very individual things. I would say just hang in there and keep doing it, and maybe you'll start to notice a flavor, maybe at some level you feel differently about the right and left sides of your body.

But I'm just speculating: you have direct access. Each person has access to relatively direct data about his or her response to the sensing, looking, and listening practice. If you notice particular things about results of your practice, you will probably go on to speculate about what that means. But don't let speculation, intellectualization, blur the actual experience. Many of the comments I have made on people's responses are based on my own experience, partly on other people's experiences, and partly on speculation. As to the degree to which they apply to you personally, only you personally the bell is ringing come to your senses will ever be able to figure that out.

I want to emphasize that. Some of my comments may not apply to you. They may be *wrong* for you, misleading for you, even if they are right for somebody else. Furthermore, things change. Maybe after a few weeks of doing this practice you will notice a difference. Maybe in a few years you will get direct experiential data on what the difference is. Maybe a particular experience will go away without ever being "understandable" in terms acceptable to your ordinary mind. There is a great variety.

This self-remembering technique of sensing, looking, and listening is not some monolithic thing designed to produce a particular experience. It is to put each one of us in better, clearer touch with our own individual, unique reality. And that's pretty neat. That is why I warn you not to freeze it. When you have some particular experience that makes sense or feels good, do not stop doing sensing, looking, and listening as a technique to become more aware of what *is* and begin trying to use it as a technique to regain that particular good feeling. Trying to use it for that purpose, to hold on to pleasure, will freeze it. This solidification, this freezing of experience, might keep you in a more desirable state than you usually are in now, but it aborts the awakening process. Flexibility is the name of the game.

DEALING WITH FEAR

STUDENT: *My father and I did that technique of sensing, looking, and listening as an exercise last night, and when I was actually focusing on sensing, looking, and listening, I became much more aware of my fear. Some of my fears became more vivid. Particularly one phobia I had as a child, which I haven't been able to overcome. It grabs me sometimes even as an adult. It's the fear of darkness.*

So I was doing my laundry, and I had to go to the basement, which is a pretty dark place, to pick up my clothing. And I was unable to go. My fear was so intense that I could not see it as a fantasy. I was so in touch with that fear. Finally, my father reminded me that I was creating my fear, that it was a fantasy. But it was so intense. That was my experience.

Is there anyone here who, as a child, was *not* afraid of the dark at some time or another? [*One person raises hand*]

You're lucky. Fear of the dark is a nearly universal fear. We get it as children. We not only have that fear, but to make it worse, most of us were told how *shameful* it was to feel that way. We are told, "You are silly to feel that way." That attitude made us feel even worse, because we were still afraid of the dark and then we were ashamed, too. Then we grow older, and the rules are quite clear: you are supposed to grow out of it. You know, inside, that as an adult you still have that fear to a certain extent, so now you have a secret shame, something you have to hide from other people. We go through life as adults faking a lack of fear but knowing that it might be there.

I can remember, still with a feeling of shame and an embarrassment at admitting this, an experience about fifteen years ago. During a period of intense psychological work on myself, I admitted to myself, after struggling for weeks and with great reluctance, that I was still afraid of the dark. I was so ashamed! I had feelings on the order of, I am a grown man, supposedly psychologically sophisticated and mature, I am on the spiritual path, and yet I am afraid of the dark! I was mad at myself, too. One night I was alone in the house, my wife and kids were away, and I said, "All right, damn it. Come on, evil spirits of the dark, or whatever you are!" I turned out all the lights, sat there in the dark, and said, "Do it! Get it over with. Come on, bogeymen, gobble me up!"

As you can tell by the fact that I'm here today, they did not get me. But for a long time I kept wondering, What is that sound? Is it dangerous? I kept thinking I was being totally silly, but I really felt afraid. Finally, some part of me got bored with being afraid, since nothing happened, and I lost most of my fear of the dark. Now I think I am still a little afraid of the dark, but it's within normal limits, it's not much of an inconvenience in life.

There is a certain reality here, of course. For most of human history, being outside in the dark at night *was* dangerous. There were things out there that could eat you. The probability was low—not too many people found a tiger as soon as they went out—but I suspect fear of the dark is genetic. I think it is programmed into our bodies. This body knows it can be eaten and is naturally suspicious of the dark. The probability may be low of being attacked or eaten on any specific occasion, but the consequences are devastating! I think there is a certain sense in which thinking you should never feel the slightest fear of the dark is unrealistic. That is antisurvival, even today. You do not, however, need to have it be overwhelming, and you should not feel ashamed of it.

You can try this mindfulness approach. First, learn to sense, look, and listen fairly well. Then, while sensing, looking, and listening, go home and lock the doors, *after* making sure the house is empty and secure. That eliminates the realistic component of fear of the dark. Now turn out all the lights and keep on sensing, looking, and listening. Of course, you cannot look very much when you have turned out all the lights, but you will have no problem feeling your body, because fear manifests as a lot of body sensation.

Can you articulate those body sensations by going into them more deeply, instead of just saying, "I feel fear"? What *exactly* does fear feel like? A lot of times breaking your experience down, through mindfulness, to experiences like it's a tension here, a trembling there, a looseness in my gut, and so forth will do much toward changing your reaction to fear. You needn't overdo it either. You can decide, I have had enough for now. I'm going to turn the lights back on now. I have done a three minute experiment and I was terrified. I didn't die, but I've experimented enough for now.

Remember you're going for *truth,* for clearer and clearer mindfulness of what *is,* not what ought to be. The better you are at sensing, looking, and listening or at classical vipassana meditation, the better you can do this exercise for dealing with fear.

Emotions have heavy body components, so by getting more into our bodies, we become more aware of emotions. The bell has sounded now. Getting in clearer touch with our emotions, with our body sensations, is part of being more alive, and of course, by being more alive, good things can come in, too, not just unpleasant things.

It's our ending time. Some people have a long way to drive home, and I've had a long day, so we'll end this session.

I find this very valuable. I like being in a room with people who are working on being present. It helps me be more present.

Keep sensing, looking, and listening as much as possible during the coming week. While it's not absolutely necessary, also try to do the morning exercise each day.

FIVE

RESULTS OF MINDFULNESS PRACTICE
Second Follow-up Session

THINKING ABOUT MINDFULNESS
VERSUS BEING MINDFUL

STUDENT: *As I work with the techniques, I have been noticing over time that often what I am doing is having the* thought *of sensing, looking, and listening, rather than actually doing it. So it is another layer of watchfulness that is going on top of that.*

What you are doing is very common. Unfortunately, it is much easier to think about being in the present than to actually be in the present. Thoughts are cheap. They come easily. They satisfy: "Gee, I'm thinking about it, so I must be doing the right thing." Actually, I suppose it is better to think about it and not do it than to not even think about it. At least there is the possibility that the thought will lead to action at some point.

STUDENT: *What I have done in those moments when it seems I am merely thinking a thought of doing it is to get down in the body sensations.*

This is good. You have a chance in this way to see how vitally important the body is in this work. The body does not *think* about being present; the body *is* present. So one significant portion of us is already here, now. If we can tune in to that body presence, we are all right. When the mind *thinks* about doing that, it might lead to tuning in, or it might just lead to more thoughts about it. Coming back to the body sensations is really where it is at. Thank goodness, we have bodies!

I think this has something to do with why in Buddhism they say that of all the various six realms of existence that they believe exist, from the hell realms to the god realms, being a human being is the best place to work for enlightenment. We have a body that can anchor us in the here and now. Was it Archimedes who said, "Give me a long enough lever, and I can move the world"? You must, however, have a fulcrum to rest that lever on. I think our mind is like a big lever, but there is usually no relatively solid place, no fulcrum, to pivot it on to accomplish things. We can use our body sensations to give it that stability, that leverage.

MINDFULNESS IN PSYCHOTHERAPY

STUDENT: *I work as a therapist, and I have been finding, especially with certain of my patients, that if I am really tuning in to my body and what is happening in the room my patients tend to be more there, too. I also am more aware of how I go in and out of being with people. The therapy session is a nice place to actually pay attention to how I drift in and out of being present, because it is fairly quiet and it is pretty easy to focus in this sensing, looking, and listening way.*

Can you give us a more specific example of how your being more there makes your patients more there?

STUDENT: *They will start talking in more concrete terms. They will start talking about more immediate kinds of experiences they are having. I have also found that both they and I take deep breaths every once in a while, or more often than normal.*

Remember, everybody, shift your eyes around a little. Do not stare fixedly. We've been away a week, and we're falling back into conventional habits that promote waking sleep.

STUDENT: *I guess that the more people are in touch with their bodies—it is true for me, too—the more easily they can talk about their feelings. I believe that I think more clearly, too.*

Another experience that I have had—this afternoon I took a walk up in the woods near our house. I love being outdoors. I was paying attention to my physical experiences, and there was a period of three or four minutes when I didn't know where I was. Suddenly, I came to and started thinking about my body again. I realized that it was fun wherever I went, that the period when I didn't know where I was was fun and it was seductive, but I wasn't in the here and now at all.

You were probably off in another world, on a fantasy jag. Fantasy jags are often wonderful. It is not that they are inherently bad. The problem is when they become automatized, when they have become the only way to exist, when they constantly, automatically take you away the bell is ringing, come to the present now, from the present situation. Then their power is destructive. It is not that fantasy is evil; it is a great talent that has gone badly astray.

Let's talk a little more about your patients coming more into the present when you are more present.

One thing you are doing as a therapist, quite aside from using specific psychological techniques and theories, is that you are providing some attention to help reduce the problems that arise from that attentional deficiency disease we spoke of earlier, the disease of a person not getting enough attention. We are all usually so spaced out in everyday life that all we give to others (and ourselves) is cheap, low quality attention and, in return, all we get is cheap, low quality attention. But I believe some part of us, some deeper aspect of mind, is pretty well tuned into what is really happening in reality. So I think that some part of your patients knows when you are actually more present in the room, in the here and now. It senses that you are there, and that has an effect on your patients.

Probably this recognition by a patient's deeper self, in turn, has an effect on you, helping you to be present even more. You are giving much better quality attention, they sense it, and they give a better quality output back. I have found in doing this kind of mindfulness training work that if, for instance, people start to space out to our so-called normal state the kinds of questions they ask may sound like important questions, but they are really off the top of the head somehow. There is an unreal quality to them, no depth.

CONNECTING WITH OTHERS THROUGH MINDFULNESS

If people sit in a meeting and stay in their bodies, however, a lot of the questions they thought they wanted to ask disappear. Those questions were relatively artificial questions based on not being present and on relatively artificial and abstract intellectual concepts, and if you are more in the here and now, they lose all their urgency. What does seem to be worth asking seems to be on a much more real level. It is not convoluted, abstract, and confused. It comes more from the heart than the head.

STUDENT: *I think people connect easier.*

The present moment is where the connection is being made, really. Suppose I say, "Let us try to have a relationship in the future." [*Laughter*] It sounds silly when we put it like that, but we do it all the time.

In practice, we tend to be stingy with our attention, stingy in an automated way. It is as if we have an implicit rule that we will give attention to people if and when they shape up properly, when they measure up to our standards. They think the same about us, so the quality attention is vaguely put off into a future that always recedes.

There's a good moral here. Let's try to be as deeply in the present as we can in this and our remaining meetings. We can get really deep at moments if we stay in the present. The level we reach will vary, but it's a real opportunity, not only to learn but for deep nourishment.

STUDENT: *Each day during the past week I have had my short moments of being aware. Sometimes it is for one minute, sometimes it is three minutes, and sometimes I fool myself that it is longer and then I realize that it is not.*

I have found several real benefits. One of them that I have begun using is sensing, looking, and listening in short periods when I am driving: then I don't want to kill the guy that cuts in front of me and stops short or signals after he has made a turn. I am able to say, even before he completes the turn, "Well, he mustn't have thought it through," or "He didn't see the light," or "Something distracted him." I can do this now, believe it or not, and that is because of this higher level of awareness. I don't leap out of the window and take his scalp! Sensing is beneficial for me and I don't have so many things moving around in my head.

When we are abstracted, off in our heads, away from sensory reality, other people become more thing-like; they become more like abstractions and so are easily put into some category, like "damn reckless driver," "someone who deserves to die," and so forth. As you are a little more in the present, other people somehow become more real. The guy who cut in front of me is a person who probably had his reasons for what he did. It was not just an annoyance to my precious sovereign self. There was actually another *person* involved in what happened. Good!

GETTING HOOKED ON BEING PRESENT

STUDENT: *I have been working on being aware as I go to bed. When I climb into bed, I go into this state again. I remind myself that I don't wish to forget. And I wake up in the morning and I want to do it some more, before I even get out of bed!*

Good!

STUDENT: *I get out of bed and all of a sudden I'm sitting on the edge of it, sensing. There may be something addicting about it. I can't put my finger on any special feeling that I have other than that I feel good.*

Is it better to feel alive or dead? Most of us would prefer to feel alive, except when it hurts a lot, and then we will temporarily choose to feel dead. Then we get in the habit of feeling dead to protect ourselves from hurt, and down we go.

Don't get attached to sensing, looking, and listening having the effect of making you feel good, though. Sometimes in doing it you see stress and suffering more clearly than before, there is that variation. But generally the *feeling tone* of being more mindful, more present—it's hard to put in words—is a *quiet* but *deep* feeling of satisfaction that you are *alive*, that you are *here*, that you are paying attention to what is going on in reality.

CONNECTING WITH HIGHER CENTERS

STUDENT: *There's even something more. I think I perceive some solutions or partial solutions to things that have been very unclear, things I couldn't reach any clarity about, but which have been important to me.*

Yes, this, too, is one of the things that can happen from this kind of mindfulness practice. You can discover that your mind is more intuitive and that it gives you useful information. It is not that it did not give you such information before so much as that you were too busy to be able to hear it before, too busy to be able to feel it. Gurdjieff said that actually people are *five-brained beings*. In addition to the body/instinctive, the emotional, and the intellectual centers, we have a higher emotional center and a higher intellectual center. Both of those higher centers are fully formed and operational now come to the present because the bell is ringing at all times, except that in normal consciousness we are completely walled off from them. It is as if you have a perceptive emotional genius and a perceptive intellectual genius in your head, seeing the life you see and coming up with wonderful insights, ideas, and possible solutions to all your problems, but you are totally deaf to their advice.

The main reason we are deaf is that we are so *busy*, going on and on and on all the time in our emotions and our thoughts, so we do not hear them. When we do quiet down a little and begin to hear them, we realize how valuable their information is: Some part of me seems to have a grasp of what is going on—how nice!

There is a very rich Eastern parable that Gurdjieff used in his teaching, that of the horse, carriage, and driver. I had wanted to introduce it in our first session, but let me tell you about it now, quoting from my book *Waking Up*, as it will be good background for dealing with this issue of developing new resources for solving problems.

There is an Eastern parable of the horse, carriage, and driver that richly illustrates our nature as three-brained beings and the problems resulting from poor development of each and from imbalance.

A horse, carriage, and driver together comprise a transportation and support system for taking a potential passenger, the Master, where he or she wants to go. The carriage provides the physical support for conveying the Master comfortably and safely, the horse provides the motive power, and the driver provides the practical knowledge for guiding the whole system to the Master's destination. The horse, carriage, and driver should be ready to go whenever the Master appears and wishes to go somewhere. Typically, though, the system does not function well.

The driver frequently lets the carriage sit out in the rain and snow when it should be garaged, so many parts are rusty or rotting. Maintenance has been poor, parts need replacement, and hazards to safe travel are present. Lack of proper usage has created further deterioration. The carriage has a built-in self-lubrication system, for example, so that the bumps of the road pump the lubricants about, but since it has sat still for long periods, many joints are frozen and corroded. Its appearance has become shabby and unattractive. The kind of "feel" for the road, important for safe and efficient driving, that would come from a well-balanced and well-maintained carriage is distorted by its poor condition.

The horse spends a lot of time harnessed to the carriage, out in the hot sun or rain and snow, when it should be in the stable. The driver doesn't pay enough attention to the horse's diet, so its food is of poor quality and it suffers from nutritional deficiency diseases. Sometimes it is neglected and not fed at all for long periods and starves; at other times it gets too much rich food. Sometimes it is groomed and cared for lovingly, at other times the driver abuses and whips the horse for no apparent reason. As a result the horse is unpredictable and neurotic, sometimes pulling the carriage too powerfully and rashly, at other times refusing to go, sometimes obeying the commands of the driver, sometimes trying to bite him.

The driver should be nearby, ready to leap to the box at the Master's appearance, prepared to guide the horse and carriage to the destination the Master commands, and is also responsible for the maintenance of the horse and carriage. Typically, though, the driver has wandered off to a tavern and gotten drunk with a bunch of other drivers. They are partying one moment and fighting the next, getting sentimental, and swapping exaggerations and lies about wonderful (but largely imaginary) journeys they have taken, or about the powerful masters they like to imagine they are serving or will serve. Actual experience and fantasy are not distinguished very well.

In the midst of this perpetual drunken revel, the driver usually does not hear the Master's call to come to the carriage, harness the horse, and take the Master to his destination. On those occasions when the call is heard, the drunken condition of the driver is more likely to get the carriage stuck or lost or crash it than to safely and swiftly convey the Master to his destination.

Is it any wonder that the Master seldom even tries to use the horse, carriage, and driver? Or that the driver, in his moments of partial sobriety, feels that some sort of important mission in his life is not being fulfilled? That the horse is full of resentment and fitful alternations of anger and despair?

There are frequent partial exceptions to the above state of affairs. Sometimes the driver is fairly sober and intelligent, but in spite of his intentions to obey, the Master can't get very far with his neurotic, half-starved horse and broken-down carriage. Sometimes there is a magnificent, well-fed, powerful, and obedient horse hitched to the carriage, but with the defective brakes on the carriage locked half the time and the driver drunk, the journey may be exciting but end up nowhere. Sometimes the carriage is of magnificent appearance and comfort, and meticulously maintained, but with the drunken driver and half-starved horse it provides only a plush ride to nowhere.

The carriage is our physical body. The horse is our emotions. The driver is our intellectual mind. The Master is what we could become if we provided for the development of our higher nature.

Now let's update this parable. As a result of your attempts to become more mindful, more present—even though your attempts are just beginning and still intermittent—the coachman is sobering up a little, not having a rowdy party with the other drunken drivers all the time. So sometimes he starts to hear the Master saying things like, "Take care of that wheel," or, "Go over there where you will find something interesting." Most of the time the results of your mindfulness efforts are not at all spectacular in ordinary terms. It is generally not as if you were to have a vision suddenly and, presto! your problem is solved. It is usually just that you casually notice that you are handling life a lot better than you were a few months or a few years before. There is more naturalness to your thoughts, feelings, and actions, a "naturalness," which unfortunately does not occur enough in nature, in ordinary life.

Keep it up!

USING YOUR ENERGY WISELY

STUDENT: *This practice has affected me strongly. A few days ago I was feeling good from doing it, and I was seeing people more clearly because I didn't react to them quickly. I could see through them, what they were doing. Then I think I burned myself out. I had so much energy that I worked very hard. Then I realized the next morning that I was extremely tired. I realized that, so yesterday I didn't do the practice. Now I am getting back to it. I wanted to share that because I am now back again to it.*

It is all right to be excited and get a lot done. Just keep track of your arms and legs, and if your arms and legs and the rest of your body say, I want to lie down for a while, I'm tired! that is fine. Lie down. Sense more deeply what it is to be tired. Get some extra sleep at night if you're tired. As well as feelings of energy, there is also the appreciation of relaxation that can come if you are in the here and now.

Think about our earlier discussion about super-efforts and moderation, about being good to yourself. See how this week goes for you.

EARNING MINDFULNESS AND THE GIFT OF MINDFULNESS

STUDENT: *I noticed that other people mentioned that sometimes they just thought out something, and the thought then occurred to me, Oh, yes, I haven't remembered myself lately, and then I remembered myself and sensed myself very briefly, and then quickly forgot to continue doing it. I also noticed that there are times when I think, Oh, I haven't sensed myself and so I'll do that, and it's a different quality than other times, where the feeling spontaneously emerges from the body. It's like I haven't thought about it: it's there, and then I think about it. It's a much stronger feeling when it happens spontaneously and I am able to remain in that state for a longer time.*

As far as instructing goes, it is easiest to talk about doing it deliberately. It's easy to talk about the little effort of will you make to sense your arms and legs. But the deliberate practice does lead to spontaneous moments of mindfulness, micro- or mini- or major awakenings. In formal Gurdjieff work, they often say that there may be periods when you make the effort to sense, look, and listen and it does not seem to work well, it feels bad, you keep forgetting, and you feel as if you are putting a lot of effort in and are getting nothing. But they say the effort you put in is never wasted, because that effort does nurture something vital. Then these experiences of apparently spontaneous mindfulness come, as gifts.

So keep up the effort!

Gurdjieff had a wonderfully paradoxical saying: "Work as if everything depends on effort. Pray as if everything depends on prayer."

Do not assume you are going to be given anything. You should work on the assumption that you will get nothing but what you put into this work: if you do not make an effort, nothing will happen. Every time you forget about sensing, looking, and listening, about being more mindful, that is so much time wasted, time that you are not alive.

There is a lot to be said for that attitude. It motivates effort, which in the long run produces results. But it is an isolating attitude. It is me against the universe and me against much of my own self that is forgetful. So Gurdjieff added, "Pray as if everything depends on prayer," because there is a higher level of reality. You can call it our *higher self* or a *spiritual* level in the universe, or *God*, whatever term is most comfortable for you, but recognize that sometimes we get blessings, we get gifts, whether our egos or superegos think we deserve them or not. It's also true that we get these gifts of awareness because, in some sense, we are prepared for them. The deliberate effort and practice has made us more receptive to being able to use this higher energy of awareness when it comes.

STUDENT: *There is a different quality.* Gift *sounds like a good word. The bell has just rung. I also notice, as I have in the past, that I will be carried away by a strong emotion and am not present, and then actually that is when I receive this gift.*

How much emotion are you feeling right now? You look quite animated. You look like there is a lot of emotional charge in you.

STUDENT: *There is a little charge.*

What is it like?

STUDENT: *It is a kind of subtle excitement . . . it's like a light . . . it feels like I'm really in myself.*

It's not like it is taking you over or pushing you off track.

STUDENT: *No, like I said, it is a different kind of excitement. It's like I'm more here.*

WHEN MINDFULNESS IS TOO MUCH

When Gurdjieff spoke about the higher emotional and intellectual centers, the centers that we normally pay no attention to, he also noted that sometimes extreme circumstances will connect us to these centers. These could be extreme stress, sometimes illness, sometimes the effects of psychoactive drugs. The usual result of this artificial connection, according to Gurdjieff, is that we almost immediately experience falling unconscious. We faint or something like that. It seems that there is so much energy there that our restricted, ordinary little "circuits" of consciousness cannot handle it, so as a protective mechanism, our consciousness faints. With this work of sensing, looking, and listening that we do with our ordinary three centers, we prepare ourselves—we increase, to continue with the analogy, the current-carrying capacity of the wires, or we brush away the things that cause short circuits. Then we can handle gifts, we can handle partial connections with these higher centers in a way that enables us to make good use of the energy, instead of getting almost literally blown away.

It is nice to see you containing that energy. I have seen that look on your face before and saw how it used to take you off base.[1] Now I can see you are staying present for it.

STUDENT: *Yes, I started doing this a long time ago and did it in a concentrated way. That period ended, but I've always tried doing it occasionally, especially when I was having an unpleasant experience.*

Maybe the timing is right now to get back into it intensely.

THE SUPEREGO STRIKES: DOING IT EXACTLY RIGHT

STUDENT: *I find that when I do become aware, it is hard for me to keep it all balanced. I'm either listening or I'm looking or I'm thinking, Oh, yes, the body. I don't know if I'm really doing it right.*

[*Ironically*] You are not keeping *exactly* 60 percent in seeing?

STUDENT: *It seems to be one after the other, rather than all three together. I don't know what to attribute it to.*

On another aspect of this work: last week was a real time of stress and problems for me. Other things constantly came up. I had to be ready to change my mind or to do something else than what I thought I had to do—like I had to work, but there were other distractions, but I allowed myself to be distracted in positive ways, rather than saying, Well, I have to work, and then getting in a bad mood because all I do is work. That was really nice.

I don't know if your superego will approve of this. It sounds like you are starting to treat yourself like a worthwhile person.

You cannot, of course, achieve "perfect" balance in sensing, looking, and listening. Reality changes from moment to moment. A loud car might go by during a lecture, then more of your attention would be drawn to that noise, to listening. It is impossible to say, for example, that 32 percent, and no more, of your conscious attention should go to hearing, although the car seems to be crashing into a wall.

We do have a certain biological bias built into our nervous systems, which basically says that anything that changes, especially if it changes suddenly, deserves more attention now, *instantly,* because it might be something that is going to eat you or it might be something that you can eat. That is part of our legacy of being biological creatures who live on a planet that has prey and predators: if something moves suddenly, it deserves, it *demands* your attention. If it moves slowly and sneakily, it deserves your attention even more. So the world we live in varies from moment to moment. So when I say 50 or 60 percent to seeing, 30 percent or so to hearing, and 10 percent to sensing, it is an approximation. The exact balance is going to change from moment to moment. The main limitation I would suggest is not doing something like crossing the street with your eyes closed so you can sense your arms and legs better.

LISTENING WITH YOUR BODY

STUDENT: *When I am listening to you I am really not at all paying attention to my arms and legs, because if I were, I would not be listening to you.*

Try a little experiment. I would like you to hear me talking to you *in* your lower legs. I would like you to feel my voice in your legs. Are you hearing me in your legs?

STUDENT: *No.*

Are you feeling your legs now?

STUDENT: *Yes. Somewhere there.*

Are you hearing my voice and feeling your legs simultaneously?

STUDENT: *Yes, now I'm getting it.*

See, that's it. It sounds pretty good. Judging from the quality of your voice and posture, it sounds like you are sensing, looking, and listening. I can't be sure, of course, you could be doing it in a purely passive way. But I think you're doing it well now.

Close your eyes for a second. Just listen to the sound of my voice and open your attention to your whole body, your body in general. Are there any places in your body in which you feel my voice more than other places? It might be a moving pattern or it might be a static pattern. Now compare that sound to loud clapping. [*Claps several times*] Is there a difference?

STUDENT: *I can hear the clapping with more vibration. Your voice I hear more in my ears.*

How conventional to hear sounds with your ears! We are taught that it is our ears that we hear with. All the authorities tell us that. Did anybody else try this while I was talking with her? Did you hear me in your legs?

STUDENT: *I heard your voice more in my body and the clapping more in my ears.*

ANOTHER STUDENT: *I felt your voice most in my solar plexus area.*

I would suggest you all get a little practice with the following meditation exercise.

Once in a while sit down for ten minutes, close your eyes, and listen to whatever sounds there are. Simultaneously, sense whatever sensations there are in your body. Don't force a connection between sounds and body sensations, but notice when there is one. I think success at this is primarily a matter of sensitization. As far as I know, everybody can do this, but you have to be sensitized.

It has several bases. One is simply that sound waves are vibratory energy and do impact on our body, so they create tiny sensations. They are very faint sensations compared with most of the gross sensations that we have from touching things, but they are there. Second, it is also a matter of where your attention is directed. Partly it may give you imaginary sensations through suggestion. I've given you a suggestion that you'll be able to hear sounds in other parts of your body, but partly it is not suggestion. At least it shouldn't remain an artifact of suggestion, because you know the emphasis here is to train yourself to focus on what actually is in the here and now, to discriminate reality from imagination.

I would like you to play with the flexibility that my suggestion and your innate and growing ability to focus your attention creates. Don't think that sounds have to be just heard in your head. By just formally meditating on hearing them wherever your body sensations happen to be at the moment, you will be sensitized to your body. It will sensitize you to listening for that particular source of information.

I notice that I've just given you a variation on the suggested meditation technique of sensing and listening, so let me make that clearer. You can do this meditation in three ways, all of which are useful. One is to formally decide where in your body you want to experience sounds, in your arm, say, or your knee or your solar plexus, whatever. Or you could systematically scan your whole body in a regular pattern, and notice whatever sensations occur as you try to hear whatever sounds are occurring there. The third is to simply follow whatever sensation is strong in your body at any given moment and notice how sounds register there, too. Try it various ways, over several different sessions.

This is a good meditation for noisy environments: the sounds become a necessary part of your technique, instead of being treated as a distraction.

STUDENT: *A deaf person doesn't hear, right?*

I don't know exactly how you mean that. Deaf people can usually feel vibrations in their bodies. I don't know how things are experienced by all deaf persons, but in general, I would think that if you stimulate a deaf person with a loud sound, they will feel it as vibrations somewhere in their body.

STUDENT: *So you are saying that one can feel the vibrations of your voice in the body?*

Partly. Sometimes you feel it as an ordinary tactile sensation, especially if the sound is somewhat loud. I do not know what the exact threshold is where the amount of energy gets so low that it really does not mechanically vibrate your body, where it's totally damped out, although I suspect that it is lower than we generally believe. It is more a question of flexibility training for us than anything else, learning to overcome a conception and becoming more sensitive, rather than the precise physics of the practice.

The first time I tried this meditation I was miserable at doing it. Every time I would hear/feel a sound someplace in my body, I would go off on a long mental fantasy of compiling a scholarly catalog of where different sounds naturally resonate in the body. This seemed, to an intellectual drunk like me, a wonderful scientific project, but I was missing the main point of the practice. The main point is to become flexible in how you conceive of yourself. You have a strong conception that you hear with your ears. It is not a bad conception: the ears are quite important for hearing. But when you get absolutely stuck in that idea, you lose some of your possible freedom.

STUDENT: *I would like to feel music. It would be emotionally satisfying.*

Put on some nice, flowing orchestral music, preferably with no vocals, and try systematically hearing it in your body. You can start by hearing it with your ears if that will help! Then hear it in your jaw or your neck, your chest or your arms. Just move it around and play with it. Like we did in the musical body exercise our first day together.

STUDENT: *There's something about hearing a good, loud something, actually vibrating my body, that I like.*

You can do what the kids do, turn up your stereo really loud, and you will feel it in other places in your body. Of course, you will probably be damaging your hearing, so I do not advise that method. I have read that most young people who are really into rock now have quite noticeable losses of hearing, even when they are still in their twenties, from having played it so loud so much of the time.

PLAYFULNESS AND SPACIOUSNESS

STUDENT: *What is the benefit of hearing your voice in my toes?*

Perhaps there is none at all. Perhaps it is the only way to do these exercises *right*. Sorry: I have a habit, maybe a bad one, of teasing other people's superegos. My own superego is another matter, of course. Mine is very serious and knows absolutely what's right and wrong.

One of my main reasons for suggesting this meditation exercise is that I do not want you to see what we're doing together as just *work*. In a vital way, it is also *play*. It is good for you! OK, that statement was for your superego. Again, superego, this play is good for you! And bringing in some playfulness is also a method of getting some spaciousness.

Sogyal Rinpoche is very good on this subject. One of the things that he talks about as part of the essence of Buddhism is spaciousness. Our ordinary mind is contracted and crunched up so much of the time. We have to do everything right. Instead of going through life all crunched up, we need to relax and have more spaciousness to do things.

I am going to give you an example of spaciousness. I want you to sense, look, and listen really deeply and be especially aware of your body while I tell you a joke. This joke is politically incorrect, dirty, and sexist, so I know I am taking a chance, but my excuse is that it's for a good cause. Really sense deeply now.

Do you know why women don't have any brains? (Notice the sensations in your bodies right now.) Because they don't have anything dangling between their legs to carry them in. (With a cosmic sense of timing, the bell rings right now.)

If you think about how jokes work, one of the things most of them do at the start is to give you a *mental set*. They throw a stereotype or set of stereotypes in front of you. You get all lined up and focused in a single direction, and then suddenly that whole framework you've bought into is pulled out from under you by the punch line, and you are mentally floating free for a moment. From being very constricted, tight, and focused, you are suddenly in a more spacious kind of state.

Recall what your bodily, emotional, and conceptual experiences were when I said, "Do you know why women . . ." For people in our culture at this time, the word *women* raises flags.

The first time I heard the joke, my body immediately tensed, my emotions flashed a warning that I might be getting into a sensitive and potentially harmful situation, my intellect got more activated to analyze every nuance of what was going to come. The words *don't have* raised my alert level even higher. Equality is what is politically correct—and that I believe in—and these two words were denying something to women.

Brains increased the tension. This was a potent area, and by then I was very identified with the bodily-emotional-mental set that had been created in me, ready for fight or flight in bodily terms—I was in dangerous territory! I was focused, constricted, set, caught up by the implications of what was going to happen, uptight.

Then presto! All of a sudden, *men* were the ones put down, those poor creatures (me included) who are slaves to their genitals. The bodily-emotional-cognitive framework I was tightly caught up in collapsed, and for a short time, before some new framework was built up and caught me, I was free, I was spacious, I was between identifications. And that is a great state. That's a good reason to laugh. It really is funny when you see the states we push ourselves into. But to see that, you have to have moments out of these constricted states.

So creating spaciousness is one of the reasons I am telling you to practice listening to sounds in your body. Instead of waiting for circumstances like a joke to loosen you up and give you a taste of freedom—which is all right, except you cannot always depend on circumstances doing it for you—I'm encouraging you to practice freedom directly.

It's weird, isn't it? You came to these meetings to learn something about really serious and important topics like mindfulness and enlightenment, and I'm telling you to practice hearing sounds in the tip of your nose. Personally, I am still looking for the path to enlightenment that is going to get me there by telling me the Big Joke some day. Anyway, I recommend that you try doing this special meditation of listening and sensing sounds in your body for ten minutes every once in a while, to sensitize yourself to your body and to sounds. It is breaking a lifetime of habits.

MINDFULNESS AND OBNOXIOUS PEOPLE

STUDENT: *Unfortunately, I am going to Boston. I am going to be visiting my mother, who's a pain in the neck.*

You will have a wonderful opportunity.

STUDENT: *The way she goes on and on, when I'm with her I don't hear a word she's saying. In my understanding, that wouldn't be hearing what she's saying with my body. That's reacting emotionally or something like that. How can I work with this situation?*

It would be better to stay here with us folks who are trying to be mindful and enlightened and all that, right? Yet your trip is a *wonder*ful, fertile situation for learning more about yourself. To spaciously observe the mechanical parts of your mind in habituated action under stress can make you full of wonder at how we let ourselves be trapped in samsara. Remember that I said earlier that when you take up this practice of mindfulness in everyday life these times when life really presses down hard on you are opportunities to see things you might never run across in years of tranquil meditation in a beautiful ashram somewhere? The more you learn about yourself, the greater your eventual freedom will be.

Your mother is going to be your trainer. Since you are going to be with your mother anyway, why not suffer *consciously,* mindfully, and get something out of it, instead of suffering unconsciously and just being uptight? Unless you prefer the ordinary kind of suffering?

Your superego, of course, will say it is good for you to suffer consciously, with the emphasis on suffering rather than learning, but watch that superego.

STUDENT: *Most of the time I have no communication with her at all, she just drives me up the wall. But there have been a few times when there was something much deeper. It amazes me. Once she shared some of her fears with me, fears about the government, about the AIDS program, about aging. We were going back and forth and saying what we were aware of. I had said that my face felt like a mask at that point. The image of a mask triggered in her the image of a movie we had just seen, in which the killer wore a mask. She started feeling all this fear, and I felt I was feeling the same fear.*

It is natural empathy that is often normally covered up. When you have more experience with practicing mindfulness, one of the things you will eventually see is how much of our lives we have all spent posturing and play acting and almost never honestly telling anyone how we feel.

It seems that we long ago decided that this world is not safe, that other people are dangerous, that I have to present a certain front all the time to keep myself safe. Then we even forgot that we were doing that. We have "deliberately" become one with our fronts. We have become totally lost in, identified with, the posturings and manipulations, and we have covered up our inner self to our own consciousness, as well as covering it up from other people. It is very nourishing to share simple kinds of statements about how we feel *now*. The exercises we did the first day had elements of that in them, that was what made them touch us deeply. Gestalt psychologists have a similar exercise that they call the *continuum of awareness,* in which you try to describe your feelings moment by moment by moment.

Sharing your feelings honestly is not to be done compulsively, of course. You do not want to walk up to every stranger on the street and share every moment-by-moment sensation, saying, "Hi there. I am feeling a flushing sensation on the backs of my ears now and I am a little unsteady on my legs. What's your name?" In situations that are safe, though, it is remarkably fulfilling: "My God, an actual human being listening to me and looking at me!"

THINKING, TALKING, AND THE SUPEREGO AS DISTRACTERS

STUDENT: *One thing I realize is that being in the present is easier for me when I am watching nature. Being in a park is very helpful; I get engrossed in the view. Just looking at beautiful, natural things seems to really bring me to the present.*

Yesterday I went to the woods with a friend. It felt pretty good. I was able to become present for a while, seeing the leaves and the patterns of things. Then we started chatting, and soon we were saying, "Oh, we have spent too much time here, let's go on," and I lost it totally with the talking.

What? Weren't you doing something productive? If you stop thinking for more than a minute you will die, and even if you do not die, you will probably miss several wonderful thoughts that will never repeat themselves. That's the kind of message I suspect your superego, and his superego, was giving.

STUDENT: *Reflecting later, I was saying to myself, How can I think this way? Paying attention to the now, sensing, looking, and listening,*

*is bringing me peace and aliveness and awareness, yet I forget all
about it in an instant and live in my thoughts and worries.*

Ordinary psychology tells us that one of the main things affecting
the way we live our lives is the pleasure principle, that we move
toward pleasure and away from pain, that we try to maximize
pleasure and minimize pain. But it is not so simple.

As we discussed last week, I love to get a massage once in a while.
The sensation of having my muscles kneaded is really neat and
pleasurable. The pleasure principle would predict that I would remain
immersed in these pleasurable sensations throughout the massage.
Yet, as I said before, my mind will get lost in thoughts within seconds,
and I will hardly feel the massage. I keep thinking and thinking. They
are almost always pleasurable thoughts, probably given that flavor
by the slightly perceived but ongoing physical pleasure. But you
would think the pleasure of a thought is much less than the actual
pleasure of a real sensation. That most intense pleasure is *here,* in my
body, *now:* why does my mind go *there, then,* someplace outside of
the present location and time? The power of the thinking habit that
draws us away all the time is quite amazing; we leave our direct
pleasure behind. After all, we think about how much better it could
be *if.* How can real time pleasure compare with what might be?

In most styles of formal sitting meditation, they will instruct you
to bring your mind back as soon as you realize it is drifting, back to
the object of your meditation. It will drift, and when you notice it,
bring it back. Most of us need to hear that instruction over and over,
because we forget. It will drift, and when you notice it, bring it back.
As you bring it back, you develop your attention muscles, your
voluntary attention muscles.

Our attention is easily captured, and our voluntary attention
muscles are weak. Practicing coming back makes them stronger.
Having attacks by your superego and your thinking mind about
drifting are part of the game at this point, but you do not always
need to fight back when they attack. If your superego says, You are
wasting your time! or, You are not doing it right! you can simply
notice that your superego said that to you, and then come right back
to the object of meditation. Again, if your superego is more persistent,
you might try mentally saying, Thank you, I heard you, goodbye,
and come back to the practice.[2]

Some people's superegos are very destructive and persistent. If yours is like that, fight it if you must, but generally fighting these voices of the superego just gets you involved with fighting them instead of practicing. Unless your superego is so destructive that some psychotherapeutic assistance might be called for, just come back to your practice. This same advice applies to sensing, looking, and listening.

Coming back to massage: because of my tendency to drift away I make massages a period of vipassana meditation, deliberately bringing my mind back from thoughts to the moment-by-moment sensation. In a strange way, it's harder to do this kind of vipassana meditation focusing on pleasure than to do it on pain. Pain is a more immediate motivator for changing your relationship to experience!

STUDENT: *When she spoke about lying, it triggered a memory I had about my experiences. There are times when my mind stops as a result of practicing, and then I notice an anxiety, a strange sensation. I worry about whether I'll be able to think normally again! Suddenly I start thinking, I don't know. The bell sounds.*

When that anxiety sensation happens, try to experience the anxiety sensation more deeply. Do not accept it as being just, Oh, I'm anxious, my thinking process might not start again, but open to it and feel it more clearly. That may or may not resolve it; that may or may not make it more clear. It does give you an opportunity to learn something more.

We can deal with that in more detail later, if you want to bring it up again, but right now it's my intuition that it's important to relate our discussion back to the earlier topic of people describing their sensations and feelings to each other, as in the exercise we did the first day.

In working on that process, I would say that, in some ways, we are doing nothing special at all. In other ways, there is something very clear and direct about it that you do not get in many, perhaps any, ordinary conversations. There is a funny sense in which, by *artificially* practicing this exercise of sensing, looking, and listening, we are being more *natural*. It is no big deal to remember yourself when you are remembering yourself, and yet when you think about the usual hysteria we live in, it is a big deal. But if anyone is worried that the usual hysteria might not come back, like the thoughts, don't worry; it is all waiting out there!

LYING

STUDENT: *Is there any effect when a person tells a lie while sensing? The body exposes people when they lie. Usually there is a movement of the eyelid, of the lips, or the hand, some body language.*

While you are describing this, at some point tell me a little lie about something, but don't tell me when you tell the lie.

STUDENT: *I was very busy today in various computer classes, and I sensed myself while I was working on a very difficult data base problem series on the Macintosh. Sensing made everything very clear, and I was very satisfied. I tried telling a lie as I was talking now, but I couldn't do it all while I was doing this sensing, looking, and listening work. I couldn't tell a lie, I was just so caught up in sensing.*

Gurdjieff made an interesting comment about this situation. When you ask people to lie deliberately, most people have a terrible time at it. That's also my own experience when asking people to practice lying. Yet Gurdjieff says that, if you want to study the psychology of ordinary life, you want to study the psychology of lies, now the reminder bell has sounded, come to your senses, because most of us lie all the time automatically, without even knowing we are lying. Deliberate (deliberate by the standards of ordinary, sleeping consciousness) lying is only a small part of all the lying that goes on in everyday life.

When we bring consciousness to lying, lying is usually a weird, awkward process. Does this mean we are living in a weird, awkward process most of the time and simply not knowing it? When I ran a group on learning self-remembering some years ago, I once gave people the assignment of telling a few little white lies each day. They were to be perfectly harmless lies that would have no real impact whatsoever on anybody. I remember that as one of the most resisted assignments I ever gave to people. Everybody forgot to do it, or simply found it impossible to do, or had great rationalizations for not doing it, or came up with wonderful moral arguments about how this hideous thing could not be done. The moral arguments were not very impressive to me.

Gurdjieff shocked people by saying that most of our morality is mechanical, conditioned. Those people who act "bad" do it because they have been conditioned to act that way; those people who act "good" do it because they have been conditioned to act that way. When Pavlov's dogs salivated at the sound of the bell, it was because they had no choice, they had been conditioned.

When you actually have a choice as to whether to do good or bad, a real choice, and you choose to do good, that counts morally. When you are conditioned so that you cannot do anything else, even if your action is good in conventional terms, that does not count much.

I can say, for example, that I am a person who is scrupulously honest, but that is partly because I have a very hard time lying. I also have honesty as one of my highest values, but I only get partial credit, as it were, for telling the truth, because I have little choice.

You might try the exercise of telling a little white lie each day and seeing what happens in your body, as well as in general. These are enlightening sorts of exercises.

REMEMBERING TO REMEMBER

STUDENT: *I have given up trying to do this sensing practice while I am on the computer. It's too hard. What I have noticed, though, is that there are a lot of opportunities at work in the transitions, in the movement from one place to another. Where I work, there are three or four different projects I am consulting on or relating with and I am moving around. I figure that when I get better at doing sensing in those places that are more fertile, then I will worry about doing it on the computer. But there is something about that kind of work that makes it most difficult for me to remain conscious.*

Your eye movements are quite restricted when working with a computer. Remember how earlier we discussed how staring fixedly at anything tends to induce waking sleep? Also, the content of what you are looking at, the ideas displayed on the computer screen, usually requires a good deal of thought to make sense of it. If you are doing something and suddenly "Fatal Error Number 2714" flashes on your screen, you have to figure out what that means fast. It is very absorbing work! You've got almost no attention energy left to devote to sensing.

The transitions are good to use. We at least have to get up to go to the bathroom several times a day and to eat, and so there are going to be some transitions in all of our lives. I use walking from one place to another at the university as a reminder to sense myself.

STUDENT: *I used to have an alarm watch. I would use that to remind me to sense, look, and listen, but after around half a day I would have automatic responses to it.*

When you would set the alarm, you would know how soon it was going to go off, so part of you would be anticipating it. If you had a truly random alarm program for your computer, it might work for several weeks before you adapted to it, simply because of its randomness. Our random bell is still working pretty well in these meetings.

(The following comment is somewhat convoluted at first, but I present it in its original form as there is a flavor of struggle conveyed that wouldn't come across if it were edited.)

THE REAL BODY AND THE FANTASY BODY

STUDENT: *I am also not always at my computer. I spend hours away from it. Because of the tense hustle and bustle of living the way I do, when I do get a chance to get away I really enjoy the quiet.*

More than in the past, I am noticing that I have periods of kinds of wordlessness, twenty seconds, something like that, and I am there, present. Then, of course, there are thoughts about the wordlessness, and then I let go of that. What I am aware of is the first question I presented to you, that is, I am in my body, but it is really not the same tangible embodiedness as at other times. I can't really say what the difference is. I know it would make a huge difference if I were doing Aikido—places where you have everything going and it doesn't work and other times it really works. There is something kind of ineffable about that. I find very much in the body, quiet, sensing, yet lots of other times it has that feeling of not quite fully there. There is not much I can do beyond that except to observe. I don't know what I could do to make it more present.

I am assuming that what is happening to you is what happens to me a lot. Let me put it this way. I make the little effort to sense, look, and listen, and for a few seconds I am clearly aware of what is going on in my body and of my immediate sensory impressions. Then a thought does not just suddenly come and snap in and take me away so much as a thought or an image starts carefully working its way around the sensations, building on the sensations. If I am sensing and am aware of a warmth in my hand, for example, I start building up little fantasies about warmth that then lead, in a very smooth transition, further and further away into fantasy, so that I lose the actual sensation over a period of a second or so, rather than losing it suddenly.

I usually find it harder to notice that kind of smooth transition than a sudden transition. So an important part of my personal work now is to try to become more sensitive to when I am starting to have a fantasy build up slowly around the actual sensation. Given the subtle nature of this kind of transition into fantasy, I don't think I'm very good at detecting it yet.

What I have done is develop something of a habit of checking sensations every once in a while to see whether I am perceiving the actual sensation or a fantasy about the sensation.

I can be clearly here in my body this moment, but if I am not making a sustained effort to stay here—if I get a little more absorbed—it seems that my actual body has what we might call the *conceptual body* or *fantasy body* slide over it. I start to "sense," as it were, imagined sensations in an imagined body instead of actual sensations in my actual body. I am now fantasizing about sensing my body when in point of fact now the bell rings, focus in on sensing the present, I have already slid over into fantasy. I have left relative awakening behind and gone back to normal, sleeping consciousness.

Then as the fantasy goes on, not even based on the fantasy body any more, elaborating itself in the there and then, it is easier to recognize. You can get better with practice—or you can at least see the problem more clearly with practice.

That's easy for me to say. Now I am trying to reflect on whether I am actually any better at detecting this slide into fantasy or not. . . . Yes, I know from my own experience that you can spend more time in touch with actual body sensations and actual sensory impressions of the moment as a result of practicing sensing, looking, and listening. That I know. Also, it really helps if you are doing something like the martial art of Aikido, where you are getting actual sensory feedback on what you are doing with your body. In general, I'd say that the body at rest is much more easily cloaked by the fantasy body than the body that is engaged in a skilled bodily interaction with somebody else or in almost any kind of physical task where you have to closely monitor the results of your actions.

STUDENT: *I think you are hitting it. You can have what you are calling the fantasy body without having the pictures or the verbalizations or so forth that alert you to the fact that something else, fantasy, is going on. It is like, something else is going on, although I feel I am totally clear and quiet.*

The image body, the fantasy body, is not necessarily a visual image, of course. It can be a tactile image, which slides itself over the actual perceived body, whose sensations are happening at the moment. This is a tricky area.

DEALING WITH FANTASIES ABOUT MINDFULNESS

STUDENT: *What do you do when you have a sense that this is happening?*

Try to come back more *precisely* to a sensation or sensations. For example, if I were listening to sounds and I drifted off into a little fantasy, once I knew I was in fantasy, I would try to come back to what is the actual quality of those sounds.

Let's say I am sitting on my back deck at home, sensing, and hearing a bird, I am fairly tuned into the actual sound qualities of this bird, but then I am off in fantasyland about how I like birds, what interesting sound qualities they have, what a great person I am to appreciate the sound of birds, and so on. Then a part of me begins to realize that I've gone away, that that is not where I want to be now. I have to tell myself Listen! Get rid of this *concept* about the bird sounds and actually *listen* to the minute variations of the actual sound. The same thing is true with body sensations, where I drift off into body sensation fantasies. I try to come back to what they actually feel like at the moment.

I put an exclamation mark after *listen,* in saying/writing this, because it does involve effort, intention. But remember what we discussed earlier about sensing, looking, and listening with a quality of gentleness: don't let your superego pick up on that exclamation mark.

I do not want to make this sound all bad. I have a tendency to talk about self-remembering in an all or nothing kind of fashion, because it is easier to present it that way. It sounds like I'm saying you are either in the present because you have some touch with body and sensory sensations or you are off in fantasyland, but actually, there are degrees in between. The degrees have to do with how easy it is to come back to what is actually happening at the moment. When you are deep in fantasy, some pretty intense or important things may happen in the world around you and in your own body and you may not notice them at all. When you are not so deep in fantasy, you come back sooner, reality doesn't have to hit you with a sledge hammer to get your attention.

I have noticed in my own practice that there are a lot of times when I do not remember to self-remember, to sense, look, and listen in a very formal way, but on the other hand, I do not slide very deep into the fantasy world. I come back fairly easily when something actually requires it. My superego can say, That's not good enough, you are just rationalizing your failures! but I think it is a lot better than being in deep fantasy all the time.

LEARNING NEW SKILLS

STUDENT: *I have found for myself that I can get in touch with sensing best when I am either resting or walking by myself. When I am doing something else I feel I am clumsy. I am more self-conscious, thinking about what I am going to do, especially when I am learning something new. When I was learning t'ai chi, for instance, I was never in my body. When I had it down, I could be more present, you know.*

I am going through exactly that same process now as I am beginning to learn t'ai chi. I am trying to remember that I am supposed to be relaxed and aware, sensing myself, but where does my foot go? Have any of you noticed that sensing, looking, and listening tends to make some of your ordinary actions more clumsy? Being mindful is using some of the energy that is usually automatically sucked up by habits and so interrupting habit patterns. Habit can become very smooth, but this sensing practice is laying the foundation for a better understanding that eventually permits more flexibility. As you get better at being mindful, it will interfere less with learning new skills.

STUDENT: *I usually work very fast, talk very fast, and do everything fast, and now I walk very slowly. Even walking to the train station takes me longer.*

You are not going to tell me you are enjoying the walk, are you? This work we are doing is not a *real* spiritual path, you understand, because it leads to pleasure, and we all know that a real spiritual path revolves around suffering!

OK, that's it for tonight. Try a few formal periods of just sensing and listening with your eyes closed. Hear the quality of the sound and feel whatever the pattern is and where it is located in your body. If it is more in one place than another, notice that. Don't try to form a directory, a set of rules, like my fantasy did: that bird sound was located in my left shoulder last time; it had better be there again. Let the birds resonate wherever they want to in your body from moment to moment.

Keep up the morning exercise and your sensing during the day, and bring in your observations, questions and problems next week.

SIX

RESULTS OF MINDFULNESS PRACTICE
Final Follow-up Session

HERE WE ARE at our last evening together.
We're going to use our random bell "teacher" in a new way tonight. We are getting somewhat used to the old way, and it may not function as effectively as an alarm clock to remind us to awaken.

Instead of physically stopping, becoming completely still and more alert when the bell rings, we will institute a new "religious" custom. The custom will be that when the bell rings, cup your hands together beside your left ear, like this, and open your mouth, as well as then freezing and using that time to observe yourself intensely.

Sounds preposterous, doesn't it? [*General laughter and agreement*]

Of course it is. We will look like a bunch of zombies in some weird religious cult. Yet the slight embarrassment that goes with it can be used to observe ourselves more intensely, so let's give it a try.

(Readers should try responding to statements about the bell in this more complex way also.)

So, what have you noticed in your practice of sensing, looking, and listening this past week?

STUDENT: *I find myself becoming more and more forgetful of it, especially in my daily life, when I'm away from this immediate workshop situation.*

Yes, there's an intensification of our efforts, of the results of our efforts, when we're here together. Also, the initial enthusiasm that we get from our first results of being more mindful tends to fade, especially since we're out in life the vast amount of the time, where there is no social encouragement for mindfulness. Has anyone else noticed this fading?

STUDENT: *I'm just not able to experience the mindful state the way I could at first. [Many nods of agreement and similar comments]*

HOLDING ON TO OLD EXPERIENCES

It looks like lots of people believe that the way we experienced increased mindfulness initially is the *right* way and now we have to hold onto that. This is in spite of my warning that this would happen and that we should go with the reality of the moment, not with what we think it should be. That's all right, I fall into doing this all the time myself.

It could be, of course, that you are making fewer and weaker efforts and so not getting results. Only you can tell that. But let's look at a different side of things.

We come to believe that increased mindfulness should feel a certain kind of way, have certain characteristics. But it doesn't have to feel a certain kind of way, even if we would like it to. That's the operation of the intellectual, calculating part of our brains: What is right and what is wrong? Am I being good? Am I being bad? It's comparing current experiences against some kind of standard of measurement, but, and I can't say it too strongly, *the experience of mindfulness does not have to stay the same.*

In fact, part of what you at first get from mindfulness practice is simply a contrast effect. When you start this work, the more spaced-out you are, the more deeply asleep you are, the greater is the contrast with the simple act of becoming present to the moment. That contrast creates great novelty, which feels good.

There is an effect of practice, even if you don't feel you are being very successful at being more mindful at any given time. When you start becoming present more often, that contrasts strongly with your usual state, the rather spaced-out state we call *normal.* It could even be that we are perhaps not becoming all that present as a result of our efforts; it's just that we are not spacing out so far so much of the time, we are not as deeply asleep: that lessens the contrast effect. As we have more and more experiences of being even a little more mindful, too, the contrast isn't so sharp, the novelty lessens, and we mistakenly begin to think our efforts aren't having much effect.

I've certainly noticed that in myself. The effects on my mind of mindfulness practice generally are not as dramatic as they were when I first started working on myself, so I have a tendency to think it's not working. But actually, while I'm still asleep most of the time, I'm not in the terribly deep sleep that I lived most of my life in.

I've also realized that this feeling that I'm not doing it well, that I'm not up to standard, is actually a serious barrier to being mindful of the actual present. It's not just a barrier in the sense of being misleading: our superegos tend to pick up on this "failure" to get results. We have to hang in there, focusing our attention on being as present and mindful as possible, whether the experience meets our standards or not.

Because of this attachment to having an interesting or exciting experience, wanting it to be a thrill, we tend to subtly alter the technique, so its no longer aimed at producing more mindfulness of what *is,* regardless of our desires, but aimed at producing an experience that will please us, please our desires, please our superegos. When this happens regularly, we've lost it, we're back into the same kind of perceptual distortion that makes ordinary mind a state of samsara, a state of illusion.

What else do you want me to say about your experience?

STUDENT: *That's it for now. Thank you.*

Is your state better now?

STUDENT: *It is.*

[*A quiet period ensues.*]

Remember to be careful about staring fixedly at anything. I see a lot of that right now. It's trance inducing. Shift your eyes, look at something, be aware, take it in, then shift your eyes.

STUDENT: *I find myself thinking the bell rings, cup your hands to your ear, open your mouth, become present. [General laughter]*

Look how silly we all look, cupping our hands to our ears! Feel the group energy it generates, the togetherness. Maybe this is how actual religious traditions are founded. So we're embarrassed, but let's use that emotional energy to sense deeply.

STUDENT: *I find myself . . . enough during the days, you know, my feelings . . . remind me of that . . . And I wonder how can I . . . that.*

I'm not following. What are your feelings reminding you of?

STUDENT: *That I'm not here. That I'm not present.*

How wonderful. Maybe.

STUDENT: *I'm not here, that's my problem.*

I presume you are not talking about those moments when you are practicing sensing, looking, and listening. I presume you have some sense of being present at those times. So you feel not here, not present, when you are not sensing, looking, and listening. Is it that you are spacing out more than ever before? Or has spacing out simply become more noticeable to you as a result of learning that you can be more present?

STUDENT: *I don't know.*

I know that is a hard question to answer.

STUDENT: *I don't know. I used to focus on awareness of being aware, but now I'm confused about that. My roommate has commented that I seemed spaced-out sometimes. I'm not sure if I know I'm aware, unless maybe somebody else can pick it up.*

Are you aware of being here now?

STUDENT: *Yes.*

I am trying to understand what you just said. Do you mean that when you practice sensing that you then remember that you don't know what you are doing?

STUDENT: *It was like that at the beginning. Now I consciously set up a time when I am supposed to remember to sense, look, and listen, but I forget. I set myself up to do it, and yet I'm not here.*

So far this sounds like normal life. [*General laughter*] Seriously, there is a resistance that builds up during the process of trying to live a more mindful life. Resistance comes with the realization that normally we are not here, not present, and that we suffer because of it. This is a painful realization, so in many ways we don't want to know that. Having had some moments of feeling more present and mindful, you have become more sensitized to not being present.

So you've become more sensitized about spacing out. I wouldn't necessarily say that you *are* spacing out more, although as your roommate commented to you, it may be a bit more obvious when you space out.

STUDENT: *Yes, it's something like that.*

As you get moments of being more in the present, you do indeed become more aware of spacing out, and that can be very, very discouraging. But don't dwell on the discouragement, in the sense of letting that feeling suck away all your energy. The thing to do when you become aware of how much you space out and get lost in fantasy is to become present. Immediately begin sensing, looking, and listening again.

The other evening I said that you have two choices when you find that your mind has drifted off into fantasy when you wanted to be present. You can berate yourself for a while about being forgetful and then start to practice mindfulness again, or you can skip the self-blaming and just start sensing again. I strongly recommend the latter. I've had considerable practice at berating myself about my failures to be present, but while it's used up a lot of my energy, I don't think it's done me a bit of good.

I wish there was some sure fire secret technique I could teach you that would help you self-remember all the time, but I haven't found anything like that. You just have to keep remembering to do it and actually do it. I wish I could just get into the habit of always sensing, looking, and listening, but this process isn't like ordinary habit; you have to transcend ordinary habit.

While there isn't a surefire technique that I know of, there are little things you can do that will help for a while or increase the probability that you will remember to make the little effort needed to be present.

One such method I discovered years ago was creating what I called *microgoals* for being present. At our stage, if you just resolve to be mindful and present all the time, you will probably forget all about it within minutes, if not seconds, and then feel like you're a failure. But if you create a goal of being mindful and present for a brief period—half a minute or a minute—you can learn to do that and so create a lot of success experiences to keep your motivation up.

I often practice such microgoal tasks when driving. I resolve, for instance, to sense, look, and listen continuously until I reach the overpass that is a few hundred yards down the road. Maybe this takes twenty seconds. I do it. Then when I reach the overpass I resolve to be present until I overtake a truck I can see ahead of me, and so forth.

The real goal is to develop more presence in all aspects of life, not just ones you set a special goal for, of course. But building up successes in these microgoals gives you practice at the skill as well as keeping your motivation up. Having lots of these microexperiences of greater presence also helps increase the contrast with our ordinary, spaced-out state, which is also motivating.

Remember, too, that using external circumstances, such as driving, to act as alarm clocks to wake you from sleep is OK, but they eventually wear out. You just get in the mechanical habit of feeling a certain way when you meet the alarm, and you're now fooling yourself about practicing mindfulness. Notice when this happens and then give up or modify that particular alarm clock.

A BRIEF NOTE ON USING GUILT

Let me add a little note about feeling guilty over not doing well at being more present. Guilt is tricky. If you are skillful, you can use the energy of small guilt feelings as energy to motivate you to try harder. But you have to be very careful in doing this. Larger amounts of guilt almost always push us off into daydreams, into samsara. So for now, I'd recommend not giving any energy to guilt about this if you can, just set microgoals, stay tuned in to your arms and legs, and be present.

So, *right now you can be here.* You don't have to feel guilt. You can practice using a microgoal technique, like sensing your arms and legs, seeing me, and listening to my voice until I reach the end of this sentence. Then try it for the next sentence, and so on.

CURIOSITY AND INTERESTINGNESS

STUDENT: *I had an experience on Saturday. I was outside in a nice field. I lay down in the field. Then I came back in and there was nothing I had to do, except just be there. I guess I was allergic to something out there in the field, and I began having severe spots and itching—just single spots, you know, on my ear and on my arm. They would go from one place to another, kind of rotate, and get stronger and weaker. I didn't let myself touch them. I'm sure they would have gone away if I'd scratched them, but I decided to try staying present. I wanted to observe all the little changes in sensation. There was a part of me that was saying, Is this a little mad, to just observe these sensations? I was doing nothing else, just observing these itching sensations and getting great satisfaction out of it!*

We could call this "How I Studied the Science of Awareness and Learned to Reach Happiness through Itching." [*General laughter*]

STUDENT: *You think this is the way to reach happiness?*

You sound like you were pretty happy about it!

STUDENT: *What I was thinking to myself was that this was weird, yet it was the most aware and happy hour I had that week.*

That's wonderful. You also did something else that was quite interesting. You went back toward your essential nature as a child, temporarily dropping your adult "shoulds." Children get fascinated by the damndest things, things that are of no importance by our adult criteria. So you stopped being an adult, with "important" things you had to do and no time to just be present and enjoy life, with a feeling that you should cure this irritation and get back to important things. Being able to do this made you more free and more creative for a while. That's wonderful.

Someday I am going to write about this, but I haven't figured out the right way to do it yet. There is something about the quality of getting *interested* in things that is one of the great satisfactions of life, one that we deny ourselves too much as adults. We have channeled our natural curiosity into utilitarian channels, which recognize only certain things as productive the bell sounds now, cup your hands. We've forgotten the joy of simply being interested in all sorts of things.

You reminded me of a wonderful story I heard over the weekend, although I'm not sure how it fits in here. A colleague at a conference was describing leading a workshop where he was trying to get people to feel more Gaia consciousness, to feel in tune with the planet, with all life. They were doing this out at the beach somewhere. One woman went off looking for her special spot, something that would feel intuitively right for doing the assigned exercise of feeling unity with all life. She found her spot in the sand dunes and started feeling a great sense of unity.

About half an hour later she was itching so badly they had to take her to the hospital. The doctor said this was the worst case of chigger bites he had ever seen. What kind of sense of unity did she have? Was she so spaced-out with this idea of unity that she did not know she was being eaten alive by the chiggers? Were she and the chiggers and the planet actually at one for a while? I am not quite sure what the moral of that story is, but it says *something* very powerfully.

Keep up that curiosity! Nourish it, it's one of the best possible things you can do for yourself.

Of course, there are many times in life when we have to yield to social pressures and discipline ourselves to focus on the task that needs to be done. We cannot just observe our itches and find them very interesting. But most of us drive ourselves to conform and be good far harder than we need to. We drive ourselves all the time. We are in the *habit* of driving ourselves all the time, so there is never time to just sit down, notice our world, notice our inner selves. Gurdjieff talked about this as the idea that we have lost our *essence,* that it has all been devoured and covered up by false personality. One aspect of what he was talking about is that we simply do not allow ourselves any time to be by ourselves and just notice: Who am I? How am I? Aren't my inner processes interesting? Look at the clever way I am making myself suffer. How interesting to feel how this itch rotates and hops! Where am I going? It is important to do that.

WHEN INTELLECT TAKES OVER

STUDENT: *My experience of the diminishedness of the experience of my environment: it doesn't seem to me to be just a matter of comparing to the previous state. It seems that my experiences are less dynamic now than right after I started doing this practice. It was more of a sensory-based experience. But now it is more a mental component, a category of "I know this." It's like dating someone for the first time, everything is so interesting, but over time it tends to be kind of boring, because it's so familiar. It's the same thing, knowing I can't do anything about this.*

You are experiencing a very common problem in this kind of mindfulness work. Your intellect is trying to take over the practice.

STUDENT: *Yes.*

You have tried it a few times, and your intellect has it all figured out. Why should you actually need to pay any attention any more once it is figured out? That is exactly the attitude that put us deep into waking sleep, into samsara, in the first place, this feeling that we have figured everything out and now we will just automatically pay attention only to what is "important."

You have to concentrate harder. You have to give more attention to trying to pay attention to actual sensory impressions, even though your intellect says in essence, I've got it all worked out. A sound happens and your mind says, in effect, That's a bell ringing; I understand bells; I don't actually have to listen to that sound, I've got the *words* for it. This is all automatized, and conditioned intellect just passes your concepts about bells on to consciousness, with very little of the actual quality of the sound getting through.

That, sadly, is the story of our life. That is the way false personality takes over and devours essence. We have words for things, concepts about experience, instead of actually having the experiences. That is not very nourishing and it is how you lose the richness of the food of impressions. You "eat" thin, tasteless abstractions about impressions, rather than the thick, juicy impressions.

You might try the little variation of the morning exercise I suggested on our first day together (in chapter 2), making a meditation out of sensing your arms and legs and just really listening to sounds, without opening your eyes, meditating that way for ten minutes before you go on to complete the morning exercise. Most of you will have to resist your conditioned intellect's desire to get it over with. It will quickly classify any sounds, dismiss them as unimportant, and want to get on to what it's conditioned to believe are important things. It is our habit. We have had umpteen years of practicing that habit, letting our intellect classify and then dismiss things, and that's it. Try just giving sounds, and sensations in general, more attention, and see what happens.

What else have people noticed in your practice?

CREATING SPACE

STUDENT: *I noticed some interesting things today when we were out to lunch.*

When you say "out to lunch," was that mentally or physically speaking? [*General laughter*]

STUDENT: *I had an appointment I wanted to get to, but the waitress disappeared for some time. I was wondering, Where is she? We need the check! So I called another waitress to find her, which she did. Everything was moving very slowly, and then when I got out to the cash register the person in front of me was moving very slowly, and then the girl doing the adding on the machine made a mistake and had to do the whole thing over! As this was happening, I sensed that it was part of something that just kind of happens. What I got was that when I was really sensing myself I had more choice. I wasn't doing it much then, but if I had, I might have not been carried along with this irritation. I'm a highly impatient person, and I probably manifested it.*

People were wasting your precious time. They should at least be punished if not killed for it, don't you think?

STUDENT: *I realized that I really had a choice. I could just let go of that impatience and anger. Then I sensed myself, and I was able to let go of it.*

That's a really important experience. You had two important things happen then. One was that by sensing, looking, and listening you gave yourself some space; you did not just get carried away automatically by the growing irritation. You gave yourself some space to consider, What do I want to do with this situation? Also, by deciding, as it were, not to forget yourself and go with it, you gave yourself time to think about the situation in alternative ways. Maybe, for example, it's not that the waitress *likes* being annoying, and that's why she deserves to die, but maybe she's new on the job the bell has just rung and isn't able to do it very fast yet. You were able to consider her as a fellow human being. Maybe you have been in situations where you were new on the job, were slow at it, and made mistakes.

That's a good observation you made, telling us something about the psychopathology of our everyday trance. We fall into these moods; we get irritated; our energy gets dulled; we have no space. We identify with and get sucked up by the emotional energy, and it's very compulsive and self-sustaining. We're on a trip and we can't get off. It's catastrophic. You could have snapped at her, added a little more to the sum of human misery, and perhaps felt bad yourself later in the day.

STUDENT: *If I had put her down, I would have felt bad. By being more mindful I realized, What good would it have done? It would have been so useless.*

In some ways I think this all-too-typical kind of experience is related to the spaciousness Sogyal Rinpoche talks about as part of the essence of Dzogchen. If you have some presence, if you are sensing yourself and your world, and are there in your body, then whatever you are doing, you are not so cramped, psychologically speaking. There is more room to maneuver in; there is less urgency and compulsiveness.

BEING MINDFUL UNDER TOUGH CONDITIONS

STUDENT: *I've had some interesting experiences. At first I felt kind of isolated when doing this sensing, and I realized I really liked to merge, you know, I like to merge into something. I felt apart in a way, a kind of withdrawal and kind of lonely.*

The last time I was really awake a lot like this, I had a very awake lover. I've really missed having someone awake to play with in that state. It brought it up when a previous questioner mentioned how good it is to be in a group like this, it's nice to have companionship.

Then I went out for Halloween, I went out to a nightclub and I practiced mindfulness for about forty-five minutes in the middle of this nightclub. To do that is just a gas! I mean, it was really empowering just to sit there, sensing my arms and legs. I mean, like every five minutes there would be these waves of energy that, like, clutch, you know, then withdraw or distract or something. For some reason, I was just in this mood, and I just sat there, you know. And then after that it was like I reached this pinnacle of embodiment and comfortableness within. And then I just lost interest, and I sort of went back to sleep.

That was a very good practice. It's interesting to compare it with formal, sitting meditation. Many of us practice some kind of formal meditation, meditation with *requirements*. We have to be in a quiet place, with nothing external bugging us, sitting in the correct posture, and then we may get experiences of feeling calm and centered, perhaps of being embodied. But this kind of calm, centeredness, and embodiedness can be very fragile. It doesn't happen if you can't sit in the correct posture, and any kind of disturbance makes it go away. Practicing in a nightclub is advanced work.

STUDENT: *My friend said, "You look so calm," and I said, "It's not easy."*

I believe I said the first day that what I'm trying to share with you is a way of mindfulness *in life,* not a way of retreating from life. It is by lifting the heavier weights that muscles begin to build. Once you choose this kind of path of more presence and wakefulness as part of everyday life, the crap life throws at you is valuable training material, not simply stress and disturbance. We can't always handle it in the "higher" way we think we should, but it is really helpful to our practice.

I can't emphasize how important this is. Ordinarily we see life as full of stresses and problems that keep us from happiness. In the worst cases, we become pessimistic and depressed about it. But if you take mindfulness as a goal, along the lines we've discussed, your perspective changes. Life becomes something like a martial arts dojo, a training center, a school. You see stresses and problems as opportunities. Paradoxically, by giving up happiness as an immediate goal and going for mindfulness, truth, you reap a lot more happiness.

SPONTANEITY AND CREATIVITY

STUDENT: *In my mind I have spontaneity hooked up with uncon- sciousness, so I am a little ambivalent for some reason about the idea of becoming more mindful and conscious. I feel like I am losing or might lose that sense of spontaneity. I feel like the whole thing of trying to be more mindful could be kind of heavy and stiff.*

That's a good observation. This is one of the dangers of this kind of work: it can get too stiff. I have seen people in some Gurdjieff groups who sense, look, and listen *very* seriously. But it's the wrong kind of seriousness; it feels like a mechanical grimness that depresses the spirit. I have an urge to go and tickle them. It's true that our situation is serious—we and the whole world suffer terribly and needlessly through mindlessness. We have to face this and deal with it, but making yourself chronically gloomy and thinking this is what mindfulness is all about is a mistake.

What is spontaneity to you?

STUDENT: *It's something that comes out of the moment, really, it's the unexpected. When it happens it gives some sort of sense of freedom.*

Is it always the same?

STUDENT: *I'm not sure.*

Although it is really related to the moment, could you see that maybe there are a number of kinds of spontaneity, and that it can come from different sources at different times? If you were in a really pissed off mood, for example, you could suddenly and spontaneously hit somebody. That might be very different from when you were in a different kind of mood and you spontaneously hugged somebody.

These kinds of mindfulness techniques will make you lose some kinds of spontaneity, that is true. In my experience, however, the kind you lose is a kind of driven, hysterical, or "pushed" spontaneity. In our and our culture's ordinary samsaric state, living in waking dreams, that driven spontaneity may be very valued, so it will feel like a loss, or your friends will notice it. Your friends will say, "You are very quiet tonight. What's wrong?" Implicitly, they are asking why you aren't hysterically singing and shouting and jumping up and down and running around like everybody else. At some psychological level, your lack of participation in common kinds of hysteria (known in samsara as "fun") is threatening; it raises questions.

There are other kinds of spontaneity that come out of a deeper level of yourself. While you may lose a certain surface, hysterical kind of spontaneity by following these kinds of mindfulness practices, I think in the long run you will touch something much deeper and more worthwhile. There is a spontaneity that comes out of our false personality, and we will tend to lose that as we calm down and become more mindful and present. But then there is a spontaneity that comes out of contact with knowing our own essence better.

As I reflect, I do not like what I just said. It sounds too artificial, somehow, it puts people down too much. But I'm talking about an important reality: check it out.

There are moments in life that are heavy, when we do feel something more deeply and it has a sad reality to it, but if you ever find yourself being rigidly serious about this practice, that is a bad sign, a very bad sign. That would be like *always* having to cup your hands together and open your mouth whenever the bell rings. Real feelings flow and change, they cover an enormous range. Freezing them through your biases and attachments, whether they then always feel good or feel bad, is not freedom, it's not learning to be mindful of what actually *is*.

HYSTERICAL "SPONTANEITY"

Let's talk about this hysterical spontaneity a little more. Can people remember experiences where you are having a good time with somebody else, but it is sort of a desperate good time, so you will not notice what is underneath? [*Many heads nod affirmatively.*]

That is the kind of spontaneity that can indeed be damaged badly by this practice. It is not a terribly useful kind of spontaneity to have, however, unless you feel that you are totally stuck in some crazy position in life and it makes the misery a little more bearable. Unfortunately, a lot of people feel that way a lot of the time. Then our operating rule for living becomes, Don't rock the boat! It may be bad now in a lot of ways, but it could be worse! But we are still pouring gasoline on the flames, as it were. Out of fear of change, we are allowing our energy to be sucked up in the processes that create our misery.

We can stop giving our energy to that kind of situation. Not because we grit our teeth and say moralistically, "I won't be spontaneous! I am going to be calm and studied!" but simply because we use a little bit of attention to sense our arms and legs, hear the sounds, and see what is actually there. Because we decide to pursue truth rather than immediate happiness. Then that kind of hysteria does not run on so strongly.

STUDENT: *One thing I already noticed along those lines . . . Wednesday night we were going to a workshop at which both of us were speaking. I was being very gay, and then suddenly I noticed that this was not really me! I was caught up in this role. My boss was there, and I realized I always act lighthearted and gay around him.*

This identification with false personality is going to cost you more as time goes on. The bell rings now, open your mouth, cup your hand to your ears, be present. It will cost you more in the sense that you see the enormous investment you have in this role that you have automatically accepted in order to keep up a certain relationship with your boss. It can be depressing to see the price you are paying. Of course, he is probably invested in it, too. At some point, if you keep practicing mindfulness, he may notice and wonder, What's wrong with her? She's not as much fun any more. Semiconscious feelings of being threatened may turn that thought into She's not doing the job right. His new view of you might be more accurate in some ways— you might get calmer—but more distorted in other ways as his defenses and his investments in you seem threatened. He is not attempting, at least to my knowledge, to become clearer about this sort of thing, to practice mindfulness. Gurdjieff warned people that they may become less interesting to their friends as they do mindfulness practice.

We get emotionally invested in our fantasies about who we are and who other people are, but in reality it helps to be in better touch with what is *really* happening. We do live in a real world here, with actual physical bodies, with things that go bump, and with other people who interact with us. The clearer the picture we have of what is actually going on, the more intelligent we can be about it—and the more joyful we can be about it. But along the way we often have to give up a lot of the essentially covert neurotic agreements we have made to maintain each other's illusions, each other's false personalities, and many of the hysterical activities we use to blind ourselves. A lot of ordinary social interaction is an implicit contract: You support my illusions, and I will support yours. Nobody rocks the boat. Of course, that does support illusions, but it carries its own high price tag.

STUDENT: *Does spontaneity go hand in hand with moment-by-moment self-awareness, or is part of the spontaneity habitual?*

Are you being aware moment by moment now?

STUDENT: *No, I am talking with my hands, waving them about, but it is automatic. I am not in much touch with my body.*

I want you to be in your body now and do something spontaneous.

STUDENT: *Once I pay attention to it, I don't feel I can be spontaneous.*

You don't feel you can be, but I don't think you actually have any data.

STUDENT: *Because that kind of spontaneity is not the same as habitual reactions.*

We walk through our ordinary life all the time with our feelings that we must be this way, we can only be that way, and so we never try any alternatives or make a space to allow any alternatives to emerge. You can organize your (false) personality in your life very rigidly to try to support your belief systems, and in many ways, it *will* support your belief systems, which will then give you the satisfaction of feeling that you are right. But you are really just keeping yourself restricted, living a rigid life. Collect some data on this. Try practicing sensing, looking, and listening for a year, and see if you are ever spontaneous when you are present in your body.

So let's remember that there are at least two kinds of spontaneity. One comes from the automatized and neurotically driven parts of our minds. It's outside the full light of ordinary consciousness, so it seems spontaneous: things just happen without our seeing the reasons for them. But it's really pretty determined behavior, the behavior of a conditioned being, of a programmed robot. That conditioning was not our choice, we are not free. The other kind of spontaneity, the deeper kind, comes more from our essence, from our spiritual nature.

It's easy to make this intellectual distinction, but in practice, any particular thing you do may be a mixture of these two kinds of spontaneity, plus other factors.

COMPULSIVE PLANNING

What would it be like to just live, to be deeply spontaneous? What a crazy idea! We go around all the time thinking, What do I do next, what I do next, what do I do next? Sometimes, though, you can just be present and let things happen. You might find that you would just do what happens next without figuring it all out, and it might be more fun.

For example, out of my own defensiveness as a child, I learned to really think ahead when talking. I always had my sentences analyzed at least ten or twenty words ahead, with an explicit map of the implications of each word and where those implications might lead me and the person I was talking to. It was like a part of me was moving into the potential future, editing everything to make sure I never accidentally got into trouble. Words with dangerous implications got edited out before I got to them in the sentence, and safer ones were substituted.

I guess in some ways it kept me out of a lot of trouble. It certainly made me very verbally fluent and able to think fast—it's a good example of how useful skills get taken over to support living in samsara. But it also reinforced the belief that the world and that people were hostile, that I had to be terribly careful all the time. It also reinforced my implicit belief that I actually could not trust myself, I couldn't just be spontaneous. I had to be edited; I had to be monitored; I had to be managed all the time.

In the course of my personal growth work, when I saw this incredibly compulsive editing process and its pernicious effects, I had to take the risk of trusting myself more, of learning to speak more spontaneously. It took me a long time to learn to just open my mouth and respond to someone without planning out what I was going to say. Sometimes what came out was embarrassing. Sometimes, in spite of being embarrassing, it was actually a lot more important than what I might have said if I had edited it. Sometimes what came out was new kinds of insights or a new kind of freedom that I would not get if I was always running scared of people's possible reaction to whatever I said.

USE A METHOD THAT WORKS FOR YOU

That is one of the reasons the emphasis in what I have been teaching is not Here are the things you should be like, here are the standards to measure up to, so much as Here is how to get more into the present, into reality, and start seeing for yourself what you and the world are really like.

That implies learning to trust yourself more, of course. If you really believed that you were basically pretty rotten, you would not want to do these mindfulness practices. But the fact that you are here working with becoming more mindful means you have some degree of trust in your deeper self. By working with mindfulness, you are reinforcing the belief that you are basically all right. That's good, because it's true. The bell rings now.

I wish we had a big mirror, so you could all see what you look like, cupping your hands to your ears at the sound of the bell and looking so serious. I'm sure I look as silly as everyone else. I notice that each person has added his own rules about *exactly* how to respond to the bell. Some people look down, some people look very religious, some people are sort of peeking out from behind their eyes, trying to see around.

This is very funny. We have to watch that this doesn't just become an automatic, habitual response to the bell, instead of a mindfulness exercise. In some ways, this kind of thing has often happened in various religious traditions. In Idries Shah's book *Caravan of Dreams* (pp. 112–13), there is a wonderful Sufi teaching story, "The Shrine," about the Mullah Nasrudin, which illustrates this.

Mullah Nasrudin's father was the highly respected keeper of a shrine, the burial-place of a great teacher which was a place of pilgrimage attracting the credulous and the Seekers After Truth alike.

In the usual course of events, Nasrudin could be expected to inherit this position. But soon after his fifteenth year, when he was considered to be a man, he decided to follow the ancient maxim: "Seek knowledge, even if it be in China."

"I will not try to prevent you, my son," said his father. So Nasrudin saddled a donkey and set off on his travels.

He visited the lands of Egypt and Babylon, roamed in the Arabian Desert, struck northward to Iconium, to Bokhara, Samarkand and the Hindu-Kush mountains, consorting with dervishes and always heading towards the farthest East.

Nasrudin was struggling across the mountain ranges in Kashmir after a detour through Little Tibet when, overcome by the rarefied atmosphere and privations, his donkey lay down and died.

Nasrudin was overcome with grief; for this was the only constant companion of his journeyings, which had covered a period of a dozen years or more. Heartbroken, he buried his friend and raised a simple mound over the grave. There he remained in silent meditation; the towering mountains above him, and the rushing torrents below.

Before long people who were taking the mountain road between India and Central Asia, China and the shrines of Turkestan, observed this lonely figure: alternately weeping at his loss and gazing across the valleys of Kashmir.

"This must indeed be the grave of a holy man," they said to one another; "and a man of no mean accomplishments, if his disciple mourns him thus. Why, he has been here for many months, and his grief shows no signs of abating."

Presently a rich man passed, and gave orders for a dome and shrine to be erected on the spot, as a pious act. Other pilgrims terraced the mountainside and planted crops whose produce went to the upkeep of the shrine. The fame of the Silent Mourning Dervish spread until Nasrudin's father came to hear of it. He at once set off on a pilgrimage to the sanctified spot. When he saw Nasrudin he asked him what had happened. Nasrudin told him. The old dervish raised his hands in amazement:

"Know, O my son," he exclaimed, "that the shrine where you were brought up and which you abandoned was raised in exactly the same manner, by a similar chain of events, when my own donkey died, over thirty years ago."

So an exercise that's originally designed to help you become more mindful can turn into habit, can turn into a venerable tradition. This one certainly won't for us, because we know it is just an artificial exercise we are doing for an evening. But sensing, looking, and listening or formal meditation practices can turn into habits that comfort but no longer aid in developing mindfulness, so be careful.

Incidentally the various books of Sufi teaching stories published by Idries Shah are quite wonderful sources of inspiration and insight.[1] Don't assume that we have extracted all of the meaning out of the donkey story by any means.

WILL THIS TAKE ME FAR ENOUGH?

STUDENT: *Is sensing, looking, and listening all you need to do to develop your mindfulness, or are there further extensions of that practice to develop awareness?*

As I have indicated before, sensing, looking, and listening is a practice that can actually work on many different levels. How it works for each particular person—how it works for *you*—is up to each person to find out. Let's focus on how it can help you be present.

You do not have to do sensing, looking, and listening to be here and now, to become more mindful of the present. A more surefire and dramatic practice to be here would be to hire someone to follow you around with a big stick and sneak up on you to beat you every time they think you have spaced out. That practice would really make you aware, it's really motivating, but whenever you slipped you would get beaten, which is not too great.

That kind of technique is actually used sometimes in advanced martial arts training. The founder of Aikido, Morihei Ueshiba, eventually told his advanced students to try to sneak up on him and hit or grab him any time of the night or day, any time they thought they might be able to do it. They tried but never succeeded; he was too alert to what was going on around him. Most of us would probably just get too paranoid to take this kind of attack as awareness training, though.

Sometimes we do a kind of "practice" that is a little like that, without being consciously aware of what we're doing. A part of our mind gives us an emotional beating, a shot of anxiety every time we do not live up to the standards we have set. You might feel guilty when you realize you've forgotten to sense, look, and listen, for example. As we discussed earlier tonight, using guilt like this is very tricky, and having it happen mechanically puts severe limits on its usefulness.

Remember, now, I'm mainly offering you in this workshop a technique for mindfulness in everyday life. But you have to see whether this practice helps you be present and mindful more often. If you find that, after giving it a good try, it makes no difference to how often you are here or to the quality of mindfulness you experience, then it is not for you. Work with something else. But if you find that it does help you expand the possible range of your consciousness, if you not only feel more present but begin acting more intelligently, if it gives you more spaciousness to exist in, then it is indeed useful.

COPING WITH STRESS THROUGH MINDFULNESS

STUDENT: *My experience with having done this sensing, looking, and listening technique a lot is that it helps more the more emotion that is going on for me at the time, especially unexpected emotions. For example, the other day at the hospital where I work there was a person who kept bugging me. She was very hostile. The situation was very stressful, the patient was going to surgery, I had to deal with the relatives who were there, so I got really caught up in it. There were these emotional outbursts. Then I sensed my body—I was aware on one level, on the natural body level—but when I sensed my body more fully, there was something very different about it, and it really grounded me into the present. It grounded me in a different way, and then I could really handle things much more effectively than I could without sensing my body.*

Most of us do not go through the day with very heavy emotional charges running through us all the time. No, actually, I'm projecting my own psychological processes on other people. Some people do experience powerful emotions most of the day. Anyway, for those of us who experience a relatively low level of obvious emotion most of the time, when a strong emotion comes, it usually sweeps us away.

Learning to sense, look, and, listen, to become more mindful, is like slowly enlarging your "experiential wiring," as we called it the other night, under calmer sorts of conditions, so that when a big charge does come, you can handle the charge much better. It does not have to sweep you away. This general enlargement of experiential capacity is why Gurdjieff talked about the Fourth Way being a way of combining the three other ways. It was not just the bodily way of the fakir; it was not just the emotional way of the monk; it was not just the insight way of the yogi. It includes aspects of them all.

If all you have on a spiritual path is insight, it is very dry. If all you have is emotion, it may be very juicy and exciting, but it can be very blind and stupid. If all you have is the will that comes from many body-development and concentrative practices, you may do stupid things with that will.

WHERE DO WE GO FROM HERE?

I have an interesting question for us now. We have a little over half an hour left, and this is our last meeting—and then what? Ordinary life goes on, without this work we have done together as a reminder of something more continuing. One answer to the question, Then what? is to just go back to sleep: except that now we may not sleep quite so comfortably. It is not that I have a particular answer I expect from you, but I am just raising the question—then what?

STUDENT: *As you know, I practiced sensing, looking, and listening for about three years after learning it from you several years ago. After the initial two years of having our group work as a support, I kept it up on my own for almost another year. It really helped me very much to bring this kind of mindfulness into my life. I was much more aware and alive than I had been before. It was especially useful at work, which is often a high stress situation.*

After our group ended and I didn't have social support, though, old habits reasserted themselves, and I gradually moved away from doing much sensing, looking, and listening. In fact, there were times when I felt it isolated me from my work colleagues and other people. So there were times when I deliberately said to myself, I have to be with these people, maybe I don't want to be so aware, so alone. It was almost like deliberately deciding to be unconscious, wanting to go back to being fully asleep. When I got to being aware, as much as I did at times, it wasn't always wonderful. Sometimes it was painful, sometimes uncomfortable. I felt things and saw things that were unpleasant. So I drifted away from doing it.

I never forgot sensing, looking, and listening entirely though—I don't think I could. It's like learning to ride a bicycle; you can't really forget. These sessions together have really reinforced my use of this technique, and reminded me of just how valuable it is.

I want to respond to that by telling you a Sufi teaching story, called "When the Waters Were Changed," from Idries Shah's *Tales of the Dervishes* (pp. 21–22).

Once upon a time Khidr, the Teacher of Moses, called upon mankind with a warning. At a certain date, he said, all the water in the world which had not been specially hoarded, would disappear. It would then be renewed, with different water, which would drive men mad.

Only one man listened to the meaning of this advice. He collected water and went to a secure place where he stored it, and waited for the water to change its character.

On the appointed date the streams stopped running, the wells went dry, and the man who had listened, seeing this happening, went to his retreat and drank his preserved water.

When he saw, from his security, the waterfalls again beginning to flow, this man descended among the other sons of men. He found that they were thinking and talking in an entirely different way from before; yet they had no memory of what had happened, nor of having been warned. When he tried to talk to them, he realized that they thought that he was mad, and they showed hostility or compassion, not understanding.

At first he drank none of the new water, but went back to his concealment to draw on his supplies, every day. Finally, however, he took the decision to drink the new water because he could not bear the loneliness of living, behaving and thinking in a different way from everyone else. He drank the new water, and became like the rest. Then he forgot all about his own store of special water, and his fellows began to look upon him as a madman who had miraculously been restored to sanity.

There is something very sad about what we have all been through in life. We live in a world where everybody has drunk the new water. I have been trying, by analogy, to remind you about the old water and giving us various exercises and practices to see if you can get some little sips of it. By sipping it together, we have given each other some social support, but now we go back out into the ordinary world where everybody is drinking the new water. It can be very lonely when we are not like everybody else, and everybody else wants us to join them in their madness.

Don't take this story too far. You should not regard everybody who is not working on mindfulness in some way as mad or bad. Be especially careful not to start giving yourself airs and thinking you're superior to others because you are working on developing mindfulness. That is one of the special hazards of this kind of work. There is an important level of truth where everybody is doing the best they can, under very difficult circumstances, and we should honor and respect all beings. But there is also a real gulf between being caught up in the trance of consensus consciousness, the spirit of the age, and trying to become more aware. The loneliness can be difficult. But never forget to honor all beings and have compassion for them, without feeding your egotistical self.

Please, it's very important to remember this. Conceit, treating others badly, will create new illusions and seriously undermine mindfulness work.

STILL, WHERE DO WE GO FROM HERE?

So what is going to happen?

STUDENT: *I'm going to go on retreat!*

That might be a great idea. Which retreat is that?

STUDENT: *Sogyal Rinpoche's.*

Good. Have you been on any of his retreats before?

STUDENT: *No.*

It should be an interesting experience for you.

STUDENT: *What gets me confused is that there is often a mixture of both help and hindrance toward developing mindfulness in being with other people. Even people in a spiritual group like Rigpa Fellowship. I want it to be consistent, that others should always inspire me to be more mindful, to always be helpful, but of course it can't be. That's what I find quite difficult. I want others and myself to always be working together on this, not distracting me. I'm already good enough at distracting myself.*

I sometimes think that I should not teach this kind of material. If I teach this kind of mindfulness-in-life material, what I should be able to do is say, "Incidentally, there is a community you can move into around the corner, where everybody is practicing this work, they are fine people and very good at being present in the here and now, and living and working with them will help everybody's individual practice, so we will all become enlightened together." But in reality, support facilities are not readily available. I fear that I may give people a glimpse of something wonderful, but then they won't be able to sustain and develop it for lack of social support.

Yet at the same time, it would be crazy in a way for me not to share with other people what I know about this kind of mindfulness, because it is so helpful! Not just in becoming more aware and intelligent in everyday life (which is actually quite a spiritual thing to do) but I think it can potentiate other genuine spiritual paths quite nicely, if used well.

In a way, there should be no problem in my recommending specific places and groups to develop this mindfulness work. I'm drawing heavily, although not exclusively, from Gurdjieff's teaching, but as I hinted at on the first day, I do not necessarily recommend orthodox Gurdjieff groups. It is not really clear to me whether Gurdjieff left a complete tradition suitable for our times or whether the people who learned from him or his disciples, and think they are carrying on his tradition, got it well enough to transmit it properly. I wish I felt fully competent to judge whether a particular Gurdjieff group was really adequate, but I am not. Some have clearly degenerated and gotten rather cultlike, although it may still be possible to learn a lot from studying from them if you're careful. Others, I just don't know.

So it's an uncomfortable place I'm in. It would not be right to just bury the knowledge I've gained, as I've gotten too much feedback that it really has been useful to a lot of people I've taught it to, even if I can't unequivocally recommend a specific group they could go on with. But I certainly wish I could. Incidentally, I've written extensively about this problem of picking a group to work with on the spiritual path in one of the last chapters of my book *Waking Up,* and I recommend that chapter for more depth here. We have so little time left to explore this further tonight, in spite of its importance.

PROBLEMS WITH EYE CONTACT

STUDENT: *One of the things that I find difficult is making eye contact with people but not getting fixated. It is very hard for me to stay in eye contact with someone for a period of time and not stare or fall into a trance or something. I guess I have a kind of negative judgment or feeling about always making eye contact with people and then looking away so that I can stay more aware in the moment. I also do the kind of work where I think it is important to stay present, and eye contact is one way of making sure I stay present. I guess I feel that about other people in relation to me also. So I struggle with that. I might be looking steadily at you and then I remember that you said not to stare steadily. It's entrancing, to be shifty-eyed and look around. I feel like I'm being bad! I guess it is rather childlike for me to feel guilty about this. I have just forgotten the instructions, I've just spaced out.*

Right, go on.

STUDENT: *Maybe it is just more of a problem with my work, because I want to be present with people, but I feel that I am not when I am being shifty-eyed or when I'm getting engrossed in other things.*

Remember, when you do look at someone, *really look*. Do not just point your eyes in some direction and then mechanically shift after a few seconds and then shift again. When you look, look more intensely, more open-mindedly, and with more genuine curiosity than you usually do. With sensing, looking, and listening, all three of these sensory functions, as well as going on simultaneously, are to be more active than they normally are. So if you look at someone and make eye contact, don't do the conventional thing of pointing your eyes there but not really letting your mind pay full attention to what you see because you don't want to get caught. On the other hand, when you look into someone's eyes, don't just get completely lost in the internal fantasies that are so frequently generated when we're in that kind of intimate contact. Actually look, and then shift.

Sometimes, of course, you have to maintain contact longer, if it would be socially inappropriate to shift your eyes after only a few seconds. On the other hand, the goal is not to be shifty-eyed all your life. Shifting your eyes consciously is a technical trick, a type of skillful means, to help prevent you from becoming readily hypnotized, but that is not the only way to prevent this kind of everyday hypnosis from happening. For instance, you can make eye contact but then sense your arms and legs even more strongly while you maintain the eye contact. You can shift back and forth, looking from one to the other of the person's eyes. If we are worried about the hypnotizing ability of other people's gazes, we can look at a spot between their eyes, instead of maintaining completely direct eye contact. Remember, it is the willful division of attention, simultaneously sensing your arms and legs while using some other sense, that is important. Bell, the bell is ringing, wake up!

You need to experiment with these techniques, too. You haven't been doing them for very long. Skill does develop with practice, so something that may at first seem impossible or too distracting or that is having undesirable side effects may become much clearer and easier with sufficient practice.

As an outstanding example, you may have a lot of trouble talking while sensing your arms and legs. That is quite normal. I still have trouble doing that, but I have gotten fairly good at talking while keeping some sensing going. There was a time when I thought it would never be possible to talk and sense something else at the same time. It was just too, too hard; my own talking was too hypnotic not to get lost in it.

HOW AWAKE ARE OTHER PEOPLE?

STUDENT: *I just feel that I have missed something here. I don't know what it means to hear that other people are not aware. How can you tell about other people being aware?*

I wouldn't worry about it. It's whether *you* are aware that matters.

STUDENT: *I thought maybe I could get a handle on this if I understood what other people have been saying about their experience of being more aware. Because, like, my problem here is that other people don't seem to forget their keys like I do!*

That doesn't necessarily mean that they are present in the here and now. It may simply mean that they have more rigid habits about some kinds of things, like compulsively remembering to check if they have their keys before going out.

I don't think it is a good idea to worry about judging how aware other people are, though. The important thing is to get more and more sensitive to the nuances of where and when *you* are, where and when *your* awareness is. That will eventually give you more feeling for other people and natural perceptiveness about whether they are really off in a daydream or relatively close to the present. Worrying about other people's degree of mindfulness at this stage of the game gets your energies going in the wrong direction.

For instance, in some Gurdjieff groups I've had experience with, the teacher creates the impression that he or she is able to tell how aware other people are. Regardless of the truth of this, sometimes one of the main results is to create a climate of fear: your teacher knows when you are being an inadequate human being, when you are failing. Teacher becomes superego.

As we've discussed, a *little* fear can actually be used as a kind of mental fuel, so people can use their fear and actually become more aware of how asleep they are and make stronger efforts. But once fear gets beyond a certain threshold—unique for each individual, and even then varying from time to time—it can fuel delusions about being present. I fear, therefore I am!

It also tends to make you become concerned about *looking* aware rather than *being* aware. It is much better to be working with yourself, trying to notice just how you and your world really are at this moment, the next moment, the next moment. For instance, do I right now hear the sounds coming form outside this room as labels (*siren*) or do I actually hear some of the sounds' auditory qualities? Do I know I have two legs and two arms because of immediate, dynamic sensation from them, or do I only have a vague thought that I am sensing my arms and legs?

STUDENT: *Why don't you do a follow-up group to this one?*

Hmm. Let me think about that. For the last several years I've done a number of one- or two-day workshops on being more mindful in life, but I've done them without any follow-up sessions. This is the first one with follow-up sessions, in which we can work with your practical experiences, that I have been able to do in a long time. We have the advantage of all living in the San Francisco Bay Area. That makes this possible.

I did a two-and-a-half-year-long group, with lots of follow-up, several years ago, but I ended it. There were many other things I needed to do, and I wasn't totally satisfied with the way things were going. Everybody was learning some important things and slowly becoming more mindful, but I wanted some kind of "more" out of it and wasn't sure how to do that at the time. Today I'm not sure whether I will do long-term groups again—at least it's not intuitively right with me just now, although that might change sometime.

One of the reasons I'm somewhat reluctant to get back into that kind of long-term teaching is that there is another whole level of complications that happen then that I don't particularly like. For example, students tend to start believing that the teacher is too good, too wise, even when you tell them differently. That creates problems. This is what psychology calls transference problems—it's discussed at length in my *Waking Up*.

I don't know. At the present time I don't want to do more follow-up. I might do a workshop like this again next year, or might not. I simply don't know. I have been very overbooked and overworked for a long while now, too. I am having fantasies about how nice it would be to have a day when I was bored. Of course, I would try to be bored and aware, sensing and savoring the sensations of boredom! So I'm working hard not to commit myself to anything else right now. I don't know how successful I'll be at that.[2]

STUDENT: *It would be nice if we could keep in contact with one another. I'll check with the organizers and see if we can mail everyone a list of each other's names and addresses.*

One possibility for something some of you could do is come to Sogyal Rinpoche's teachings.[3] As I said the first day, I have not been representing Sogyal Rinpoche or the Rigpa Fellowship in what I've taught in our time together, even though I have done this workshop as a benefit for the Rigpa Fellowship. I have taught from my personal knowledge of modern psychology, Gurdjieff's ideas, and other experiences of mine, material I have acquired considerable confidence in. But I have not been representing myself as any kind of authority on Tibetan Buddhism, as I'm not as sure about the quality of my understanding about some key points. But it does seem appropriate, given our question, What next? for me to indicate why I've been studying with Sogyal Rinpoche for a number of years and am highly supportive of his work.

A main personal reason I am involved is because the Dzogchen aspect of what Sogyal Rinpoche teaches seems to me to have a great deal to do with developing mindfulness of the moment; thus it builds on and, in important ways, extends my previous work. It also has important elements that the more standard kind of Gurdjieff work, as I know it, doesn't. The devotional element is particularly important to me.

I am a person who needs to stimulate my devotion, my caring and compassion for others, otherwise this mindfulness work gets too abstract. I have always been too intellectual and too cold a person, so my personal path requires that I develop these other aspects of myself, develop (to put it the way Gurdjieff would) my emotional brain, my heart, and my body brain, not just my intellect. Sogyal Rinpoche is a very compassionate and devoted person and also emphasizes these aspects of Tibetan Buddhism, so putting a lot of energy into his style of work is right for me at this time in my life. Needless to say, I have enormous respect for Sogyal Rinpoche and what he teaches.

On the other hand, there are things in Tibetan Buddhism, as Sogyal Rinpoche teaches it, that drive me to distraction! There are some long (six to eight hours) ceremonies (*tsoks*), for example, which I deliberately absent myself from, as they make me bored and angry with devotion rather than helping me. Intellectually, I know it is a beautiful, inspiring ceremony filled with rich teachings, and some Western students find it very fulfilling, but it just isn't my style. What may be an inspiring and effective practice for one person may be uninspiring and counterproductive for another. For better or worse, I am a quite independent person and so I do considerable picking and choosing in what I practice.[4]

Tibetan Buddhist teachings, as I know them, also do not have enough about educating the body brain, but I've gotten that information from other sources. So I recommend Tibetan Buddhism as a path to try if you are interested in developing mindfulness, but it may not be suitable for many people.

The Dzogchen tradition that Sogyal Rinpoche represents is, I think, a very high-level tradition that can take you a long, long way, probably all the way on the journey to enlightenment. I say "probably" just so you'll remember that I'm not qualified to make high-level judgments about enlightenment, even though I have become too much of an authority on endarkenment and obstacles to growth!

I think work in the regular Gurdjieff tradition can be the bell sounds, cup your hands to your ear and be present quite valuable. I was involved in orthodox and unorthodox Gurdjieff work for some time and found it very valuable. I also found what for me were certain deficiencies that made me not stay involved with it. Whether those things would be important to other people or not, I don't know.

STUDENT: *What particular Gurdjieff groups were you involved with?*

I was involved with the Gurdjieff Foundation and also with a couple of unorthodox groups, "independents," as they like to call themselves. But for all the opportunities, I must emphasize, beware of Gurdjieff groups! Gurdjieff work sometimes attracts people who are power mad. Since Gurdjieff was hard on people and didn't suffer fools gladly, some people thus seem to think that being nasty to other people is the way to wake them up. I don't think the answer is really so simple.

I certainly continue to practice the morning exercise and the sensing, looking, and listening work, both fundamentals of Gurdjieff work, as my main personal practice. I can't do it as well without the social support of others doing that work, but it is still very valuable. Its effects in making me more mindful of my own feelings, my more spacious self, and the world around me are sometimes fairly obvious, sometimes subtler. Generally for me the outcome of mindfulness practice is not obvious until I suddenly notice that something important in me has changed for the better in a quiet sort of way. I am not sure what else to say at this point.

DZOGCHEN AND EVERYDAY MINDFULNESS

STUDENT: *Since you have been studying Tibetan Buddhism, how would you correlate your understanding of Dzogchen with what you have been teaching us?*

I have deliberately avoided doing that because I feel I am not adequately expert on Dzogchen. I go through phases when I think I understand the essence (as opposed to the innumerable technical aspects and teachings of the tradition) of Dzogchen quite well, but then on other days I think I don't understand much about it. When I think I understand it, I think that it is basically a matter of increasing your mindfulness in all things, in all aspects of life, with the added gift of a kind of "contact high," as people said in the seventies, a kind of transmission of glimpses of the highest possibilities. For instance, in Sogyal Rinpoche's translation of His Holiness Dudjom Rinpoche's *The Prayer of Calling the Lama from Afar*, we have lines like

Since pure awareness of Nowness is the real Buddha . . .

or

By relaxing in uncontrived Awareness, the free and open natural state,
We obtain the blessing of aimless self-liberation of whatever arises.

It's my experience that self-remembering, as I've taught it here, does lead to an "aimless self-liberation" of at least some things—that is, being in a mindful condition allows a lot of psychological disturbance to just pass through without catching you up. Mindfulness allows many neurotic disturbances to just pass, without activating your psychological machinery and habits and creating more and more disturbance. There is much richness in Dzogchen that goes beyond that, however, but I do not feel I have a solid enough grasp of Dzogchen to want to teach about it.[5]

As I said, there is also a ceremonial side of practice that doesn't work well for me, even though it may work well for some other people. I tend to mix and match, working with the aspects of Sogyal Rinpoche's teachings that resonate with me and giving little attention to the other aspects. Rinpoche seems to tolerate this in me, so I suppose I am not doing it too badly.

So how much Dzogchen I really understand, I don't know. The hypothesis I go on for the moment, my best current understanding, is that more and more mindfulness of what *is* at the moment—and a clear distinction between that and what we believe ought to be and what we are conditioned to think and so forth—is really the heart of the Buddhist Dzogchen tradition.

DISTORTING MINDFULNESS PRACTICE

STUDENT: *I have a question about a way I sometimes change this exercise. It seems my motivation or the intention I put into it is very important. When I experience some kinds of feelings I like to avoid, sometimes I realize semiconsciously that I'm using sensing, looking, and listening to avoid feeling and expressing certain emotions. Instead of being in better touch with the emotion, as a result of becoming more mindful, I try to bring my attention into sensing my body as a way of avoiding the emotion, selectively intensifying neutral body sensations, using them as distraction. There is something very sticky about doing this, and it doesn't seem to work too well.*

Don't be too hard on yourself. We are not up to a skilled level of proficiency in doing this kind of mindfulness work. We've just started. Of course, we are going to tend to do it more when we are feeling an unpleasant emotion, and we are going to tend to twist the technique around as a way of getting out of dealing with negative emotions.

So what you do in that case is observe the way you are twisting it around, getting away from the emotion instead of simply being present to what is. You are bound to get caught in doing some of this. Rather than put excess energy into berating yourself for this "failure," though, it's better to continue to observe yourself when you are distorting the sensing process and see what you can learn from such observations. That works better in the long run than simply being hard on yourself because you are not doing it up to some level of exalted standards.

I LIKE FANTASIES AND MEMORIES AND THINKING!

STUDENT: *What I find is that it is hard for me to put the three together, the sensing, looking, and listening. It is like when you are learning how to drive and forget to press the gas pedal at the same time as switching the gears and using the steering wheel. I don't know how to do the three of them together. It seems so automatic and so artificial when I am doing it that I forget one of the three. I might be remembering to sense my legs and listening, but then I realize that I am forgetting to look. So then I add looking but realize later that I forgot to sense my body almost as soon as I started looking. It is really very difficult, especially when I am walking.*

I went to a place called Wilbur Hot Springs, a very peaceful environment, and took lots of walks. When I am walking it seems particularly artificial to do this kind of exercise, because it becomes even boring. I ask myself, What am I doing, looking at a beautiful landscape? I find a lack of excitement. Instead, when I am here or in a peaceful room and I do it as a form of practice, like a form of meditation, then it is easier to focus. When I am walking, I get distracted by everything. Everything reminds me of something from the past, and I start engaging in those types of thoughts and forgetting the experience. It is really difficult.

I am a little confused by what you said. At first I thought you were saying that to do sensing, looking, and listening while you are walking makes it boring, but now I just heard you say that when you are walking everything reminds you of something else and you are totally lost from the present. It sounds like you really need to do sensing, looking, and listening to appreciate the beauty around you.

STUDENT: *I just feel that I am not really present when I am walking. My thoughts are fun. I know they are fantasy, but they are fun. Like today, I looked up and saw a beautiful field that reminded me of years ago when I was in a field like that in Spain with my cousins, and so that brought a lot of happiness, even though it had nothing to do with reality. It was just thinking of the past.*

I am not against happiness.

STUDENT: *I don't think I am really focusing on what is really here.*

Again, the thing is to learn the skill to be *able* to be here. You were mentioning learning how to drive, but you don't want to drive every second the rest of your life. It is a good thing that you know how, because there are times when you really need to drive. The main focus for us has been to learn *how* to be more present and to refine that skill. When I read a novel I don't want to be here; I want to get lost in the novel. Of course, I don't lie down in the middle of the road to read a novel; I do my reading in the bell is ringing now protected environments, where is doesn't matter that I'm not very aware of exactly what is happening moment by moment.

STUDENT: *So what you are saying is that it is okay, that it is still good practice to get lost in your thoughts while you are walking or when you are trying to look, listen, and—I forgot the other one.*

That's not what I said, no. You should practice so that you *can* sense, look, and listen in *any* activity of life. Then, when you know you *can* do it, when you can be really mindful in the midst of any circumstances, it is fine to do other things at times. You are then making a genuine choice. If you tell yourself that you're choosing not to be mindful when, in point of fact, you're not able to be very mindful, you're just kidding yourself.

Don't be too rigid about this. It is not that you should never have another thought until you master this sensing practice in all areas of life. You couldn't do it if you tried anyway. It is most important to practice this exercise in areas in which you find it difficult to do it, though—walking in your case—so that you develop the skill. Then, if you want to walk through a beautiful valley while only thinking of past valleys and it makes you happy, that's all right with me.

GURDJIEFF GROUPS

STUDENT: *I saw the film about Gurdjieff's life,* MEETINGS WITH REMARKABLE MEN, *and I was fascinated by the sacred dances shown. Is it possible to go to the monastery shown in the film to learn those dances or other things? I like the idea of going on a retreat in a monastery, too.*

You probably can't go to that monastery. The film was largely shot on location in Afghanistan, and the film crew got out of there just before the shooting war started. I don't think the more serious kind of shooting is all over yet. Of course, Gurdjieff said that shooting wars can be very useful times to learn to sense, look, and listen. There is something very motivating to being really present when you know the bullets are flying around. Be in touch, know when to duck, or die! Anyway, that monastery was just a filming location, not the actual source of Gurdjieff's teachings. There are monasteries around where you can do retreats, especially Catholic ones. Some are organized retreats with instruction; others are just room and board and you set up your own retreat and practice schedule. I know several people who do that once in a while and find it very useful.

STUDENT: *How do you learn those sacred dances?*

Those particular exercises are unique to the Gurdjieff work, developed by Gurdjieff himself as a result of what he learned in his travels in the East and his attempts to come up with mindfulness practices that would be effective for Westerners. Usually you have to be in one of the Gurdjieff Foundation groups to get instruction in them, although some other Gurdjieff groups have them. They are very meaningful exercises, and they are very difficult to learn, deliberately so. They are attention training processes, which push you to your limits and beyond.

If anyone is interested in orthodox Gurdjieff groups, you will have to make some effort and use a little ingenuity to contact them. They don't advertise, and finding them is a test. The feeling is that if you're not motivated and clever enough to find them, you're not interested enough to really do that kind of work anyway. On the other hand, some others advertise widely, feeling the idea that you have to make a test of finding them is not useful. I imagine both ways have advantages and disadvantages, and can see the arguments on both sides.

STUDENT: *Can you share your opinion about these groups? There are other classes in this area. I've seen four or five groups advertised.*

I generally wouldn't want to make any statements about any of them, primarily because I know very little about most of them, and so I don't want to express an opinion based mainly on hearsay. But if you're interested in getting involved with *any* spiritual group, I strongly recommend you read or reread the cautionary notes in my book *Waking Up* about getting involved with any long-term group work.

STUDENT: *What is the foundation you have mentioned?*

When Gurdjieff died, the crucial question was who was going to carry on his work. As so often happens when a great teacher dies, after a while, several different students said, in effect, "I got the real transmission of knowledge and power, and those other people really didn't get it, or only partly got it, so follow me. My way is the authentic way." The Gurdjieff Foundation of America is one of those ways. Some of these various branches do seem to have respect for each other, though. It's not all dissension by any means.

The Foundation, of course, considers itself the authentic tradition, which carries on with Gurdjieff's blessing. They are probably the biggest single group. I think of them as the orthodox, mainstream Gurdjieff tradition. From my personal experience, they have a lot to offer. In other ways, I feel they can be rather rigid. My opinion, were I more informed, would probably be the same about some of the other Gurdjieff groups, although I suspect some may have become dangerously corrupted.

There really is no central, objective directory that compares all these various groups and says group X is the most genuine tradition, group Y is not authentic, and group M charges only 5 percent of your income and is the Consumer's Union Best Buy on the Gurdjieff tradition. I wish there was really high quality information like this, but while it's easy to compare washing machines and toasters, we are not talking about some simple, straightforward evaluation process. And how can sleeping people evaluate whether someone else is awake enough to awaken them? For instance, a charlatan or a well-meaning teacher whose opinion of himself or herself went well beyond his or her actual attainments might treat you in ways that your ordinary self would consider bad, but might not a genuinely awake teacher do the same if it had a high chance of awakening you? If I knew a highly probable way to give you the greatest gift of all, awakening, would I care that it involved a lot of ordinary suffering? Is this a rationalization for a sadistic streak in me? This is a very tricky area.

Some people have argued that Gurdjieff never intended to set up a continuing tradition, that his work was an experiment carried out on behalf of a secret brotherhood of awakened people from Asia to test Western culture to see how ready we were for real teachings. But then the people who say that tend to be invested in their own teaching organizations. How much of this idea is sound and how much is commercial rivalry I do not know.

I'm a practical and woefully unenlightened person, and I have no way of knowing the truth about secret organizations of enlightened people and what their intentions were and are. For me, if you can learn something from the techniques of being more mindful, of quieting the insane chatter of ordinary consciousness, if you become more present and insightful from any kind of personal growth or spiritual work, if you have become more kind, you have gained something of enormous value. It certainly helps to have organizational and social support in trying to grow, but *all* organizations are dangerous. All organizations have the tendency to turn into cults. Read Arthur Deikman's marvelous book on this, *The Wrong Way Home*. All organizations have the tendency to seduce you into selling out your actual capacity for greater awareness for the illusions and satisfactions that come from achieving acceptance and prestigious positions in the group, thus exploiting our natural social needs for friendship and acceptance. That is the way life on earth is. Again, if you get serious about joining a Gurdjieff group—or any spiritual group for that matter—the bell is ringing, or *any* group, I strongly recommend that you study the chapter in *Waking Up* on making a "spiritual commitment contract."

There are a million things we haven't been able to cover in our brief time together, but we've covered the basics of mindfulness in everyday life. The reports you've given of your experiences in practicing them are encouraging signs that many of you are off to a good start. Go! Work as if everything depends on work. And Godspeed! Work as if everything depends on prayer. I hope that whatever path, or paths, you find has heart for you and that the tools we have studied together help you on your journey.

The sounding of the bell a moment ago is perfect timing. We have reached the end of our time together, and that reminder to come to the present, to be mindful, is a better note to end on than anything else I could say.

NOTES

CHAPTER 1: WE ARE MINDLESS ROBOTS . . . WHO CAN CHANGE

1. Those interested in contacting the Rigpa organization for information about Sogyal Rinpoche's teachings can use the following addresses, current as of 1994.

    United States: Rigpa, P.O. Box 607, Santa Cruz, CA 95061-0607.
    Telephone: (408) 454-9103.

    Australia: Rigpa, 12/37 Nicholson St, Balmain, NSW 2041.
    Telephone: (02) 555-9952.

    England: Rigpa, 330 Caledonian Road, London N1 1BB.
    Telephone: (071) 700-0185.

    France: Rigpa, 22 rue Burq, 75018 Paris. Telephone: (1) 42 54 53 25.

    Germany: Rigpa, Hasenheide 9, 10967 Berlin. Telephone (030) 694-6433.

    India: Dzogchen Gompa, Dhondenling, P.O. Tibetan Settlement, Kollegal Taluk, Dist. Mysore, Karnataka State.

    Ireland: Dzogchen Beara, Garranes, Allihies, West Cork.
    Telephone: (027) 730 32.

    Netherlands: Sint Agnietenstraat 22, 1012 EG Amsterdam.
    Telephone: (020) 623 80 22.

    Switzerland: Rigpa, P.O. Box 253, 8059 Zurich. Telephone (01) 463 1547.

2. Note to the reader. I can't make this book ring a bell at random intervals, but I want you to benefit from being able to do this practice. I could just have *Bell* printed in the text at random places, but your peripheral vision would spot it well ahead of your conscious mind getting to that part of the text and that would lessen the surprise effect. To eliminate this anticipation, I will insert the phrase *the bell is ringing* or variations of it, without quotation marks or capitalization, throughout as a continuous part of the text.

    The instant you see it, STOP! Take a few seconds to just be as still, physically and mentally, as possible. Be aware of the sensations in your physical body, the sensations reaching your senses from the world around you, your internal state. Perhaps put the book down (slowly and sensitively) for half a minute and be present to the world around you and your inner state.

A good analogy would be if you were alone in a forest at night and you heard a twig snap. You would become instantly alert, listening, sensing/feeling with your whole being for a few seconds. Don't take the analogy too far, though. You don't have to feel afraid, become physically tense, or mentally analyze, What is it? Just take in what *is* for those few seconds.

3. Because students at various workshops have frequently wanted to get a copy of this random bell tape, I have had Psychological Processes Inc. produce three random bell tapes, with different patterns and bells, so they can be interchanged to slow adaptation to them. Information is available by sending one dollar for a catalog to PPI, P.O. Box 8385, Berkeley, CA 94707.

4. The body-centered person was called Man Number One, the emotionally centered one Man Number Two, and the intellectually centered person Man Number Three. Unfortunately, a lot of confusion has been caused by Gurdjieff's using numbers here, for if four is better than three, then we automatically tend to assume that three is better than two and two better than one. In point of fact, the three basic types of people are just different, one is not inherently superior to another.

5. Please note I am using *nirvana* in the popular, escapist sense here, not in its proper meaning.

6. This interview, under the title "Talking Tantra: An Interview with Robert A. F. Thurman," appeared in the Fall 1991 issue of *Inquiring Mind: A Semi-Annual Journal of the Vipasssana Community*. I also recommend subscribing to *Inquiring Mind* for those interested in meditation and/or Buddhism, as it is a vigorous, informative, and stimulating journal. Write them at P.O. Box 9999, Berkeley, CA 94709 and enclose a donation of ten dollars or more.

7. A copy of the musical body cassette tape used in the workshop, with the exercise directed by me and with special music by the group Geist, can be ordered from Psychological Processes Inc. Send one dollar for a catalog to PPI, P.O. Box 8385, Berkeley, CA 94707.

On a personal note, I feel awkward about this and other footnotes indicating that something of mine, even if relevant to this book, can be purchased from PPI. Am I some kind of snake oil salesman or huckster? Rationally, though, these various books and tapes that PPI stocks are of use to people and it's the only convenient way to find most of them, so I'll have to learn to deal with my feelings of awkwardness.

Chapter 2: Mindfulness Exercizes

1. I'm not sure Gurdjieff knew about genuine kundalini yoga traditions, however, so take this story as an example of what can go wrong, not as the last word on kundalini yoga.

2. A tape recording of me leading the listener through the morning exercise procedure is available from PPI.

3. Heinlein's book *Stranger in a Strange Land* had a great impact on many of us in the sixties. It was first published by Putnams in 1961.

4. Information on this unusual form of psychotherapy, which I personally found very helpful, can be found in Robert Hoffman's *Getting Divorced from Mother and Dad: The Discoveries of the Fischer-Hoffman Process* (New York: Dutton, 1976).

Chapter 3: Deepening Practice

1. This questioner had learned the sensing, looking, and listening practice as a member of an experimental mindfulness training group that I had set up some ten years before this workshop, so she spoke from long experience.

2. The enneagram is a fascinating and rich source of ideas about personality structure—the false personality—that I have found very useful in my personal work, although to date there has been almost no scientific work on its validity.

   The most accessible book published to date is Helen Palmer's *The Enneagram: Understanding Yourself and the Others in Your Life* (San Francisco: Harper & Row, 1988). Other useful books are:

   Beesing, M., R. J. Nogoseko, and P. H. O'Leary. *The Enneagram: A Journey of Self-Discovery.* Danville, New Jersey: Dimension Books, 1984.

   Leviton, R., Trademarking the new age: Can spiritual and intellectual ideas be copyrighted? *East/West Journal,* March 1991, 33–37.

   Lilly, J. and J. Hart. "The Arica training." In C. T. Tart (ed.), *Transpersonal Psychologies.* New York: Harper & Row, 1975.

   Naranjo, Claudio. *Ennea-Type Structures: Self-Analysis for the Seeker.* Nevada City, California: Gateways/IDHHB, 1990.

   Riso, D. R. *Personality Types: Using the Enneagram for Self-Discovery.* Boston: Houghton Mifflin Company, 1987.

3. Note that the questioner is a member of the Rigpa Fellowship.

Chapter 4: First Follow-up Session

1. This beautiful prayer, translated from the Tibetan by Sogyal Rinpoche, is given as the ending dedication to this book.

2. This questioner was a student in my Awareness Enhancement Training in the 1980s, a group that focused on Gurdjieffian training.

CHAPTER 5: SECOND FOLLOW-UP SESSION

1. The commentator was a student years before in my Awareness Enhancement Training group, where we practiced self-remembering techniques. See my book *Waking Up* for information on that group.

2. My superego, for instance, is very incensed to discover in the course of editing this manuscript that I have already said similar things about massages and superegos before. How dare I be repetitious here! Thank you, superego, but most of us really do need to hear the instructions and ideas many times before we get them.

CHAPTER 6: FINAL FOLLOW-UP SESSION

1. Idries Shah has published many books about the Sufis, particularly about the teaching stories that they consider to be a timely way of increasing wisdom in the West. The following books are highly recommended.

The Sufis. Garden City, New York: Doubleday & Co., 1964.

The Exploits of the Incomparable Mulla Nasrudin. New York: Simon & Schuster, 1966.

Caravan of Dreams. London: Octagon Press, 1968.

The Book of the Book. London: Octagon Press, 1969.

Wisdom of the Idiots. London: Octagon Press, 1969.

The Dermis Probe. London: Johnathon Cape, 1970.

The Way of the Sufi. New York: E. P. Dutton & Co., 1970.

Tales of the Dervishes: Teaching Stories of the Sufi Masters over the Past Thousand Years. New York: E. P. Dutton & Co., 1970.

Thinkers of the East. London: Jonathan Cape, 1971.

Reflections: Fables in the Sufi Tradition. Baltimore: Penguin Books, 1971.

The Magic Monastery: Analogical and Action Philosophy of the Middle East and Central Asia. New York: E. P. Dutton & Co., 1972.

The Subtleties of the Inimitable Mulla Nasrudin. New York: E. P. Dutton & Co., 1973.

The Hundred Tales of Wisdom. London: Octagon Press, 1978.

Learning How to Learn. London: Octagon Press, 1978.

A Perfumed Scorpion. London: Octagon Press, 1978.

Seeker After Truth: A Handbook of Tales and Teachings. San Francisco: Harper & Row, 1982.

2. If there were enough people interested in the San Francisco Bay Area, and if my intuition told me it was right, I might start a long-term mindfulness training group. At the time of this final editing in January, 1994 I think the probability is fairly high of doing this, perhaps through the auspices of the Institute of Transpersonal Psychology, Palo Alto, California, starting in late 1994 or in 1995. If you are interested in that, or in brief mindfulness workshops in other geographical areas, write me at the Department of Psychology, University of California, Davis, California 95616. I'll write back about brief workshops, and I will keep letters expressing interest in a long term Bay Area group on file if and until the time is right.

3. For those interested in this possibility who do not live in the San Francisco Bay Area, Sogyal Rinpoche travels between centers in France, England, Germany, Australia, the East and West coasts of the United States, and other areas. Information about these centers and his teaching retreats can be obtained by writing to the Rigpa Fellowship. Other Tibetan teachers have also begun to teach Dzogchen in the West in recent years. You can inquire about them by writing the Office of Tibet, 107 E. 31st St., New York, NY 10016.

4. As I do the final editing on this manuscript, I notice that I am somewhat uncomfortable being described as a *student* of Sogyal Rinpoche's. I am, of course: I have been studying with him (as well as some other lamas) for ten years. Yet in some of the circles in which I move, to be described as the student of any spiritual teacher could imply that you are a mindless follower, a disciple, or a devotee, such that, for the sake of emotional fulfillment, you only use your intellectual faculties to rationalize what you irrationally believe. Such an implication would be inaccurate in describing my relationship to Sogyal Rinpoche and to the Dzogchen teachings, however.

    I have enormous respect for Sogyal Rinpoche, both as a person and as a representative of the Dzogchen tradition, and have benefited enormously from our contact. I have never been much of a "follower" of anything, though, and I approach Buddhism and Dzogchen from the perspectives of my own varied work and background as, among other things, psychologist, scientist, Aikidoist, student of Gurdjieff's ideas, husband, father, grandfather, American citizen, and on and on. Attempts to fit Dzogchen ideas and practices into my own perspective undoubtedly create distortions and difficulties at times, and enrich my understanding at others.

    At times I am genuinely envious of those who find a teacher they feel such total confidence in that they can just put all their own being and views aside and take in the new ideas wholesale—it seems to speed their learning. But I've never felt *total* confidence about any teacher, even though I've had great respect for and have learned from many. I do not know to what degree this stems from some fundamental inability to completely trust on my part, and/ or having enough maturity to not fall into transference relationships, and/ or being comfortable in (and perhaps too attached to) my intellectual independence, but this stance is my past and current reality. It is clear that whoever I am, complete honesty about it is the only right and sensible course. I hope the few remarks I have made about Buddhism and particularly about Dzogchen are accurate, but they are my interpretations, not the teachings of a lineage. The positive side of my independence—positive for my various teachers over the years—is that none of them should be blamed for any mistakes I make!

5. In the year and a half between making this statement in the workshop and the final editing of this book, I have, I hope, developed a little more understanding, so I will assay a comment on an important difference between the essence of the Dzogchen teachings and what I have been teaching in this and other mindfulness training workshops.

In our ordinary state, consensus consciousness, our attention and energies are automatically captured by various psychological programs—psychological machines, as it were—that distort our perceptions, thoughts, and feelings and our knowledge of who we really are. We are far too often enchanted, absorbed, and lost, and we suffer a great deal because of this lack of contact with reality. We identify with the contents of our samsaric consciousness. The drama of the moment is *me* most of the time. As I quoted in the beginning dedication,

> HO! Mesmerized by the sheer variety of perceptions,
> Which are like the illusory reflections of the moon in water,
> Beings wander endlessly in samsara's vicious cycle.

The horror is that it can indeed be endless!

The kind of mindfulness training presented in this workshop, drawing heavily from Gurdjieff's practices, as well as almost all forms of classical meditation, is based on a deliberate psychological dualism, a splitting off of one part of the mind from the rest. Instead of "I" being totally identical with the current contents of experience, you become an observer, an observer who is somehow apart and can so observe the fluctuating contents of experience. You thus weaken your otherwise automatic identification with ongoing experience. It's as though you learn to say to yourself things like, This strong anger is only a small, transient portion of me rather than all of me; it is something I, the observer, can (learn to) look at objectively, or, This pain, this pleasure, this moment of boredom, this taste, this sight, this attraction, this aversion, and so forth—these are all small, passing parts of me, not the whole.

This deliberate creation of an observer is, incidentally, not at all the same as the conditioned dissociation and withdrawal that occurs through the operation of psychological defense mechanisms, although there are some tricky potential interactions here.

Since the observer is of a different nature from and more spacious than ordinary "I," this is a tremendous accomplishment. Instead of being pushed around by the changing world and our conditioned reactions all the time, we develop a kind of spaciousness, a calmness, and an inner, nonconditional kind of pleasure and happiness. This gives us more flexibility and intelligence in dealing with life and a mental development that lets us discover more and more about our true nature, our essence. It also, in a paradoxical way, makes life more vivid, not less vivid.

From a Dzogchen point of view, this kind of mindfulness development is indeed a great accomplishment but—and this is a big *but*—the dualism inherent in the approach keeps us from full enlightenment. Our ultimate essence *is* the nature of mind, which is not separate from anything or anyone else. The observer, no matter how useful, is still a construction, a fabrication, that keeps us from seeing the ultimate nature of mind by supporting, even if very subtly, the attraction, aversion, and ignorance that create the psychological state of samsara in the first place. To put it rather inadequately (I'm pushing my limits of understanding here) Dzogchen is about a mindfulness that transcends the observer and has no limits or fabrications.

Obviously, this is not an easy accomplishment. Years of practice may bring momentary glimpses of the state of rigpa, and, it is hoped, these will get longer with practice. To rest in this nondualistic nature of mind, to relax into your true nature, is, from the perspective of Dzogchen, to attain full enlightenment.

I shall not attempt to explain this further, but I will note that the kind of mindfulness training explained herein, and in classical Theravadin meditation practice, strikes me (from an inherently deluded, dualistic perspective?) as an excellent foundation for Dzogchen practice, while being an easier place to start work on oneself.

EXTENDING MINDFULNESS TO EVERYDAY LIFE

This appendix is a reprinting of an article of mine of the same title that appeared in the *Journal of Humanistic Psychology* 30, no. 1 (Winter 1990): 81–106, and is reproduced here by permission of the journal.

SUMMARY

The great spiritual traditions agree that the cultivation of mindfulness is central. Without mindfulness we live in a state of distorted perceptions and fantasies, acting inappropriately with reference to our own true nature and the reality of the immediate situation, and consequently creating stupid and useless suffering. This article is oriented toward those readers already convinced of the value of cultivating increased mindfulness, so I shall not attempt to prove its value here: I have discussed this elsewhere (Tart, 1986), as well as the way modern psychological knowledge supports it. Although the traditions advocate developing mindfulness in all situations of life, advocacy, skillful training, and emphasis are not the same thing. Much traditional Buddhist practice, in particular, effectively puts its emphasis on formal sitting without engaging in extensive and specific training for mindfulness in everyday life. Because traditional Buddhist practice is a major influence on people interested in meditation, the apparent lack of means for generalizing mindfulness to everyday life can be a serious problem for many Westerners, especially because most of us want to enliven all of life through our growth practices, not retire to a life of solitary meditation. This article discusses ways in which elements of a less well-known mindfulness cultivation tradition, the Gurdjieff training, may be used to increase mindfulness in everyday life situations and to facilitate the generalization of mindfulness from intensive meditation sessions to everyday life. Some specific training exercises are presented, as well as the principles of devising such exercises.

A basic theme of humanistic and transpersonal psychologies is that people live in a limited, indeed *constricted,* subset of their full potential. This is especially true for those of us who are overintellectualized: We are too often unmindful of our embodied and feeling nature. In addition to specific defense mechanisms that block awareness (repression, rationalization, etc.), we do not pay clear, mindful attention to the richness of ongoing experience.

Mindfulness, a feeling of clarity of experience, of "presence," is central in Buddhist mind-training practice (see, for example, Dhiravamsa, 1975; Goldstein, 1987; Goldstein & Kornfield, 1987; Kornfield & Breiter, 1985; Solè-Leris, 1986). During a Buddhist practitioners meeting I attended last year, a student discussed the fact that although she could develop a great deal of mindfulness during a retreat, this mindfulness disappeared rapidly as she left the retreat and was difficult to generate in everyday life. She wanted more mindfulness, but because she could not spend her life on retreat, what could she do? This is a common problem among beginning (and even more advanced) meditators.

This article is a discussion of some possibilities for more effectively extending the mindfulness developed in traditional Buddhist (or similar) practices into everyday life, based on three key themes: (a) the potentiating effect of group work on mindfulness, (b) the psychological principle of generalization, and (c) practical experience drawn from another spiritual growth tradition, the Gurdjieff work, which focuses on developing mindfulness in everyday life. I believe it will be of general interest to all who already know the value of and seek greater mindfulness in life and of special interest to those trained in meditative disciplines like Buddhist *vipassana* (insight, mindfulness) meditation, who might want to adapt some techniques from modern psychology and the Gurdjieff work in order to make the traditional meditative disciplines more effective in contemporary society. Our focus is practical as well as theoretical, so principles for designing exercises for enhancing mindfulness in life will be discussed and several exercises given.

First let us clarify the term *mindfulness,* as it tends to be used in several ways in much spiritual literature.

MINDFULNESS

In one sense, mindfulness refers to a clear, *lucid* quality of awareness of the everyday experiences of life. Much of ordinary life is spent in abstractions and fantasies about what might happen or abstractions and fantasies about what has happened. We seldom live in the present, the only fully real moment. If you are eating an ice cream cone and become more vividly, mindfully aware of just what that tastes like right now, instead of being lost in thoughts about past and future ice cream cones, leading on to thoughts far removed from ice cream cones, you are being more mindful.

In another sense, mindfulness refers to a clear quality of awareness as applied to deeper and more subtle processes of the mind. For example: As I attempt to be clearly and directly aware of my ongoing bodily sensations while practicing vipassana meditation, I might suddenly note that there is a covert belief or bias operating at the fringes of my awareness but exerting some control over that awareness. Perhaps it is a belief that certain kinds of body sensations are "better" or "more meditative" than another kind. This may lead to the insight that covert biases are generally operating in all of my life experiences. I have been mindful in the second sense of the word, seeing a more subtle level of mental functioning.

In a third sense, mindfulness refers to what we might call *awareness of being aware,* to full self-consciousness. I do not mean self-consciousness in the ordinary use of the term to mean feeling awkward and inhibited because of internal doubts, or because of superego processes, but rather self-consciousness in the sense of not *being completely* absorbed in or *totally* identified with the content of ongoing experience: some part of the mind, a "neutral observer" or "fair witness,"[1] remains aware, in a relatively objective way, of the nature of ongoing experience as related to immediate here and now existence. As I sit here typing, for example, I can be completely absorbed in what I am writing, such that only strong sensory stimuli can manage to attract my attention, or I can *remember myself,* to use Gurdjieff's term: thus, a nonordinary part of myself is aware that most of me is absorbed in the writing task but I simultaneously know that I am sitting in a bouncing van on my way to the university, portable computer in my lap, hearing other conversations on the periphery of my awareness, having a body with many sensations in it, and so on. I am mindful in the sense of being clearly aware of what is happening while simultaneously being aware that I am aware of these things. I remember myself.

In a fourth sense, mindfulness can be described as a continuous and precise awareness of the process of being aware, such that a thought is recognized at the time as a thought, a perception as a perception, an emotion as an emotion, a fantasy as a fantasy, and so on, rather than mistaking a thought or emotion or fantasy for a perception.

In practice the four senses of mindfulness mentioned above often overlap. Too, verbal definitions can only point at mindfulness, not adequately capture it. My focus in this article becomes the question: How can we maintain some or all aspects of mindfulness outside a retreat situation, in the complexity and turmoil of ordinary life?

I have been attempting to cultivate mindfulness, especially the self-remembering kind, for a number of years, with varying degrees of success.[2] One of the most interesting observations I and others doing this practice have made about it is that it is not at all difficult to be mindful in most circumstances. A tiny effort, a small shift of attention is all it takes. What is difficult is to *remember to make* that effort!

Both Buddhism and the Gurdjieff work emphasize that our minds are ordinarily driven and controlled by the circumstances we find ourselves in, so that in practice we live mindlessly in *samsara,* or a kind of waking dream, instead of mindfully in the here and now. Buddhism frequently expresses this in terms of the influence of past karma determining our fate. Gurdjieff expresses it as the *mechanical-ness* of ordinary life, that we are best understood as *machines* driven by outside forces. Such mindless experiencing and acting leads to maladaptive behavior, which in turn creates useless suffering and more mechanical karma. Modern psychological discoveries lend strong support to this position (Tart, 1986), although they do not operate within a mindfulness framework. While the long-term goal of both disciplines is to develop a continual mindfulness that is *independent* of outside circumstances, our focus here is on the development of mindfulness for those of us at the beginning of the path, where external circumstances are important in aiding or hindering our work. We begin with a consideration of some of the effects of working in a group.

POTENTIATING EFFECT OF GROUP WORK

When you are surrounded by other individuals who are also trying to be mindful, it reminds you of your own intention to be mindful and you make the small effort required to be mindful far more often. An analogy used in the Gurdjieff work is that these others serve as "alarm clocks" to help awaken you. On the other hand, when you are surrounded by individuals who are ignorant of or uninterested in mindfulness, not only are you not reminded to make efforts at mindfulness yourself, you are subjected to the kinds of hypnoticlike interpersonal influences that induce and reinforce the state I have called *consensus trance* (Tart, 1986), the relative mindlessness of everyday life, living in samsara.

Consider an example from a retreat, based on my own and others' experience. You are sitting, doing vipassana meditation, with your eyes open. But you have wandered off into some fantasy for the last few minutes with no mindfulness whatsoever. A woman seated across from you takes a moment to roll her neck to relieve some discomfort. The sight of her moving interrupts your fantasy. You may start on another fantasy after a moment, or during the period of interruption, you may remember that you are at a retreat and that your intention in being there is to be mindful, not to fantasize. You make the effort to become more mindful, then continue sitting mindfully. This is what we might call a basic-level *reminding function* of group work: The perceptual reality of being in the group reminds you of your purpose.

There is a higher-level reminding function that can happen in a group practicing mindfulness, though. To continue our example, the sensory stimulation of the woman rolling her neck may not only interrupt your fantasy but you may notice a certain *nonordinary* quality of her movement, perhaps a certain deliberateness or slowness, that makes it likely that she is not only stretching, she is stretching *mindfully*. This direct observation of apparent mindfulness by another group member is even more likely to remind you to become mindful yourself rather than to again wander off into fantasy. Once you have become dedicated to being mindful, there is a certain sense in which mindfulness becomes contagious.

The degree of mindfulness you experience at a retreat, then, is a function of the intensity of your own practice, but at our beginning level, it is also strongly affected by this reminding function of the others in the group. This is a generalization, of course, and individual cases may vary. If you are very well established in your own mindfulness practice, it is not as important. My own experience of Gurdjieff work and group meditation situations has suggested that group reminding is an important factor for almost everyone, even for those whose own practice is well established.

The importance of group potentiation of mindfulness can be further appreciated if we consider the nature of most group interactions in ordinary life.

Suppose we are talking with several co-workers at the office. On the surface level we are friendly, but on another level we may be rivals competing for promotion. As a result, our conversations have hidden agendas, such as an implicit contract that we will focus on the surface friendliness and not notice the hidden rivalries in order to smooth our interaction, thus avoiding the extra stress that would be generated through open rivalry. A second hidden agenda might be to preserve our own self-concept about not being aggressive. A third might be to spy out information about our rivals' intended actions that might be useful to us. An atmosphere of friendliness might make it more likely that a rival would be lulled and say more than he or she might say if he or she remembered our rivalry. A fourth hidden agenda might involve demonstrating our own superiority by being relaxed around a rival.

Such a situation, although conducive to a biased, self-centered kind of ordinary attentiveness, is not conducive to a general, even-handed mindfulness, to equanimity, to remembering yourself and accurately observing *all* there is to be observed in reality. Unless you are very practiced at maintaining mindfulness, you will automatically avoid general mindfulness, thus avoiding immediate tension by suppression and repression. This apparent immediate gain does not take account, of course, of the long-term costs. As I have discussed in detail elsewhere (Tart, 1986), most ordinary interactions are reinforcements and deepenings of the state of consensus trance we live in, quite aside from their ostensible content.

A major reason mindfulness fades quickly after leaving a retreat, then, is that we lose the reminding functions that other retreat participants perform and we are subjected to other ordinary "reminding functions," reminding us of the "normalcy" and social desirability of mind*less*ness.

Now let us consider an important psychological principle, *generalization*.

GENERALIZATION OF SKILLS

Generalization was first formally identified in Ivan Pavlov's well-known experiments on classical conditioning. A hungry dog would hear the sound of a bell; half a second later the sound would be followed by some food. After repeated pairings of the bell sound followed by food, the dog would salivate at the sound of the bell alone. The bell was called the *conditioned stimulus:* conditioned because a dog does not normally salivate to the sound of a bell. *Stimulus generalization* of conditioning referred to the fact that stimuli other than the bell might also elicit salivation, especially if they were like the bell. A bell of a slightly different pitch would elicit much salivation, a scratching sound almost none. The greater the resemblance of the new and originally conditioned stimuli, the more likely the conditioned response would arise.

Conditioning was interpreted as a mechanical response not involving consciousness at the time of Pavlov's work and for most of psychology's subsequent history, reflecting the mechanistic worldview then (and still too much) in vogue. In higher animals we can also view the same process as *learning:* The dog, or a human in a similar situation, reaches an understanding that the bell will be followed by a reward, and the thought of the reward elicits a bodily response and associated mental responses. For example, you hear a telephone bell and get up and answer the telephone. This is a learned response: There is no "natural" genetically coded response that tells us that a bell sound is to be followed by picking up an object and saying hello to someone who is not physically present!

Stimulus generalization applies to conscious learning. If we learn to produce a certain mental attitude or overt response to a specific stimulus situation, we are likely to produce that attitude to a very similar situation, produce it somewhat to a fairly similar situation, and not produce it at all to a clearly different stimulus situation. Generalization can aid recall. A practical application, for example, is that students who have difficulty remembering relevant knowledge when they take tests are often advised to study for the test in the same classroom where they will be tested. The identicalness of the testing room (stimulus array) and the studying room makes it easier to recall needed information than if that information were associated with the sensory context of some other room.

Note that I do not believe that mindfulness per se can be conditioned in the sense that mindfulness will occur automatically given a certain stimulus situation identical or similar to one in which mindfulness has been cultivated before. When I am feeling frustrated about the difficulty of being mindful, I often wish that I could be automatically and continually mindful, but in my personal experience, mindfulness almost always involves a small but *deliberate* effort. It does not happen by itself. But conditioning can *remind you* that you want to make the effort to be mindful. Thus, conditioning can function as a reminding factor just as group work can.

Consider the typical meditation retreat situation now. It is intentionally designed to be very different from everyday life. We hold a retreat at a place designated as a retreat center; we see only fellow meditators, people playing an unusual social role, around us; we sit in special meditation postures through the day; when not meditating our usual social interactions are very circumscribed. This specialness gives the retreat situation definite advantages for learning various aspects of mindfulness.

When we are initially learning mindfulness, for example, we can deal with only so much distraction: too much and we usually learn nothing. So ordinary distractions (social conversation, phone calls, mail, decision making, reading novels, everyday work concerns, and so forth) are minimized or eliminated. Internal psychological distractions still have to be dealt with, but the sheer amount of distraction is less, and there is a better chance of coping and going on to experience periods of mindfulness.

The qualities that make the retreat situation so good for initially learning mindfulness are, unfortunately, poor ones in terms of generalizing the practice of mindfulness to everyday life. That is, the reminding functions discussed above, which the people and physical settings of the retreat situation have during the retreat, become mostly inoperative in ordinary life. The retreat situation is too different for mindfulness (or being reminded that we want to be mindful), as a specific response, to generalize to everyday life. We do not sit in meditative postures or walk slowly and mindfully during the ordinary day, so we do not have the special postural sense or conditioned/learned movement style as a reminding factor. We have not practiced mindfulness in social conversations, in business affairs, in phone calls, during decision making, while reading mail, and so on, so it is not surprising that these situations do not make it easy for us to be mindful.

ADAPTING BUDDHISM TO CONTEMPORARY CULTURE

The problem of lack of generalization of the reminders to practice mindfulness of a retreat to everyday life is, I suspect, partly rooted in historical and cultural traditions that must be skillfully modified if Buddhism is to have a widespread effectiveness in Western culture.

Historically, Buddhism in the East has, by and large, been nurtured and institutionalized as a monastic culture. Lay Buddhists would occasionally visit a monastery for special practice, but the core of Buddhist practitioners were monks and nuns. *Life was one long retreat for core practitioners.* There were few problems of generalizing from the special mindfulness practices to ordinary life because there was almost no separation: Monastic life *was* ordinary life for the core practitioners.

It is not the case now, however, and probably will not become so, that monastic Buddhism will be the main form of Buddhist practice in the West. Western lay practitioners expect to meditate, to become mindful, to achieve some degree of enlightenment. For maximum effectiveness, I believe we will have to develop skillful ways of modifying retreat training procedures to aid the development of mindfulness in situations that span the range from special retreat to ordinary life situations, so the skill of developing mindfulness generalizes more readily to everyday life.

GURDJIEFF WORK

G. I. Gurdjieff was one of the first people to try to adapt Eastern spiritual practices to forms more suitable and effective for contemporary Westerners. Born somewhere between 1872 and 1877 in Alexandropol, the area we now call Armenia, he was exposed to both Eastern and Western cultures as a child, and he spent much time around the turn of the century traveling in the East. Although he deliberately made it difficult for others to trace the sources of his teaching—he wanted people to test the ideas he presented and personally verify their usefulness rather than accept them because of his personal charisma or because they came from the mysterious East—he obviously had considerable contact with Buddhist, Hindu, Sufi, and Eastern Christian sources. His main theme was that man was "asleep," in samsara, living a life with perception, thought, and feeling badly distorted by automatized beliefs and emotions. "Waking up" to higher levels of consciousness was the only worthwhile goal.

Gurdjieff's main practices, *self-observation* and *self-remembering,* were intended to produce increasing degrees of insight and mindfulness in everyday life situations. I shall briefly describe these practices. Greater practical detail can be found in my book, *Waking Up* (Tart, 1986), or in traditional sources such as Nicoll (1984), Ouspensky (1977), Speeth (1976), or Walker (1974). Although Gurdjieff felt that occasional special retreat and training situations were useful, he noted that ordinary life is where we live, so mindfulness must be developed and applied there. Indeed, the technically simplified situation of a retreat could even hinder the development of a capacity for full mindfulness, because many of the stimulus situations that trigger our automaticity and mindless mechanicalness are absent in the retreat, and so we cannot practice dealing with them mindfully.

To illustrate: you have little social interaction with others in a retreat, and what interaction there is is usually positive and considerate. In ordinary life, however, others frequently treat us inconsiderately and sometimes actually attack us emotionally and verbally. To facilitate mindfulness training in this kind of stress situation, Gurdjieff actually provided free room and board to a Russian refugee at his training center, a man who had no interest whatsoever in Gurdjieff's work (Peters, 1964). But this man had an outstanding virtue for training mindfulness under stress: he was one of the most inconsiderate, annoying, irritating people one could hope to meet! He was, to use Carlos Castaneda's term, a "worthy opponent" for students working on developing mindfulness under stress. On one occasion, when his students banded together to play cruel practical jokes on this man until they finally got him so angry he left, Gurdjieff drove to Paris to find him and paid him to return!

SELF-OBSERVATION AND SELF-REMEMBERING

Self-observation is necessary because we live in samsara, in a state of constant illusion and self-deception. Since this state is an active, *dynamic* state, rather than simply a collection of simple bad habits, it often cannot just be changed, in Gurdjieff's view, by intending to change it. You must understand it *thoroughly* before attempting any major changes, otherwise these changes may backfire. This is similar to the modern psychological view that some of our problems are expressions of deep conflicts, so if you just work on the particular expression, the conflict may come out somewhere else. Self-observation is a practice of trying to observe neutrally the manifestations of your mind, being a *fair witness* or *objective observer* of yourself. The process is difficult, of course, as we tend to identify with our thoughts, feelings, and actions and so justify them rather than observe and study them objectively. If worked with sufficiently, however, a great deal of knowledge about the functioning of our ordinary mind—what Gurdjieff called *false personality*, because so much of it was conditioned in us by society and others, rather than being our own choice—can be built up. Then changes can be made that will result in great increases in available energy, as that energy will no longer be automatically wasted in the workings of false personality, in ordinary consensus consciousness.

Self-remembering is somewhat similar to (and facilitates) self-observation. Basically, it involves deliberately splitting off a small part of your awareness to monitor the rest of the operation of your mind in general, thus producing mindfulness. While self-remembering ultimately involves self-awareness of everything that is happening, internally and externally, the more practical version for beginners is to focus clearly on external events while simultaneously keeping some body awareness. This body awareness acts like an anchor in the here and now. Because body sensation exists in the here and now, it thus inhibits getting lost in thought or fantasy or becoming totally absorbed by external stimulation at the cost of losing contact with yourself. It is similar to returning to following the breath in vipassana meditation when you find you have drifted off in thought.

This is a simplified description of a rather sophisticated process, so I refer interested readers to the sources mentioned above for more detail.

PRACTICE IN GURDJIEFF WORK

Self-observation and self-remembering are intended to be practiced in every aspect of ordinary life. Like meditation, it is not easy for beginners. While only a small effort is usually called for to be mindful in this way, *remembering to make the effort* can be difficult. Success in either or both practices (and they can often blend into one another) is very rewarding. Any ordinary action, such as brewing a cup of tea, can become an ordinary-yet-extraordinary action if done mindfully. Gurdjieff work can be very useful in bringing mindfulness and its inherent satisfactions into ordinary life.

To see some of the possibilities in Gurdjieff-type workdays, especially in light of our interest in generalizing mindfulness to everyday life, I will describe a few aspects of a typical such workday, drawing from my own and others' experience. Note that this is an example of highlights—I have compressed several hours of experience into a couple of pages of description—and actual mindful experience is much more temporally dense.

Note that the usefulness of the following description, as that of most of this article, depends on the degree to which the reader already values the cultivation of mindfulness and the degree to which personal experience has demonstrated that it is not an easy thing to cultivate. Without some background here, the following description may sound like making a big deal out of perfectly ordinary actions. On the other hand, it might stimulate the reader who has not begun to value and practice mindfulness to do some self-reflection.

A typical day of intensive Gurdjieff work begins with awakening in the morning. Almost at once, a few minutes are devoted to a body-scanning exercise (see Tart, 1986, chap. 18), somewhat like the *sweeping* method of one contemporary form of vipassana. This morning exercise has multiple functions, but two primary ones are to start the day off with consciousness of what is happening in your body and to remind you that you intend to be mindful through the day. This morning exercise leads directly into self-observation and self-remembering.

Washing, dressing, eating—all are to be taken as occasions for self-observation and self-remembering. Traveling to the workday site is another such occasion. I mention these briefly, but they are just as potentially rich ground for self-observation and self-remembering as the more organized work later.

You arrive at the workday site, mindfully check an assignment roster and see, for example, that you are assigned to a building crew that is shingling the side of a building. You have never shingled a building before: perhaps that is why you have been assigned this particular task. Remembering to be mindful of at least some of your body sensations as well as clearly aware of the external world, you walk (perhaps just slightly slower and more mindfully than normal) to the tool shed and check out a hammer and box of shingling nails. Others are going to and from the tool shed, carrying various tools and supplies, so you must stay aware of exactly where they are and where you are—it would not be genuinely mindful to "feel" mindful inside and then bump into someone who was carrying a sharp tool!

At the shingling site several others are already at work. A woman you know tells you she is in charge of the shingling crew and gives you instructions as to just what to do and how to do it. If you are a man, this could be a particularly rich situation for practicing self-observation and self-remembering. Suppose, for example, you are a man with some deep feelings of insecurity. Do you notice a resentment that you, a man, are getting orders from a woman? Orders about traditionally male work? Is there a feeling of embarrassment that you are a man but do not already know how to do this traditionally male work? Does your awareness tend to identify with a feeling of resentment at getting orders from a woman? Might a funny internal *flavor* to this resentment suggest it is covering over the less pleasant feeling of embarrassment?

Can you remember yourself sufficiently while making these observations to avoid identifying with these feelings as they occur? That is, can you be mindful enough that you can act from a clearer, more mindful place, remembering yourself, your (nonordinary) self that is here to learn about itself and how to practice mindfulness? Can you pay full attention to the instructions so they do not need to be given again, for example? If you need to ask for clarification, can you do *only that,* without any hidden games in your words expressing, say, resentment?

Now you begin nailing on shingles, still observing and remembering yourself. Or have you forgotten to do either? If so, as in meditation, you gently bring your attention back to that task. Now you begin nailing on shingles. Is there enough attention on the necessities of the task that your nails are going in straight? Without cracking shingles? Is your body in a comfortable, efficient posture? Does it have unnecessary strains? Are there any emotional tones associated with those body strains, such as resentment from the previous interaction you are still identified with and that are surfacing in another way?

Suppose you are not able to be very mindful and concentrate on the shingling: your mind is still replaying a quarrel with a friend from the previous day. Because you are attempting to be mindful and concentrate on the shingling that you are doing in the here and now, though, the replay of the quarrel does not run as mechanically, as automatically, as usual. You are more aware of it. You are at least more mindful than usual; perhaps you will have some insights into normally invisible aspects of how you feel when you are angry.

Another group member walks by, someone toward whom you feel an immediate dislike. There is something about him or her that is mindful, though, reminding you that you are trying to practice mindfulness, so you do so. Immediately you see your feeling of dislike more clearly and realize it concerns a quarrel with someone at work last week who physically resembles the group member who walked by, and you see the process of projection in action.

Suppose you are able to be fairly mindful. It is a beautiful day, your shingling is going well, you enjoy the movement of the work, and the mindfulness you are creating adds a quality of subtle joy and light to existence. Suddenly a messenger appears and tells you to stop shingling, go to the front yard, and get instructions on how to water the rose bushes. Now there is a rich opportunity to observe possible attachment. Are your mindfulness and good feelings dependent on shingling? On your success at it? Have you gotten attached to it? Do you think it's a better job—more appropriate to who you think you are or what you deserve—than watering roses? If subtle (or not so subtle) feelings like this run through you, can you still practice self-observation and self-remembering?

Suppose the message is that you are to join the kitchen cleaning crew and function as supervisor, telling others what needs to be done. How will you handle this authority? Can you observe the kind of emotional intoxication that authority may bring? If that happens, can you be mindful of the feelings behind the need to identify with the authority? Can you remember yourself sufficiently, be mindful enough, not to let those feelings affect the way you tell someone to sweep the kitchen stairs? Can you say something like, "Bob, sweep the kitchen stairs and put the sweepings in the garbage can" and have it be a completely clean communication, meaning nothing but what it says, without any covert messages like "I am the boss here, recognize my authority by doing what I say"?

And so the day goes on. You may do a single task all day (what happens to your mindfulness without the benefit of novelty, when you are tired, cold, or bored?) or switch frequently. There will probably be brief meetings where some kind of talk will be given by the teacher about practicing mindfulness, or questions may be asked. Can you maintain mindfulness while asking a question? Being with others who are speaking mindfully can stimulate deep mindfulness on your part. You may take a coffee break, which is also an occasion to practice mindfulness. The time comes to go home: do you let your mindfulness go like a burden and lapse back into the apparently comfortable mechanicalness of everyday thought, feeling, and action?

If you do, can you observe it and learn from it? The workday never stops; it just changes its form.

Obviously, the Gurdjieff workday situation, although special and different from ordinary life, is much more like ordinary life in many ways than the classical meditation retreat. You do talk to others, take and give orders, make some decisions, wash the dishes, water the garden, and so on in ordinary life, so the practice in mindfulness in the workday can generalize to ordinary life situations more easily than practices in the classical meditation retreat. You still have to make the effort to be mindful, but ordinary life can frequently remind you of the work situation in which you have practiced mindfulness, and you can be mindful again. This may be a mindfulness that is deeper than it might have been from your unaided efforts, as it is connected with an earlier mindfulness in a workday situation—that is, mindfulness can sometimes cumulate around specific areas.

GURDJIEFF WORK AND BUDDHISM

In terms of range of potential experience and growth, Buddhism and Gurdjieff work are both systems that claim they can lead people to a degree of enlightenment well beyond ordinary functioning. I deliberately say *claim,* as I have not personally experienced the higher ranges of either discipline and so cannot speak with any authority there. In terms of my personal experience with the beginnings of both paths, the varieties of mindfulness engendered by both paths is similar in some ways, different in others.

Both paths advocate mindfulness in *all* areas of life, and so in principle overlap greatly. I have received some training in Zen, in several forms of Theravadan Buddhism, and in several forms of Tibetan Buddhism. From my limited experience of Buddhist practice, I note that the emphasis is on mindfulness generated in formal meditation, that is, in a technically simplified, quieted, nondemanding situation. Consequently, I can be mindful of very subtle aspects of experience after the "noise" of my ordinary mind quiets down. Gurdjieff work, on the other hand, is mostly practiced in the noise of ordinary life. Consequently, there are less of these insights into very subtle aspects of mind (although they are not lacking), but more insights into the normally hidden dynamics of how I relate to the world and other people, a class of insights much less frequent, in my experience, in formal Buddhist meditation.

I am not really concerned with comparing Buddhism as the formal system of Buddhism with Gurdjieff work as the formal system of Gurdjieff work, however. It is the cultivation of mindfulness per se and its consequent effects of psychological and spiritual evolution that is important. Accurate observation of what is actually happening here and now is the essence, with what conceptual system it fits into being an important, but secondary, question. Both Gurdjieff and the Buddha instructed their students to investigate the truth of psychological and spiritual matters through their direct, mindful experience and to not accept any teachings on faith alone.

Thus the central thesis of this article is that for us beginners the incorporation of some Gurdjieff-type work would probably be generally useful in helping mindfulness cultivated in retreats and meditation sessions generalize into everyday life more effectively as well as in cultivating mindfulness in everyday life in a direct way. Similarly, the introduction of some periods of Buddhist vipassana type meditation into traditional Gurdjieff work would probably aid that process in developing comprehensive mindfulness.

Such incorporation of new elements into a tradition is experimental work. It should be done as mindfully as possible, the results assessed as carefully as possible, and adjustments made as necessary.

I end this article on a practical note by describing some general rules for creating special mindfulness exercises and then presenting several particular exercises that could be introduced into traditional Buddhist retreats near their end as experiments in helping to transfer mindfulness into everyday life.

GENERAL RULES FOR DESIGNING MINDFULNESS EXERCISES

First, there is really only one rule for designing mindfulness-training exercises, namely, to be *mindful yourself in all things and experimentally try various practices to help others to be mindful.* Any action can be used as a mindfulness exercise in this general sense. The word *experimentally* is important here, as it means you check how well various procedures work as objectively as possible, rather than being wedded to some conceptual system. Because always being mindful tends to be too vague for most of us and so easily forgotten, we can be helped in the initial development of mindfulness by using much more specific exercises.

Second, these are contrived *exercises,* not rules on how to live. Both students and instructors should remember this, because it is too easy to get caught up in a system of ideas and turn technical practices into "teachings" and rules.

Third, mindfulness exercises usually sound silly to the intellectual mind. Thus the proper way to evaluate them is to practice them, not simply read about them and form a judgment.

Fourth, contrived exercises will work only temporarily, then they will gradually wear out. Mindfulness exercises provide an opportunity to practice mindfulness, but mindfulness is a small effort you must make yourself. Because of the novelty and/or tension-inducing characteristics of an exercise, your activation level goes up and mindfulness is easier, but that novelty will wear off after a while. Sometimes the usefulness of an exercise can be stretched by modifying it, but eventually the exercise should be abandoned. This time of usefulness differs for different individuals, so there are no hard and fast rules here. I have personally found some exercises to lose their special stimulation value for me in minutes; others work for years of intermittent use.

Fifth, doing an exercise for a specified interval and clearly stopping it will allow it to be used again at a later time. Trying to be mindful in the specified way all the time or for an unspecified period of time will wear out the exercise fast.

Sixth, the mechanics of the exercise are not the same thing as the mindfulness it is intended to help induce. Do not kid yourself that going through the motions of an exercise is in itself being mindful. When you find yourself doing one of these mindlessly on repeated occasions, that is a good indication to drop the exercise for the time being.

Seventh, a moderate amount of tension (physical, intellectual, or emotional) can be helpful in mindfulness exercises, as mindfulness will convert that tension into free energy that can intensify awareness. Too much tension, however, can activate people's automatic defense mechanisms too strongly, grabbing all attention, and making mindfulness very difficult. There are considerable individual differences here. An exercise that is relaxing and easy for one person may cause considerable nervousness in another.

In practice, I often arrange mindfulness exercises in a series, starting with easy, low-tension ones and gradually increasing the tension to higher levels. This also allows participants to observe the kinds and qualities of tension that interfere with their mindfulness. When tension is deliberately increased, it is wise to allow a safety valve, an option for a person to say he or she has become too tense to practice mindfulness and withdraw to a more passive role.

Let us now look at some specific mindfulness exercises. I have arranged them from what I feel is roughly easiest to hardest, but the order will not be the same for everyone.

THE THRESHOLD-CROSSING EXERCISE

The basic form of this exercise is one used at the Green Gulch Zen Center near San Francisco. Be mindful whenever you approach a doorway, and control your pace so you first step across the threshold with the foot nearest the hinge on the door. Doorways thus serve as a reminder to be mindful. Ordinary life is full of thresholds to cross, so this generalizes easily into everyday life.

A difficulty with exercises of this type, which call for a particular behavioral response as well as mindfulness, is that the behavior eventually becomes automated and conditioned. How quickly this happens varies from person to person. As the behavior becomes automated, there is a strong tendency for your mind to have a *fantasy* about being mindful in that situation instead of actually being mindful.

As with other mindfulness exercises, it is a good idea to stop the exercise once automatization starts to happen, so as not to reinforce fantasies about mindfulness. Or you may make the exercise more complex. In this instance, once you notice a tendency for mindless automatization, you might add a rule like doing it this way on Mondays, Wednesdays, and Fridays, using the opposite foot on Tuesdays, Thursdays, and Saturdays, and just letting whichever foot happens to be in front go through first on Sundays.

Another and especially useful way to deal with automatization of mindfulness exercises is to use exercises that give you sensory *feed-back* about whether you are actually being mindful or not. Many of the practical work tasks done in Gurdjieff workdays do this, for instance. If you are nailing something together and not really being mindful, you will bend more nails and leave more hammer marks on the wood. I have also found the Japanese self-defense art of Aikido very helpful this way. When I am standing on the mat daydreaming about how aware I am, my partner's grab for me or punch at me seems quick and startles me. When I am actually being mindful and present, there is much more time to handle the situation smoothly.

THE AUTO EXERCISE

As Westerners, we not only spend a great deal of time in automobiles, we have very strong feelings toward them. An outside observer might be led to believe that automobiles are an object of religious veneration among many Americans, with all sorts of cults having formed around them. Thus training awareness around automobiles is useful for transferring mindfulness skills to everyday life. The following type of exercise is useful near the end of a retreat, when most participants will leave the retreat to get into a car.

Instruct the retreat participants who have their cars parked outside to stand up. Those without cars should then pick a driver they will work with, preferably someone they do not know well. The driver and his companion(s) should not exchange any words during this exercise.

Each driver should then walk mindfully (and at slightly less than a normal rate of walking) outside to their car, accompanied by their companions without cars. They should stop near the car, looking at it mindfully, noting any internal reactions they have toward it.

Now mindfully walk close to the car, close enough to touch it, but do not. Be mindful. Now touch the car, gently, affectionately, appreciatively, as you would touch a baby or a lover. Be mindful of what you experience. The driver should mindfully put the key in the lock and make a mindful resolution to come to his senses and be mindful every time this key touches this lock for the next two weeks. (Resolving *while* mindful to be mindful in future situations similar to the one you are in is helpful.) Before unlocking the car, however, the driver should then mindfully remove the key and hand it to the companion he least knows and then mindfully turn away and walk back to the retreat hall. A most interesting set of feelings to be mindful about is likely.

The companion or, if alone, the driver, should now get in the car and mindfully look around the interior. Then sit in the driver's seat and look ahead as if driving. Put the key in the ignition, turn it far enough to turn on the ignition, but not the starter. Turn it off, remove the keys, and leave and lock the car. If the driver is doing this, he should make a mindful resolution to come to his senses and be mindful every time this key touches this lock for the next two weeks. If this is being done by a companion who has no car of his or her own, this person should make a mindful resolution to become mindful every time he or she has a key of any kind in his or her hand for the next couple of weeks.

The companion mindfully returns to the meditation hall and quite slowly walks toward the driver, car keys in hand, and returns them.

THE SOLITAIRE MINDFULNESS TECHNIQUE

There is a kind of solitaire card game, a slightly modified version of the very popular Klondike solitaire, that I played frequently as a child.[3] While needing to keep busy through some stressful waiting periods recently, I discovered that it can be an excellent mindfulness-training technique. The very idea of playing cards to cultivate mindfulness has some shock value in itself!

I find Klondike solitaire an excellent mindfulness-training exercise at an intermediate level of difficulty, excellent for transferring mindfulness to ordinary life. Other forms of solitaire games would probably work as well.

The game itself requires that you pay attention to what cards are up and their numerical and color relations to each other. You must be alert to potential plays, because it is a disqualifying error to skip a possible play. You must occasionally make strategic decisions about which of two or more possible moves is better. You must deal the cards properly and play through the remainder of the deck (by threes) over and over again until you either win or are stuck with no further moves. The physical world around you may provide distractions from the game, but you must not miss plays. Compared to classical vipassana meditation, considerable activity of physical motion, counting, and decision making is added, thus moving closer to life.

To work on paying adequate attention to the game and playing to win, while maintaining mindfulness, is very rich, but not as overwhelming as ordinary social interaction. Observations of transient mental and emotional phenomena that apply in many areas of life is possible in this rich situation, as I will illustrate by describing a typical experiential sequence for me.

I am mindful that I am sitting at a table, seeing the room around me, hearing the sound the cards make as I shuffle them, feeling the coordinated hand motions necessary to shuffle them. I must count out the first seven cards to form my playing field. The count tends to develop an inertia and rhythm of its own: Can I remain mindful, or do I get pulled into the counting activity so much that I lose track of my immediate sensory impressions? Impatience to get the game set up manifests, urging me to deal faster. Can I remain mindful and keep an even pace? Or might I deal faster but still try to be mindful during the faster deal? Could I deliberately deal slower as a way of increasing my impatience, so I can better observe it? Can I remember to be aware of the tactile qualities of each card as I deal it, being mindful of the fact that I am aware of these qualities, that I am directing my attention to be mindful?

I finish dealing and see that I have no aces to go up top and all black cards up; nothing can play on anything else. A flash of disappointment wells up! Can I stay mindful of this emotion, perhaps taste its flavor precisely? I start going through the remaining deck by threes, and red cards that play on the black cards on the playing row start turning up. I get excited, mindfulness starts slipping as my attention gets constellated into the good feeling that I am on a winning streak! The touch of the cards, the sound they make as I play them, and my peripheral field of vision all start to narrow and become lost. Oops, stay mindful with that feeling. A little attention and again I feel the cards in my hands, hear their sounds, see the table I am sitting at while still feeling the excitement over the idea of a winning streak, see my attraction to the excitement, remain mindful that I am experiencing these things.

But after the initial run nothing plays for a while. My thoughts tell me that I am going to be stuck; I will lose this hand. The disappointed feeling starts sucking my attention in, but I see the feeling and manage to maintain mindfulness. Yes, the disappointing feeling is associated with a desire to hurry, be less aware, get it over with if I am going to lose anyway. I lose mindfulness for a minute again and come back just in time to see that a run of plays has again excited me. I am going to win! Lose mindfulness for half a minute in the attachment/absorption in the idea of winning, then manage to get mindfulness back. I remember, Doesn't Buddhism say something about the transience of feelings? Each was eternal when I lost mindfulness and was absorbed in it, yet I see they come and go like the wind as the play of the cards changes.

If I am making this sound exciting, it can indeed be when you are mindful enough to see this rapid play of emotion!

This solitaire play situation is parallel to much human interaction. You are engaged in "games," structured interactions with rules. The initial "deals" of the games excite or depress you, your spirits rise and fall with the momentary course of the interaction, and mindfulness and absorption come and go. The "emotional stakes" are generally much higher when you are playing with another human, though, instead of in this artificial situation with a deck of cards.

A more advanced form of this exercise would involve actual two-person card games, so the human interaction component is added.

HERE AND NOW REPORTING AND WITNESSING

A useful exercise for learning to cultivate mindfulness during interpersonal interactions is derived from a Gestalt psychology exercise known as the *continuum of awareness,* here presented with some modifications that make it more mindful for both participants.

People are asked to choose a partner, preferably someone they do not know well. It is much harder to do well with friends or lovers, because of the implicit contracts we have about keeping the relationship within certain limits.

The partners sit opposite each other so they can look at each other's faces and bodies. A traditional meditative posture is fine, as are more informal postures. The partners choose who will start in the role of talker, with the other in the role of neutral witness.

At a signal from the group coordinator, the talker is to begin talking continuously, with the aim of being continuously aware of whatever he or she is experiencing *in the present moment* and describing it aloud to his or her partner. The emphasis is on describing what you are experiencing *now*, not associations or analyses. For example, as I write, I am aware of the touch of the keys against my fingers, of a frustration that description is slower than experience so that I cannot describe *all* of my experience, of a swollen feeling in my fingers, of a tension in the small of my back, of a "quiet" analytical thought that wanted me to have a broader scope of experience, of wondering what the person sitting beside me must think about what I am doing, of remembering a fear that comes up in this exercise that I might have a socially unacceptable thought about my partner to whom I am describing my ongoing experience, such as a sexual thought about the partner, and so on. Note that the last experience I reported is on the borderline between a here and now experience and drifting off down memory lane or into formal analysis.

The hardest form of this exercise is to call for continuous reporting of *all* ongoing experience, because we do have social taboos that are not completely overcome just by instructing participants to report on everything. Thus in introducing the exercise I usually add a qualifying instruction that if the talking partner has an experience that he or she fears is too unacceptable to communicate, he should say "censoring," and go on with reporting the next experience, such as, "There is tension in my legs, censoring, I feel embarrassed that I'm censoring, I feel my face flushing, I feel embarrassed at being embarrassed, my foot itches," and so on.

The role of the talker is deliberately difficult, for we are attempting to train mindfulness under conditions of interpersonal interaction. The tension can actually be used as a kind of energy for deep mindfulness, though. The role of the listener, the neutral witness, is also difficult. The instructions to the listener are to stay present, listen to and observe the talker attentively, and *give no social feedback of any kind*. That is, the listener cannot nod, smile, frown, look sympathetic, or say *anything*. The listener must sit perfectly still, looking at and listening to the talker. This is a skill that most people must learn. As they learn it, they will find not only that their skill at mindfully listening improves, but a whole host of internal psychological reactions occurs that can lead to important insights. A listener may find, for example, that he has an enormous compulsion to nod agreement, and being mindful of the feeling tones associated with that compulsion can lead to the discovery of important aspects of early conditioning.

I generally have the partners talk for about five minutes in this way, then I call time and have them switch roles.

A mindful discussion by the group and sharing of experiences to this exercise can be quite useful.

EXPERIMENTAL APPLICATION

Both Buddhism and the Gurdjieff work are powerful and sophisticated paths for developing mindfulness. I am not advocating that either be replaced by the other but that each may be able to profit by experimenting with adapting some techniques from the other. Here I have emphasized that Gurdjieffian mindfulness techniques that are practiced in situations that closely resemble ordinary life may be useful in helping to generalize the mindfulness developed in traditional meditation retreats into everyday life.

I stress that this is an experiment, and a long-term experiment. Straightforward borrowing may or may not be appropriate; some techniques may need modification and successive adaptation. I have presented some general principles and some specific exercises that I have designed from my own experience in teaching an experimental form of the Gurdjieff work (Tart, 1986). I look forward to hearing from teachers who adapt some of these to see how helpful they are.

Notes

1. The quotes around these terms are to remind us that I refer to a *process* that is difficult to describe verbally and not to a fixed sort of *thing* that the use of nouns implies.

2. As a scientifically trained writer, conditioned to the norms of the scientific subculture, I find it awkward to refer to my own experience frequently, especially because I do not consider myself particularly adept at formal meditation or Gurdjieffian mindfulness. In the study of mindfulness, however, the investigator is the primary instrument, and it would be silly and misleading to depersonalize the writing.

3. In Klondike solitaire, you deal out seven cards in a row, the first (leftmost) face up. Then you deal six in a row on top of cards two through seven, again first card face up, and so on, until you have dealt out one card, face up, over the original seventh card. This is your playing row or tableau. Aces play above this row and you play cards on them that match suit and number sequentially, that is, two of diamonds on the ace of diamonds, and so on. Meanwhile, on the original piles you play down red on black by number, and so on. The aim is to get all 52 cards up on the aces. In the most difficult version of Klondike solitaire, cards are turned up from the remaining pack one by one to see if they play either red on black down on the tableaux or directly up on ace piles. If not, they go down in a pile, and because there is only one pass through the pile, needed cards can easily be irretrievably buried. The modification I use is to go through this pile by threes over and over again until I am stuck.

References

Dhiravamsa (1975). *The way of non-attachment: The practice of insight meditation.* Wellingborough, Northamptonshire: Turnstone.

Goldstein, J. (1987). *The experience of insight: A simple and direct guide to Buddhist meditation.* Boston: Shambhala Publications.

Goldstein, J., & Kornfield, J. (1987). *Seeking the heart of wisdom: The path of insight meditation.* Boston: Shambhala Publications.

Kornfield, J., & Breiter, P. (eds.). (1985). *A still forest pool: The insight meditation of Achaan Chah.* Wheaton, Ill.: Theosophical.

Nicoll, M. (1984). *Psychological commentaries on the teachings of Gurdjieff and Ouspensky.* Boston: Shambhala Publications.

Ouspensky, P. D. (1977). *In search of the miraculous: Fragments of an unknown teaching.* New York: Harcourt Brace Jovanovich.

Peters, F. (1964). *Boyhood with Gurdjieff.* New York: Dutton.

Solè-Leris, A. (1986). *Tranquility and insight: An introduction to the oldest form of Buddhist meditation.* Boston: Shambhala Publications.

Speeth, K. (1976). *The Gurdjieff work.* Berkeley, Calif.: And/Or Press.

Tart, C. T. (1986). *Waking up: Overcoming the obstacles to human potential.* Boston: Shambhala Publications.

Walker, K. (1974). *A study of Gurdjieff's teaching.* New York: Samuel Weiser.

RECOMMENDED READINGS

This appendix lists some of the more useful books on Gurdjieff's ideas, a few more general writings of mine that supplement and expand the themes in this book, some books on learning formal meditation, and some books on Dzogchen. This is only a small selection of what is available. If you get very interested in this sort of material, you will find more references as you read. What follows is partly based on the recommended readings in my book *Waking Up,* with additional information on Dzogchen, states of consciousness, and meditation.

I want to emphasize, however, that reading is only a small part of the process of understanding yourself and beginning to awaken. It is helpful to have some intellectual framework, but only if that intellectual framework is a provisional tool for working with deeper experiential data. The map can be a useful guide to the territory, but the map is not the territory. Indeed, having a good map when you are too far from the territory is dangerous, for we are easily charmed by clear maps and think we know too much.

Note too that Gurdjieff's work was intended to be passed on primarily by direct contact between teacher and student, so the books are often deliberately incomplete.

Several times I have stressed that you should not accept the ideas in this book just because they seem clear or clever or appealing or because they come from people (including me) who are supposed to be authorities on consciousness. Test them for yourself, modify them as needed, and accept only what works out in your experience. Even then, make such acceptance provisional: if your further experience doesn't fit with the ideas, they may need to be revised. Be particularly wary if you find yourself passionately defending any idea, as such an action often indicates that at a deeper level you are not at all sure about it yourself and are afraid to look at it clearly. This same advice applies to all the readings cited here.

BOOKS ABOUT THE GURDJIEFF WORK

For most of us, books about Gurdjieff's ideas and practices are easier to begin with than Gurdjieff's own writings. Opinions vary greatly among people who espouse Gurdjieff's ideas as to the authenticity and usefulness of the various books in this category, however. Some use the criterion that having studied directly with Gurdjieff is prerequisite to writing an accurate book, and they judge later books by their consistency with the writings of such direct pupils and Gurdjieff's own writings. This makes a fair amount of sense. Others feel that this attitude tends to become dogmatic and is an attempt to preserve an ideological purity that fossilizes what should be a living teaching. This also makes sense.

In making a selection of readings, I assume that almost any book by any person (including me and including Gurdjieff) will be a mixture of wisdom and error, and it is up to the reader to discriminate. The books I mention below are such mixtures, but I believe they have in them much more wisdom than error. I also have some bias toward books that focus on the psychology, rather than the cosmology, of Gurdjieff, as I can understand and validate the psychology but not the cosmology. The ones listed here have been useful to me and will, I hope, be useful to you. The editions cited are generally the most recent at the time of writing.

My *Waking Up: Overcoming the Obstacles to Human Potential* (Boston: Shambhala Publications, 1986) is my primary recommendation if you have benefited from the material in this book. The style is more formal, but I'm told the writing is clear—indeed, a University of California committee reviewing my work commented that since it was readily understandable it couldn't have any real scientific value! (I am not making this up.) *Waking Up* covers a lot not touched upon here.

In Search of the Miraculous: Fragments of an Unknown Teaching, by P. D. Ouspensky (New York: Harcourt Brace Jovanovich, 1977) is generally considered one of the best and most comprehensive expositions of many of Gurdjieff's ideas. Gurdjieff approved the book as being an accurate exposition of the ideas he was teaching at the time Ouspensky studied with him. I have returned to it many times for clarification. It is not an easy book, but it is well worth attempting to master. It presents Gurdjieff's cosmological theories, which may be profound or incorrect: I cannot tell which.

In reading this book, note that Ouspensky did break with Gurdjieff and so indeed presents fragments, not a complete system, as he honestly indicated in the book and in its subtitle. Ouspensky was a brilliant intellectual, probably in the unbalanced way described in chapter 14, and I believe the break came when he could no longer deal with the emotional aspects of Gurdjieff's work. Try to compensate for the overly intellectual tone of the book as you read it.

Ouspensky also wrote a much shorter introduction to Gurdjieff's work, *The Psychology of Man's Possible Evolution* (New York: Random House, 1981). I recommend reading this before starting *In Search of the Miraculous*. When you are familiar with these two books, you may want to read Ouspensky's *The Fourth Way: A Record of Talks and Answers to Questions Based on the Teaching of G. I. Gurdjieff* (New York: Random House, 1971).

Another brief introduction to Gurdjieff's ideas is a chapter by Kathleen Riordan (now Speeth) in my *Transpersonal Psychologies* (El Cerrito, Calif.: Psychological Processes, 1983). She later expanded this chapter into a small, excellent book, *The Gurdjieff Work* (Berkeley: And/Or Press, 1976).

John Bennett spent some time working with Gurdjieff as well as studying other sources of psychological and spiritual teaching. His books have impressed me as intelligent and honest attempts to understand Gurdjieff rather than just a repetition of Gurdjieff's ideas. His major work, *Gurdjieff: Making a New World* (New York: Harper & Row, 1976), is a combination of the presentation of some of Gurdjieff's ideas with historical background for those ideas and speculation about their meaning.

Robert de Ropp's *The Master Game: Pathways to Higher Consciousness beyond the Drug Experience* (New York: Dell, 1968) is a useful introduction to Gurdjieff's ideas in the context of the psychedelic revolution of the late 1960s; it thus gives a broader context than the usual Gurdjieff book. There is a strong streak of negativity toward ordinary people running through de Ropp's writings, which may need to be filtered out in reading. When I read de Ropp's autobiography, *Warrior's Way: The Challenging Life Games* (New York: Delacorte, 1979), I understood the roots of his attitude and admire his personal triumph over the horrors life can put in our way.

Maurice Nicoll was a psychologist who trained with Carl Jung before becoming involved with Gurdjieff's ideas. His five volumes of *Psychological Commentaries on the Teaching of Gurdjieff and*

Ouspensky (Boston: Shambhala Publications, 1984) are valuable and stimulating. He was also interested in the relation of Gurdjieff's ideas to early and esoteric Christianity and put forward some ingenious ideas about their relationship in *The Mark* (Boston: Shambhala Publications, 1985) and *The New Man* (Boston: Shambhala Publications, 1984).

Michel Waldberg's *Gurdjieff: An Approach to His Ideas* (London: Routledge & Kegan Paul, 1981) is a useful and brief introduction, as are Kenneth Walker's *A Study of Gurdjieff's Teaching* (New York: Samuel Weiser, 1974) and Jean Vaysse's *Toward Awakening: An Approach to the Teaching Left by Gurdjieff* (San Francisco: Harper & Row, 1979).

For the reader who wants to track down everything written about Gurdjieff, the authoritative reference work is *Gurdjieff: An Annotated Bibliography* by J. Walter Driscoll and the Gurdjieff Foundation of California (New York: Garland Publishing, 1985). With 1,146 references to English-language references to Gurdjieff, 581 in French, and some miscellaneous ones in other languages, this is as complete a scholarly reference as we could hope for. Many of the references are merely passing mentions, but all the substantial references are there. The evaluation of some of the references as misleading or worthless from the authors' point of view sometimes comes through the attempt at scholarly neutrality.

GURDJIEFF'S OWN WRITINGS

Gurdjieff gave the inclusive title *All and Everything* to a series of three books that were intended to be an exposition of his major teachings. The first volume of the series was entitled *Beelzebub's Tales to His Grandson* (New York: Dutton, 1978). Written as an allegory, it takes the form of stories by a very high cosmic personage/ "devil"/angel, Beelzebub, told to his grandson to illustrate the way the universe works, particularly with reference to humanity on earth.

In writing this volume Gurdjieff tried an experiment based on the idea that the harder you work for something the more you appreciate it. He would write a chapter and read it to his students. If they understood it, he would rewrite it to make it more difficult. Full of elaborate, multisyllabic words invented by Gurdjieff, this is a difficult book. I have heard stories that Gurdjieff decided in later life that this experiment hadn't worked—students did not necessarily have a better understanding because of the deliberate difficulty. I am not sure whether you should force your way through it if it doesn't speak to you. In some branches of the Gurdjieff work, it is treated like a sacred gospel whose every word is absolutely true. This has the negative effect of making those who don't clearly understand it feel guilty and inadequate.

The second volume of the series, *Meetings with Remarkable Men* (New York: Dutton, 1969), is very readable. You can breeze through it like you would an interesting novel or as a allegorical account of some of Gurdjieff's travels, but it has deeper levels.

Life Is Real Only Then, When "I Am" (New York: Dutton, 1982) is the third volume of the series and very provocative. I would suggest this as later reading, after you gain thorough familiarity with Gurdjieff's work.

Views from the Real World (New York: Dutton, 1975) is a collection of talks by Gurdjieff as recollected by his pupils.

The Herald of Coming Good: First Appeal to Contemporary Humanity (New York: Samuel Weiser, 1971) strikes me as one of Gurdjieff's experiments that he quickly decided wasn't going right, as he withdrew it almost immediately. Of primarily historical interest.

RELATED WRITINGS OF MINE

The following recommended readings deal with psychological possibilities that fit with the theme of waking up developed here and in the book *Waking Up*.

A more formal scientific presentation of my understanding of the mind, particularly as mind manifests in various altered states of consciousness, is presented in my *States of Consciousness* (originally published by Dutton, 1975, now in print with Psychological Processes). This book will be of particular interest to psychologists and researchers as well as the reader looking for a systematic conceptual tool for understanding states of consciousness. *Altered States of Consciousness* (originally published New York: John Wiley & Sons, 1969; third edition by Harper San Francisco, 1990, available from Psychological Processes) is a collection of research articles on topics like hypnosis, dreaming, lucid dreaming, meditation, and psychedelic drug effects. I considered revising it a couple of years ago but found almost all of the articles in it too useful and still timely to be worth revising. *Transpersonal Psychologies* (originally published by Harper & Row, now in print with Psychological Processes) develops the psychological and parapsychological background for taking spiritual development seriously and has chapters by several authorities that present the psychologies inherent in a number of major spiritual systems (Buddhism, yoga, Gurdjieff, Sufism, Christianity, and the Western magical tradition).

READINGS ON MEDITATION

If I do any further extended work with groups, I shall add formal sitting meditation practice to the teaching of mindfulness in everyday life. There is a depth of insight possible in sitting meditation that is not easily gotten in sensing, looking, and listening in the midst of the action of life, although this deep insight does not readily generalize into everyday life, as discussed in appendix 1. The two practices complement each other beautifully, though.

Meditation is best learned from a good meditation teacher, such as Sogyal Rinpoche, but for those who do not have ready access to one, I strongly recommend Shinzen Young's "Five Classic Meditations" (San Francisco: Audio Renaissance, 1989). Shinzen is one of the best meditation teachers for Westerners I know of, and this tape gives guided meditations to get you actually started practicing. While this is a commercially produced tape, many of Shinzen's lectures on meditation and guided meditations, as well as information on his teaching and retreat schedule (he is an excellent meditation teacher), can be gotten from the Vipassana Support Institute, 4070 Albright Avenue, Los Angeles, CA 90066, telephone (310) 915-1943.

A list of readings, oriented toward learning practically the skill of various kinds of meditation, is given below. Also included are a few readings that are more conceptually oriented, but which are quite interesting and accessible. I have put a double asterisk in front of those I feel are especially useful for learning to meditate.

**Benson, Herbert. *The Relaxation Response*. New York: Morrow, 1975.
Benson, Herbert. *The Mind/Body Effect: How Behavioral Medicine Can Show You the Way to Better Health*. New York: Simon and Schuster, 1979.

Blofeld, John. *The Tantric Mysticism of Tibet: A Practical Guide*. New York: E. P. Dutton, 1970.

Bodian, Stephan, Jack Kornfield, Frances Vaughan, Swami Ajaya and Arthur Deikman. If the Buddha had been a shrink. *Yoga Journal,* no. 88 (September/October 1989), 42–55.

**Brunton, Paul. *The Notebooks of Paul Brunton.* Vol. 4, Part I: *Meditation.* Burdett, N.Y.: Larson Publications, 1987.

Carrington, Patricia. *Freedom in Meditation.* Garden City, N.Y.: Anchor, 1977.

Chogyam, Nagpa. *Journey into Vastness: A Handbook of Tibetan Meditation Techniques.* Worcester: Element Books, 1988.

Deikman, Arthur J. 1963. Experimental meditation. *Journal of Nervous and Mental Diseases* 136, 329–373. Reprinted in Charles T. Tart (ed.), *Altered States of Consciousness.* San Francisco: Harper & Row, 1990.

Deikman, Arthur J. 1966. Deautomatization and the mystic experience. *Psychiatry* 29, 324–338. Reprinted in Charles T. Tart (ed.), *Altered States of Consciousness.* San Francisco: Harper & Row, 1990.

**Dhiravamsa. *The Way of Non-Attachment: The Practice of Insight Meditation.* Wellingborough, Northamptonshire: Turnstone Press, 1984.

Emmons, M. L. *The Inner Source: A Guide to Meditative Therapy.* San Luis Obispo, Calif.: Impact Publishers, 1978.

Epstein, Mark. 1987. Did Freud unconsciously use meditation techniques? *Common Ground 5* (no. 2): 7.

**Fontana, David. *The Elements of Meditation.* New York: Element, 1992.

**Fontana, David. *The Meditator's Handbook.* New York: Element, 1992.

**Goldstein, Joseph, and Jack Kornfield. *Seeking the Heart of Wisdom: The Path of Insight Meditation.* Boston: Shambhala Publications, 1987.

**Goldstein, Joseph. *The Experience of Insight: A Simple and Direct Guide to Buddhist Meditation.* Boston: Shambhala Publications, 1987.

**Goleman, Daniel. *The Varieties of Meditative Experience.* New York: Dutton, 1977.

**Goleman, Daniel. *The Meditative Mind: The Varieties of Meditative Experience.* Los Angeles: Jeremy P. Tarcher, 1988.

Govinda, Anagarika. *Creative Meditation and Multi-Dimensional Consciousness.* Wheaton, Illinois: The Theosophical Publishing House, 1984.

Gyatso, Gesche Kelsang. *Light of Bliss: Mahamudra in Vajrayana Buddhism.* London: Wisdom Publications, 1982.

**Gyatso, Tenzin (the Dalai Lama). *Kindness, Clarity and Insight.* Ithaca, N.Y.: Snow Lion Publications, 1984.

Harding, Douglas E. *On Having No Head: Zen and the Re-Discovery of the Obvious.* London: Arkana Paperbacks, 1986.

Hendlin, Steven. *The Discriminating Mind: A Guide to Deepening Insight and Clarifying Outlook*. London: Unwin, 1989.

Hirai, Tomio. *Zen and the Mind*. Tokyo: Japan Publications, 1978.

Hopkins, Jeffrey. *Compassion in Tibetan Buddhism*. Ithaca, N.Y.: Snow Lion Publications, 1980.

Johansson, Rune. *The Psychology of Nirvana*. London: Allen & Unwin, 1969.

Johnson, Willard. *Riding the Ox Home: A History of Meditation from Shamanism to Science*. London: Rider & Company, 1982.

**Kabat-Zinn, Jon. *Full Castrophe Living: Using the Wisdom of Your Body and Mind to Face Stress, Pain and Illness*. New York: Delacorte, 1991.

Kornfield, Jack. *Living Buddhist Masters*. Santa Cruz, Calif.: Unity Press, 1977.

**Kornfield, Jack, and Paul Breiter. *A Still Forest Pool: The Insight Meditation of Achaan Chah*. Wheaton, Illinois: The Theosophical Publishing House, 1985.

**LeShan, Lawrence. *How to Meditate*. Boston: Little, Brown, 1974.

Levine, Stephen. *Who Dies? An Investigation of Conscious Living and Conscious Dying*. Garden City, New York: Anchor Press/Doubleday, 1982.

Lipman, Kennard, and Merrill Peterson. *You Are the Eyes of the World: Longchempa*. Novato, Calif.: Lotsawa, 1987.

Miller, O. *A sharing of breaths: An Eastern approach to illness and dying*. The Quest, Autumn 1991 65–69.

Mullin, Glen. *Selected Works of the Dalai Lama III: Essence of Refined Gold*. Ithica, N.Y.: Snow Lion Publications, 1985.

Murphy, Michael, and Steve Donovan. *The Physical and Psychological Effects of Meditation: A Review of Contemporary Meditation Research with a Comprehensive Bibliography (1931–1988)*. Big Sur, California: Esalen Institute, 1988.

Naranjo, Claudio, and Robert Ornstein. *On the Psychology of Meditation*. New York: Viking Press, 1971.

Norbu, Namkhai. *Dzog Chen and Zen*. Nevada City, Calif.: Blue Dolphin Publishing, 1986.

Norbu, Namkhai. *The Cycle of Day and Night: An Essential Tibetan Text on the Practice of Dzogchen*. Barrytown, N.Y.: Station Hill Press, 1987.

Owens, Clair Meyers. *Zen and the Lady: Memoirs—Personal and Transpersonal—in a World in Transition*. New York: Baraka Books, 1979.

**Patanjali (translated by Alistair Shearer). *Effortless Being: The Yoga Sutras of Patanjali*. London: Unwin Hyman Ltd., 1989.

Progoff, Ira. *The Practice of Process Meditation*. New York: Dialogue House Library, 1980.

Roberts, Bernadette. *The Experience of No-Self: A Contemplative Journey.* Boston: Shambhala Publications, 1982.

Russell, Peter. *The TM Technique: An Introduction to Transcendental Meditation and the Teachings of Maharishi Mahesh Yogi.* London: Routledge & Kegan Paul, 1976.

Shafii, Mahammad. *Freedom from the Self: Sufism, Meditation and Psychotherapy.* New York: Human Sciences Press, 1985.

Shapiro, Deane. *Precision Nirvana.* Englewood Cliffs, N.J.: Prentice-Hall, 1978.

Shapiro, Deane. *Meditation: Self-regulation Strategy and Altered States of Consciousness.* New York: Aldine, 1980.

Shapiro, Deane and Roger Walsh (eds.). *Meditation: Classic and Contemporary Perspectives.* New York: Aldine, 1984.

**Shearer, Alistair and Richard Lannoy. *Effortless Being: The Yoga Sutras of Patanjali.* London: Unwin Hyman Ltd., 1989.

Sogyal Rinpoche. *Dzogchen and Padmasambhava.* Berkeley: Rigpa Fellowship, 1989.

**Sogyal Rinpoche. *The Tibetan Book of Living and Dying.* San Francisco: HarperSanFrancisco, 1992.

Solé-Leris, Amadeo. *Tranquility and Insight: An Introduction to the Oldest Form of Buddhist Meditation.* Boston: Shambhala Publications, 1986.

**Suzuki, Shunryu. *Zen Mind, Beginner's Mind: Informal Talks on Zen Meditation and Practice.* New York: John Weatherhill, 1970.

Tart, Charles T. 1972. A psychologist's experience with transcendental meditation. *Journal of Transpersonal Psychology* 3, 135–140.

Tart, Charles T. Meditation and consciousness: A dialogue between a meditation teacher and a psychologist. *Noetic Sciences Review,* 1988, no. 8, 14–21.

Tarthang Tulku. *Gesture of Balance: A Guide to Awareness, Self-healing and Meditation.* Emeryville, Calif.: Dharma Publishing, 1977.

**Thich Nhat Hanh. *Being Peace.* Berkeley, Calif.: Parallax Press, 1987.

**Thich Nhat Hanh. *The Miracle of Mindfulness: A Manual on Meditation.* Boston: Beacon Press, 1987.

Walker, Susan (ed.). *Speaking of Silence: Christians and Buddhists on the Contemplative Way.* New York: Paulist Press, 1987.

Walsh, Roger. Meditation research: The state of the art. In Roger Walsh and Frances Vaughan (eds.), *Paths Beyond Ego: The Transpersonal Vision.* Los Angeles: Jeremy P. Tarcher.

West, Michael A. (ed.). *The Psychology of Meditation.* Oxford: Clarendon Press, 1987.

Wilber, Ken, Jack Engler, and Daniel P. Brown. *Transformations of Consciousness: Conventional and Contemplative Perspectives on Development.* Boston: Shambhala Publications, 1986.

Yeshe, Y. T. *Light of Dharma: A Commentary on the Three Principle Paths to Enlightenment.* London: Wisdom Publications, 1984.

Zahler, Leah. *Meditative States in Tibetan Buddhism: The Concentrations and Formless Absorptions.* London: Wisdom Publications, 1983.

READINGS ON DZOGCHEN

I do not feel I understand Dzogchen well enough to give any kind of authoritative guide to readings on it, but I will enthusiastically recommend Sogyal Rinpoche's 1992 best-seller, *The Tibetan Book of Living and Dying,* which was published by HarperSanFrancisco.

To give you some feeling for this book, which I find quite inspiring and which contains the essence of Dzogchen teachings, here is a review of the book that I wrote for the *Institute of Noetic Sciences Review.*

> *What is it I hope for from this book? To inspire a quiet revolution in the whole way we look at death and care for the dying, and the whole way we look at life, and care for the living.* —SOGYAL RINPOCHE

This is the most important book I have reviewed for IONS members, but I must start with some words of warning. First, this review is about death. Parts of you may not want to read it, and your mind can come up with good reasons for skipping onto something else. There are so many more important things to do, aren't there? But it's also about the quality of your life, for if you won't deal with your mortality, you cannot have more than a partial life, a shadow of a life. As this book says,

> If we look into our lives we will see clearly how many unimportant tasks, so-called "responsibilities" accumulate to fill them up. One master compares them to "housekeeping in a dream." We tell ourselves we want to spend them on the important things of life, but there never is any time. Even simply to get up in the morning, there is so much to do: open the window, make the bed, take a

shower, brush your teeth, feed the dog or cat, do last night's washing up, discover you are out of sugar or coffee, go and buy them, make breakfast—the list is endless. Then there are clothes to sort out, choose, iron, and fold up again. And what about your hair, or your makeup? Helpless, we watch our days fill up with telephone calls and petty projects, with so many responsibilities— or shouldn't we call them "irresponsibilities"?

As a second warning, I cannot be completely objective about this book as I have my personal fears of and problems with death—and life. Like most of us, I have a theoretical interest in death and what might happen after death. My interest is theoretical in that I seldom reflect on death with all my faculties, especially my emotions, but just with my intellect. Intellect is cool and distancing. Why not be cool and distant? Despite knowing better, I tend to automatically think of death, as most of us do, as something that happens to others, not to me personally.

Though I seldom think about it I also know that tuning out reality—my death, my life, in this case—in any fashion is costly. But I can put off thinking about death to some vague future time, can't I?

I had planned to review Sogyal Rinpoche's book last weekend but other, important tasks (conveniently?) intervened. Well, I know about my automatic tendencies to avoid anything unpleasant, and I try to work against it. I also pray each day that whatever is higher in our universe will guide me to learn what is important, even if I'm avoiding it. Perhaps it was a coincidence, or perhaps an answer to my prayers, but Sunday morning I suddenly had a severe pain in my abdomen and ended up taking my first ambulance ride to an emergency room. It seemed to me that I probably had some obstruction of the bowels that would require surgery. While the odds were good that I would survive, *I* could die in surgery. Was I ready for *my* death? Not anywhere near to the degree I would like.

My pain turned out to be due to a kidney stone passing: death was put off into the vague future again. Well, thank you, universe, for this reminder to live life fully, to keep working on understanding my deeper mind, and to be ready for death. I suppose a few hours of severe pain is a cheap price for such a good reminder. But I hope I can get by with more gentle reminders in the future!

Now, my final warning. I cannot write here in a completely objective manner, as only a scientist who has studied relevant areas and can so give an unbiased report on the book. I *am* a scientist who has studied relevant areas, but since hearing Sogyal Rinpoche lecture a decade ago, I have regularly attended retreats of his, for I felt that what he was teaching and embodying was important to my (and others') spiritual development. So I am not detached from the book and its author. On the other hand, no friend has ever suggested that I tend to become a mindless devotee of anyone. I have had several spiritual teachers for whom I have great respect, but I maintain my independence of thought and belief, as doing that is important in the role I see for myself of trying to bridge spiritual traditions and the scientific world. So I may be biased in this review in ways I'm not aware of, but it would be quite remiss of me not to bring *The Tibetan Book of Living and Dying* to your attention.

Sogyal Rinpoche is what Tibetan Buddhists call a *tulku,* a being so highly enlightened and evolved that at death, instead of passing beyond our ordinary worlds with their suffering to realms of ultimate bliss, he or she deliberately chooses to reincarnate here in order to continue helping others find the way to enlightenment. This tulku idea is what the pragmatic and scientific parts of my mind call "fancy stuff" or "mythological gloss," and I am not too comfortable with it. I have no way of verifying the truth or falsity of this, and the idea of a tulku tends to create, in most Western minds, grandiose (and infantile) fantasies about a magic being who will solve your problems for you.

On a more realistic level, Sogyal Rinpoche is a man I have known and studied with, a teacher of Tibetan Buddhism, particularly a teacher of Dzogchen, a tradition of developing a deep mindfulness that leads to ultimate enlightenment. I can't say much about enlightenment from personal experience, but I can say that Sogyal Rinpoche is a very intelligent, knowledgeable, dedicated, and compassionate man, and a pioneer in attempting to bring the essence of Tibetan Buddhist understandings to us in a way Westerners can understand and use. In spite of my need for independence as a scholar and scientist, in spite of my psychological defenses and resistances, I have learned a great deal from studying with him, and so I can say that *The Tibetan Book of Living and Dying* is one of the most important books ever published. If you want a better death—and just as importantly, a better life—I cannot recommend this book too highly. Let's sample some of the book.

Most IONS members are well aware of how lopsided the development of our culture has been, of the dominance of materialism and scientism at the expense of the human spirit. As Rinpoche points out,

> Sometimes I think that the greatest achievement of modern culture is its brilliant selling of samsara [living in a state of illusion] and its barren distractions. Modern society seems to me a celebration of all the things that lead away from the truth, make truth hard to live for, and discourage people from even believing that it exists. And to think that all this springs from a civilization that claims to adore life, but actually starves it of any real meaning; that endlessly speaks of making people "happy," but in fact blocks their way to the source of real joy.

Now let's look more specifically at death. In the Tibetan Buddhist cosmology, the time of death is what we might call one of *high leverage*. Normally we identify our consciousness with our body, which patterns and constrains it. As the body and brain break down and consciousness goes through various stages of freeing itself from the body (discussed in detail in the book), deliberate and healthy actions of consciousness can have a much greater effect in moving you toward liberation and/or a much better new incarnation than similar actions during ordinary life. That's the high leverage. By the same token, unskilled, maladaptive actions can make things worse. Thus, there is a great deal of practical as well as spiritual—as if we can really separate these two categories—advice in the book on preparing for death, helping others prepare, and acting skillfully during the dying process. *The Tibetan Book of Living and Dying* is much more practical and useful than the old classic *Tibetan Book of the Dead* in this way—and you don't have to be a Buddhist to benefit from the advice.

While the word *death* in the title strongly attracts (and repels) our attention, the way we live our life has enormous effects on how we die and what goes on afterward. The best preparation for death is to become more and more enlightened in this life. Sogyal Rinpoche frankly amazes me in the way he has distilled in this book the essence of years of his teachings on how to live and recognize one's inner essence, one's *rigpa*.

Whatever label we put on ourselves—Buddhist, Christian, agnostic, and so on—there is a spiritual reality that is our common heritage simply by virtue of being human. If only we had support for discovering our deep nature:

> Despite this massive and nearly all-pervasive denial of their existence, we still sometimes have fleeting glimpses of the nature of mind. . . . I think we do, sometimes, half understand these glimpses, but modern culture gives us no context or framework in which to comprehend them. Worse still, rather than encouraging us to explore these glimpses more deeply and discover where they spring from, we are told in both obvious and subtle ways to shut them out. We know that no one will take us seriously if we try to share them. We can be frightened by them, or even think we are going mad. So we ignore what could really be the most revealing experiences of our lives, if only we understood them. This is perhaps the darkest and most disturbing aspect of modern civilization—its ignorance and repression of who we really are.

You do not have to accept everything in this book—I don't—but it calls to and supports something deep in our nature.

I cannot really review *The Tibetan Book of Living and Dying* in a comprehensive way: there is too much in it to summarize, such as the gentle yet profound instructions on Dzogchen meditation, and much of the material is of a kind my heart responds to and wants to understand and practice, without being able to yet. I can only tantalize you with a few more glimpses.

Reflecting on the social and planetary consequences of our rejection of death, Sogyal Rinpoche notes:

> I am reminded of what one Tibetan master says: "People often make the mistake of being frivolous about death, and think, 'Oh well, death happens to everybody. It's not a big deal, it's natural. I'll be fine.' That's a nice theory until one is dying."
>
> One [type of person] views death as something to scurry away from and [an]other as something that will just take care of itself. How far they both are from understanding death's true significance!

All the greatest spiritual traditions of the world, including of course Christianity, have told us clearly that death is not the end. They have all handed down a vision of some sort of life to come, which infuses this life that we are leading now with sacred meaning. But despite their teaching, modern society is largely a spiritual desert where the vast majority imagine that this life is all that there is. Without any real or authentic faith in an afterlife, most people live lives deprived of any ultimate meaning.

I have come to realize that the disastrous effects of the denial of death go far beyond the individual: They affect the whole planet. Believing fundamentally that this life is the only one, modern people have developed no long-term vision. So there is nothing to restrain them from plundering the planet for their own immediate ends and from living in a selfish way that could prove fatal for the future.

This book is also unique in giving many glimpses into the life of a person who was raised to be a spiritual teacher in a now endangered culture that was pervaded by spirituality. I will end this review by quoting the beginning of the first chapter, describing Sogyal Rinpoche's introduction to death:

My own first experience of death came when I was about seven. We were preparing to leave the eastern highlands to travel to central Tibet. Samten, one of the personal attendants of my master, was a wonderful monk who was kind to me during my childhood. He had a bright, round, chubby face, always ready to break into a smile. He was everyone's favorite in the monastery because he was so good-natured. Every day my master would give teaching and initiations and lead practices and rituals. Toward the end of the day, I would gather together my friends and act out a little theatrical performance, reenacting the morning's events. It was Samten who would always lend me the costumes my master had worn in the morning. He never refused me.

Then suddenly Samten fell ill, and it was clear he was not going to live. We had to postpone our departure. I will never forget the two weeks that followed. The rank smell of death hung like a cloud over everything, and whenever I think of that time, the smell comes back to me. The monastery was saturated with an intense awareness of death. This was not at all morbid or frightening, however; in the presence of my master, Samten's death took on a special significance. It became a teaching for us all.

Samten lay on a bed by the window in a small temple in my master's residence. I knew he was dying. From time to time I would go in and sit by him. He could not talk, and I was shocked by the change in his face, which was now so haggard and drawn. I realized that he was going to leave us and we would never see him again. I felt intensely sad and lonely.

Samten's death was not an easy one. The sound of his labored breathing followed us everywhere, and we could smell his body decaying. The monastery was overwhelmingly silent except for this breathing. Everything focused on Samten.

Yet although there was much suffering in Samten's prolonged dying, we could all see that deep down he had a peace and inner confidence about him. At first I could not explain this, but then I realized what it came from: his faith and his training, and the presence of our master. And though I felt sad, I knew then that if our master was there, everything would turn out all right, because he would be able to help Samten toward liberation. Later I came to know that it is the dream of any practitioner to die before his master and have the good fortune to be guided by him through death.

As Jamyang Khyentse guided Samten calmly through his dying, he introduced him to all the stages of the process he was going through, one by one. I was astonished by the precision of my master's knowledge, and by his confidence and peace. When my master was there, his peaceful confidence would reassure even the most anxious person. Now Jamyang Khyentse was revealing to us his fearlessness of death. Not that he ever treated death lightly: He often told us that he was afraid of it, and warned us against taking it naively or complacently. Yet what was it that allowed my master to face death in a way that was at once so sober and so lighthearted, so practical yet so mysteriously carefree? That question fascinated and absorbed me.

Samten's death shook me. At the age of seven, I had my first glimpse of the vast power of the tradition I was being made part of, and I began to understand the purpose of spiritual practice.

Practice had given Samten an acceptance of death, as well as a clear understanding that suffering and pain can be part of a deep, natural process of purification. Practice had given my master a complete knowledge of what death is, and a precise technology for guiding individuals through it.

Four audio cassettes of selections from *The Tibetan Book of Living and Dying* are now available from Audio Literature, San Francisco. I will also recommend a few other books on Dzogchen:

Chogyam, Nagpa. *Journey into Vastness: A Handbook of Tibetan Meditation Techniques.* Longmead, Shaftsbury, Dorset: Element Books, 1988.

Lipman, Kennard, and Merrill Peterson. *You Are the Eyes of the World: Longchempa.* Novato, Calif.: Lotsawa, 1987.

Norbu, Namkhai. *The Crystal and the Way of Light: Sutra, Tantra and Dzogchen.* New York: Routledge & Kegan Paul, 1986.

Norbu, Namkhai. *The Cycle of Day and Night: An Essential Tibetan Text on the Practice of Dzogchen.* Barrytown, N.Y.: Station Hill Press, 1987.

Rangdrol, Tsele Natsok (translated by Erik Pema Kunsang). *The Mirror of Mindfulness: The Cycle of the Four Bardos.* Boston: Shambhala Publications, 1989.

Reynolds, John (trans.). *Self-Liberation Through Seeing with Naked Awareness.* Barrytown, N.Y.: Station Hill Press, 1989.

Sogyal Rinpoche. *Dzogchen and Padmasambhava.* Berkeley: Rigpa Fellowship, 1989.

ENDING DEDICATION

By the power and the truth of this practice, may all beings have
   happiness, and the causes of happiness,
May all be free from sorrow, and the causes of sorrow,
May all never be separated from the sacred happiness which
   is sorrowless,
And may all live in equanimity, without too much attachment and
   too much aversion,
And live believing in the equality of all that lives.

—traditional prayer, perhaps attributable
to Shakyamuni Buddha himself,
as translated by Sogyal Rinpoche

INDEX

Resistance, 153
Responsibilities, 233
Retreats, 83–84, 184, 204–206
Reynolds, John, 239
Rigidity, 163
Rigpa, 11, 42, 189, 195
Rigpa Fellowship, 8, 11, 106
  addresses, 189n1:1
  devotion and, 90–91
Riordan, Kathleen, 225. *See also*
  Speeth
Riso, D. R., 191
Roberts, Bernadette, 231
Robot, 11, 86
Rose, 28–29
Routines, 100
Russell, Peter, 231
Russian Orthodox Christians, 20

Sacred dances, 184–185
Samsara, 49, 61
Samten, 237–239
Sanity, 172
Sarmouni Brotherhood, 21
Scanning the body, 135
Science, 18
Scientism, 17–18, 94
Scurvy, 28
Secondary gain, 116–117, 163
Secret service, 20
Security, 70
Self, 115–117
  as illusion, 31
  deep, loss of, 62–63
Self-defense, 34
Self image, 12
Self-consciousness, 199
Self-esteem, 70
Self-liberation, 181
Self-lubrication system, 128
Self-observation, 32, 206, 207,
  209–212. *See also* Mindfulness
Self-remembeirng, 206, 207–208,
  209–212. *See also* Mindfulness;
  Sensing, looking, and listening

Sensation, 44, 62
Senses, 26
Sensing, looking, and listening, 56–57,
  104–106, 169–170, 182–183. *See
  also* Mindfulness
  dealing with fear, 118–120
  emotions and, 170–171
  exercises, 38–39, 54–56
  experiences, 57–58, 99–100,
  125–126, 153–154, 159–161
  "hearing" with the body, 133–136
  physical activities and, 148–149
Sensing the body, 14
Sensory feedback, 215–216
Seriousness, 38–39, 161
Sexism, 4, 209
Shafii, Mohammad, 231
Shah, Idries, 168, 171, 192
Shame, 99, 119
Shapiro, Deane, 231
Shearer, Alistair, 230, 231
Shifty-eyed technique, 56, 144,
  174–176
Shoulds, 156
Sin, 17
Six realms of existence, 122
Skills, 33
Sleep 2–3
  degrees of, 148, 152
  deprivation, 84
Slowing down, 100
Smell, 88
Sobriety, 129
Social contract, 69, 73
Social feedback, 220
Social support for mindfulness, 72–73,
  171, 173–174
Sogyal Rinpoche, 42, 179, 181, 193n3
  *Tibetan Book of Living and Dying,
  The,* 232–239
  transference and, 91–92
Solè-Leris, Amadeo, 198, 222, 231
Solitaire mindfulness exercise,
  217–219